THE
Pro Football Fan's
COMPANION

THE
Pro Football Fan's
COMPANION

How to Watch the Game Like an Expert

RALPH HICKOK

MACMILLAN • USA

MACMILLAN
a Simon & Schuster Macmillan Company
1633 Broadway
New York, NY 10019

MACMILLAN is a registered trademark of Macmillan, Inc.

Library of Congress Cataloging-in-Publication Data available
ISBN   0-02-860439-3

10 9 8 7 6 5 4 3 2 1

Printed in the United States of America

Designed by George McKeon

Contents

1

A Brief History

In 1969, the National Collegiate Athletic Association celebrated the 100th anniversary of college football.

Wrong!

Of course, it's hard to blame the NCAA. A centennial is so much fun, why not celebrate it a few years too soon? But the Rutgers-Princeton game of November 3, 1869, supposedly the first "football" game and the reason for the centennial celebration, was a soccer match.

And soccer might now be a major college sport, except for a bunch of stubborn Harvard players who preferred their own strange version of football. It was called "the Boston game," and its informal rules allowed a player to handle the ball and to pass it to a teammate. He was even allowed to run with it, so long as a defender was chasing him. As soon as pursuit stopped, he was supposed to stop, too.

When the Intercollegiate Football Association was formed in 1873 to standardize the rules of soccer, Harvard refused to join. The Harvard captain, Henry Grant, wrote in a rather snotty letter to the Yale captain, "We even went so far as to practice and try the Yale game. We gave it up at once as hopeless."

A few colleges, notably Princeton and Yale, played soccer for a while. Harvard, meanwhile, couldn't find any opponents. Word must somehow have reached Montreal, because early in 1874 McGill University challenged Harvard.

McGill proposed a two-game series, the first game to be played in Cambridge under Harvard's "Boston Game" rules, the second to be played in Montreal under McGill's rules for Rugby football.

The Harvard players didn't think they'd be allowed to take any time off to go to Montreal, so they suggested playing both games in Cambridge. McGill agreed.

On May 14, about 500 spectators paid 50 cents apiece to watch the first game. McGill players were smartly dressed in Rugby uniforms, but the Harvard players had simply thrown on white shirts and dark trousers, though they did wear red (some sources specify magenta, of all colors) kerchiefs around their heads so they could identify one another. It took Harvard only 22 minutes to score the three goals required for victory.

The following day, the teams played Rugby. Though the egg-shaped ball was new to Harvard, the players caught on fast and the result was a scoreless tie. Afterward, Harvard used the gate receipts to throw a banquet for both teams.

If graffiti had been in back then, someone could have spray-painted "Harvard Loves Rugby" on John Harvard's statue. The Boston game was no longer in favor; one Harvard publication referred to it as "the somewhat sleepy game played by our men."

That fall, the Harvard faculty surprisingly allowed the team to go to Montreal to play a Rugby match against McGill. Harvard won 3–0 and there was another banquet. Those post-game banquets, featuring sumptuous menus, extensive wine lists, and many toasts, all paid for by the fans, could undoubtedly have made any sport popular among college students.

Harvard got its comeuppance in June of 1875, losing 1–0 to Tufts College from nearby Medford. Though little noted nor long remembered—especially not by Harvard—this was the first Rugby match between colleges from the United States. Since Rugby eventually evolved into American football, maybe that Tufts victory over Harvard should be remembered as the first intercollegiate football game.

Or maybe not. The question arises: When *did* Rugby become American football? It's not easy to answer. A real purist might choose the year 1906, when the forward pass was finally legalized. An even purer purist might opt for 1912, when the present scoring system was finally established.

My answer would be (in fact, is) 1880. To understand why, we have to return to November of 1875, when Harvard and Yale played what amounted to a Rugby match at New Haven. Harvard won 4–0 before a crowd of about 2,000 spectators. More important, one of the Yale players was a freshman halfback named Walter Camp.

Shown here as captain of the Yale football team in 1879, Walter Camp innovated rules changes that turned Rugby into American football. *Courtesy Yale University*

Camp liked order and efficiency. He spent most of his life running a clock factory in New Haven, which tells you something. He must have enjoyed Rugby, since he was on the Yale team for six seasons, including two while he was in medical school—he finally dropped out because he couldn't stand the sight of blood—but he also must have felt it was a bit too disorderly.

Rugby, like soccer, field hockey, and ice hockey, is essentially a continuous action sport. Control of the ball is always tenuous. When a player is tackled, he's supposed to release the ball so that someone else, from either team, can pick it up. If he doesn't release it, or if the ball goes out of bounds, possession is decided by a messy procedure called a "scrum," short for "scrummage," a variant of "skirmish."

In a scrum, the ball is placed between the opposing teams, and the linemen struggle against one another, while the backs hover behind them, waiting for the ball to appear. Eventually, one line prevails and a back can snatch the ball from the ground to start play again.

To Camp's orderly mind, this was chaos. In 1880, he came up with a better idea: Replace the scrummage with a scrimmage. Camp changed just one letter in the word, but he changed the entire nature of football.

With the scrimmage, a team controlled the ball. When a player was tackled, the teams lined up on opposite sides of the scrimmage line and the player could then "snap" the ball, with a quick backward action of the foot, to a teammate behind him, setting play in motion again.

This was a revolutionary change. Given undisputed possession of the ball and a lapse of time before play resumed, a team can plan what to do next, instead of depending entirely on spontaneity and instantaneous decisions in the heat of action. And this is what sets American football apart from soccer and Rugby.

The scrimmage presented one big problem, though. There was no limit on how long a team could control the ball. If you've watched football at all, in person or on television, you've seen games in which the quarterback takes the snap from center and simply kneels down to run time off the clock, usually near the end of the game when his team has a lead.

After the scrimmage was introduced in 1880, a team could do something like that for an entire half. That's exactly what happened in the 1881 Yale-Princeton game at the Polo Grounds, before 10,000 bored spectators. Both teams were undefeated and the crowd was there to see one of them win the championship.

Neither team even tried to win the championship. After four minutes of the first half, Princeton simply held on to the ball by using simple runs into the line that gained nothing and risked little. Yale received the kickoff to start the second half and did exactly the same thing until the game ended in a scoreless tie.

It was called the "block game." And it was very, very dull.

Princeton's newspaper accurately declared, "The block game is not football," and suggested that a team, on its third down, should be forced to kick or give up the ball.

Walter Camp duly noted that. But, as usual, he had an even better idea. At the spring meeting of the Intercollegiate Football Association in 1882, he proposed a rule requiring a team to gain 5 yards or lose 10 yards in three downs in order to maintain possession, and the rule was adopted.

The five- or ten-yard rule, as it became known, created the "gridiron." Football fields were marked with chalk lines at 5-yard intervals to help the referee decide whether a team had gained 5 yards or lost 10 in its three downs.

The rule also ended the block game. There was just one other little problem to be solved: When a football game ended, nobody knew what the score was.

Scoring had been a problem all along. In Rugby, a touchdown doesn't count for anything; it simply gives a team a free kick for a field goal. And, in Rugby, a field goal can also be scored on a drop kick when a player is running with the ball.

Harvard had felt, from the beginning, that a touchdown should count for something. In fact, the only real concession that Harvard made when the "concessionary rules" were adopted for the 1875 game against Yale was to give up on the touchdown.

That hurt in the second Harvard-Yale game in 1876. Harvard scored two touchdowns but missed both free kicks, and Yale won on a field goal.

After the 1876 season, there was a long argument about scoring. Columbia, Harvard, Princeton, and Yale were the only schools in the IFA at the time. They finally agreed on a rule.

Read it: "A match shall be decided by a majority of touchdowns; a goal shall be equal to four touchdowns; but in case of a tie a goal kicked from a touchdown shall take precedence over four touchdowns."

Now read it again. If you understand it, you're a better person than I am, Gunga Din.

There was another problem with scoring. The safety got its name because, when a team was backed up near its own goal line, a player could simply run back into the end zone with the ball and touch it down. His team would then gain possession of the ball at its own 25-yard line, safely out of danger. Camp didn't like that; he felt that a safety should count somehow in the scoring.

In 1881, Camp sort of won that argument, and the scoring rule was amended to read "four touchdowns shall take precedence over a goal kicked from the field; two safeties shall be equal to a touchdown."

That sure made it a lot clearer, didn't it? Despite the clarification, though, several games ended in lengthy arguments about exactly who had won. They went something like this:

"Our two touchdowns and the goal from touchdown and four safeties beat your goal kicked from field and only two safeties."

"Did not."

"Did too."

"Did not."

Well, you can probably imagine the rest of it.

Once again, Camp rode to the rescue. And by now, it's hard not to picture him riding a white horse and wearing a white hat, if not gleaming armor. He set up the first real scoring system, adopted in 1883. It awarded 1 point for a safety, 2 for a touchdown, 4 for a goal following a touchdown, and 5 for a goal from the field.

So, in 1883, the point-after was worth four points.

A lot of other changes took place during the next twenty years. Much of it was the process of tinkering with the rules to try to get the right balance between offense and defense. The point system in particular underwent a lot of tinkering, with a touchdown continually rising while the value of the goal kicks was dropping. The present system of 6 points for a touchdown, 3 for a field goal, and 1 for the conversion wasn't reached until 1912.

This 1807 "View of the Buildings of Yale College" shows top-hatted students kicking a football in the foreground. *Library of Congress*

In addition to his work as a rules maker, Walter Camp helped create American football as the unofficial coach of the Yale team. In 1882, he devised the offensive system that became standard for many years, with seven men on the line of scrimmage, a quarterback, two halfbacks, and a fullback. In fact, it was a primitive version of the T formation.

He also devised the first system of calling signals in 1882. Yale had four plays, each designated by a sentence. (Teams didn't begin huddling to call plays until about 1920, so the defense could hear the quarterback's signals quite clearly.) One sentence was "Look out quick, Deac," which meant that the quarterback would take the snap and toss the ball to a halfback for a run to the right. Another was "Play up sharp, Charley," which was the same play in the other direction.

There was a refinement. The defense would certainly soon catch on to what the offense was about to do if an entire sentence was used each time. But Camp used sixteen different words in the four sentences, and any word or combination of words from a sentence also designated the play. So the word "look" or the word "quick" or the phrase "out, Deac" all meant a toss to the halfback for a run to the right.

Camp also came up with football's first game plan. In 1883, when Yale and Princeton played for the college championship, Princeton had the sport's first great kicker, Alexander Moffat, who could boot field goals with either foot. He had beaten Harvard that year with five field goals, three with his right foot and two with his left, ranging from 38 to 46 yards.

At the time, teams did a lot of punting, often on first or second down. To keep the ball away from Moffat, though, Camp went to a ball control attack, running on first and second down and even on third down if there wasn't much yardage to be gained. It worked: Moffat kicked only one field goal, while Yale scored two goals and two touchdowns to win the championship.

It might be interesting, at this point, to take a quick look at a game of the 1880s. The modern fan would recognize it as football—that is, American football, not soccer or Rugby—but it would seem like a very strange version of the sport. (Probably because it was.)

Before the game, there was a coin toss, but the team that won the toss almost always chose to kick off. The kicker could kick the ball away to the other team, but usually he would simply "dribble" it a short distance, pick it up, and lateral it to a teammate. After the player with the ball was tackled, the two teams lined up for a scrimmage at the spot where he was downed.

Players didn't crouch or use a three-point stance. Offensive linemen stood straight up, well apart from one another, their feet spread, arms extended, hands closed into fists, and the defensive linemen stood opposite them, toe to toe and nose to nose.

The "center-rush" or "snapper-back" was turned sideways, his foot on top of the front point of the ball. Directly behind him, two to three yards back, was the quarterback. The halfbacks were spread wide, five to seven yards deep, while the fullback was directly behind the quarterback and about ten yards behind the line of scrimmage.

There was no huddle. When his team was ready, the quarterback called the signal for the play. Yale, as noted, used a sentence, or part of a sentence, as the signal. Princeton also used a short sentence, but the first letter of the sentence indicated the play: If "W" was the signal, the sentence might be "Watch out on the right." Harvard used both letters and sentences in some fashion, but within a couple of years the Harvard team began using numbers.

As soon as the offensive signal was given, the snapper-back stepped down hard on the front end of the ball to deliver it, on one bounce, to the quarterback—something like snapping a tiddly-wink. Linemen immediately began sparring with one another. "It was the heyday for a good boxer

and the slugger type of player, for there was no penalty for rough work," A. A. Stagg recalled. There was no attempt to block, as we know blocking; an offensive lineman simply tried to keep his counterpart from penetrating into the backfield.

The quarterback wasn't allowed to run with the ball immediately after receiving the snap, so he almost always lateraled it to a halfback. After getting the lateral, the halfback would usually try to go wide around end, with an eye out for any opening that might develop inside.

The other backs trailed the man with the ball, ready to receive a lateral when he was tackled, or about to be tackled. (The quarterback could run with the ball after it had been touched by another player.) As in Rugby, a play often included as many as a half-dozen laterals before it was over.

Although teams were using the running attack to control the ball more consistently in 1883, the punt on first or second down was not unusual, especially if a team had a comfortable lead or was deep in its own territory. The fullback, as noted, was usually the punter, but a halfback might at times punt the ball on the run. If a defensive player called for a fair catch, he made a heel mark on the spot and was entitled to a free kick—a return punt or, if he was close enough, a drop kick or place kick at goal. His team could also elect to start a scrimmage from the spot.

One of the most peculiar sights for a modern fan would be the "maul-in-goal," which was taken straight from Rugby. It arose from the fact that a player actually had to touch the ball to the ground after crossing the goal line for it to count as a touchdown. Defenders could attempt to prevent him from touching it down by grabbing the ball and trying to wrestle it free. If a defender then got possession of the ball, *he* would generally touch it down to get a safety—although he could also kick or run it out. The maul-in-goal often went on for several seconds before the touchdown or safety was made.

The goal kick after touchdown was also very different from our simple conversion. The scoring team had an option. The ball could be brought out from the point where it had crossed the goal line to any distance, for a place kick or drop kick. Or someone from the scoring team could punt the ball out from directly behind the spot where it had crossed the goal line; a member of his team could then make a fair catch and attempt the goal. The punt-out was usually chosen if the ball had crossed the goal line near the sideline, since the punter could kick the ball toward the middle of the field, giving his team a better angle on the goal kick.

A game lasted an hour and a half, with two 45-minute periods and a 10-minute break between. But there were no timeouts, even for a dead ball. If the ball went out of bounds or crossed the goal line, the referee kept his stopwatch running. There was also no limit on the amount of time the offense could take to start a play. If a quarterback felt his players needed a rest, he could delay until the referee specifically told him to call his signal, which might take a minute or more.

The players wore no special protection, and the sport was rough, but it was not nearly as brutal as it was to become during the next decade. There were very few high-speed collisions and most contact was simply one man against another—an offensive lineman sparring with a defender, a defensive player attempting to tackle the runner. Players suffered plenty of bumps and bruises, cuts and scratches, but serious injuries were rare. In most of the games recorded during the period, all of the starters played the entire ninety minutes.

In a mere eight years, American football had been created by college students and a few young alumni. The three major evolutionary changes in the transformation of Rugby into this new sport were the scrimmage rule, the "five-or-ten yard rule," and the numerical scoring system, all of which had been proposed by Walter Camp, who was to become known as "the father of American football."

Another change took place, not at first because of new rules, but because of the American way of ignoring rules when they obstruct progress. Rugby has a rule against "interference." A player running ahead of the ball-carrier isn't allowed to interfere with a defender.

That was also the rule in American football for many years, but no one paid much attention to it. It began, probably, in the 1879 Princeton-Yale game. Interestingly, Walter Camp was the referee. In a scoreless tie, a Princeton player ran down the field with a teammate on each side to screen him from tacklers until he got close enough to kick the winning goal.

Referee Camp allowed the kick, but warned Princeton's captain that guarding the runner in such a way was illegal. After sleeping on it, he must have changed his mind, because Camp's Yale team began using the same kind of play later that season.

Within a few years, teams were sending blockers ahead of their runners, not just alongside them, and officials completely ignored the infraction. That led, within a short time, to "mass momentum" plays.

The most famous of them was Princeton's flying wedge, which was just about what it sounds like. Ten players formed into a V, locking their arms together to create a wall, with the ball-carrier tucked snugly inside to be escorted to the end zone. The flying wedge wasn't always as effective as it must have looked on the blackboard. Pudge Heffelfinger of Yale, who will re-appear a little later as the first known professional football player, defeated the wedge by simply jumping over it and landing on top of the poor, unsuspecting runner.

But, with the mass momentum principle established, all kinds of plays were built around it. Every time a new rule was adopted to prevent that sort of thing, teams found a loophole. And the body count mounted.

In 1905, eighteen high school and college players were killed playing football. A group of thirteen colleges voted on whether they should get rid of football or reform the rules to prevent that kind of mayhem and manslaughter. Reform won by an 8–5 vote.

The most important rule change in 1906 was the legalization of the forward pass. Walter Camp, who had been in the vanguard twenty-five and more years before, now found himself bringing up the rear. He was against the idea, but he was out-voted. The new rules also required the offensive team to have at least six players on the line of scrimmage and increased the yardage required for a first down from 5 to 10. The rule allowing a team to keep the ball by losing 10 yards was abolished.

The trouble was, the rules-makers were so suspicious of the forward pass that they did almost everything possible to keep teams from using it. The passer could be no more than 5 yards to either side of the center, the ball couldn't be thrown more than 20 yards beyond the line of scrimmage and, unkindest cut of all, the other team got possession if the pass was incomplete.

Incidentally, that rule about where the passer could be created a very strange looking football field, to modern eyes. Now there were chalk lines running the length of the field, at 5-yard intervals, to help officials decide whether the passer was within 5 yards of the center when he threw the ball.

Some writers have said this new marking created the "gridiron." Those writers have never seen a gridiron (the real thing, not the football version). This new marking actually created something like a very long chessboard.

These much heralded changes really didn't help much, but it took a while for anyone to realize that. After all, reform had taken place, so there couldn't be any more problems.

But thirty-three college players were killed in 1909, mainly because blockers were still allowed to lock their arms together while escorting the runner down the field. So rules were passed banning interlocked interference and requiring the offense to have at least seven players on the line of scrimmage.

The changes that made American football almost what it is today took place before the 1912 season. The distance between the goal lines was chopped down from 110 to 100 yards, but the field itself was lengthened to 120 yards by adding the end zones. That was important, because up until then a forward pass was incomplete if it was caught beyond the goal line.

The offense was given four downs instead of three in which to gain 10 yards for a first down; the 20-yard limit on the forward pass was removed; the business about an incomplete pass giving possession to the other team was scuttled; and the only limitation on the passer was that he had to be at least 10 yards behind the line of scrimmage. That got rid of the elongated chessboard and restored the good old gridiron. The present scoring system was also established in 1912.

A single professional game led to another important set of rules changes in 1933. The Chicago Bears and Portsmouth, Ohio, Spartans finished the 1932 season in a tie for first place and a championship game was scheduled for December 18 at Wrigley Field in Chicago.

But bitter cold, biting winds, and a couple of blizzards hit Chicago during the week before the game. George Halas, president of the Bears, suggested that the game should be played indoors at Chicago Stadium. The Spartans agreed.

It was an odd setting. The home of hockey's Black Hawks, the stadium wasn't big enough to hold a football field. The field for the championship game was only 80 yards long from end line to end line, and the sidelines were right up against the stands. The goalposts, which were 10 yards behind the goal line at the time (as they are now, again), were moved to the goal line.

A special rule was adopted to have the ball moved 10 yards toward the center of the field if it went out of bounds. Until then, the ball was put back into play just barely inside the field and the offensive team had to waste a down just to get closer to the field's center.

The teams played a scoreless tie until late in the fourth quarter, when the Bears intercepted a pass and had a first down at Portsmouth's 7-yard line. The great Bronko Nagurski smashed for 5 yards, then carried the ball twice more without gaining anything.

On fourth down and goal from the 2, Nagurski went charging toward the line again, but he suddenly pulled up and threw a touchdown pass to Red Grange, who was standing all alone in the end zone.

The rules of 1932 said that a passer must be at least 5 yards behind the line of scrimmage when he threw the ball. The Portsmouth coach argued that Nagurski's pass was illegal, but the touchdown stood. Chicago got a safety in the closing minutes to win 9–0.

When the NFL held its annual pre-season meeting in 1933, Halas joined with George Preston Marshall of the Boston Redskins and Joe Carr, president of the league, to propose three rules changes:

1) Moving the goal posts from the back of the end zone to the goal line; 2) Legalizing the forward pass from anywhere behind the line of scrimmage; 3) Moving the ball 10 yards in-bounds after every out-of-bounds play. All three changes were adopted, resulting in an immediate increase in offense, scoring, and excitement.

Although rules are changed virtually every year, most of the changes are relatively insignificant tinkerings that don't mean a great deal to the average fan.

But there was one more big change needed to create pro football as we know and love it. Like the temporary changes that were forced by cold and snow in Chicago, only to become permanent after the season, the free substitution rule was originally caused by outside circumstances. Only, in this case, it was not a mere winter storm, but a world war.

It may seem strange that pro football should decide to try free substitution at a time when manpower was short because of World War II. But most of the available players were too old to be drafted. The great Bronko Nagurski, for example, returned to the Chicago Bears at the age of thirty-eight, after five years of retirement.

It would be tough for these geezers to go out there for sixty minutes, as they had in the good old days, and free substitution allowed them to go to the sidelines frequently to get some rest and perhaps sip some Geritol.

(Of course, not all of the players were ancient. Some of them were simply unfit for military service. For example, Irv Comp, Green Bay's chief passer during the war years, had only one eye.)

The rules-makers had no idea that free substitution would eventually lead to the two-platoon system, kicking specialists, special teams, situational substitution, and 47-man rosters.

Oddly, coaches didn't see the possibilities right away, either. The first to make a move toward the two-platoon system was Fritz Crisler of the University of Michigan in 1945, and he did it only out of desperation. Most of his players were too *young* for the draft, and Michigan was going up against an Army team that was loaded with talent, so Crisler decided to train some of his young linemen to play offense and some others to play defense. Michigan lost 21–14, but that was much closer than anyone had expected it to be.

In 1947, Michigan went all the way to the two-platoon system and finished second in the country. Other teams quickly followed suit. Colleges did away with free substitution in 1953, but pro football didn't. The wire services finally began picking offensive and defensive All-Pro teams in 1951.

So we've arrived at football pretty much as it is played today. Now let's step back in time once more and see how professional football came into existence.

Until about 1890, football was almost exclusively a college sport, ruled by the "Big Three," Harvard, Princeton, and Yale. But athletic clubs were proliferating across the country at that time, and many of them organized football teams. "Amateur" teams, of course—as far as the record shows, anyway.

The most important, for our purposes, was the Allegheny Athletic Association. Allegheny is now part of Pittsburgh, but at the time it was a separate city. Two of the chief organizers of the AAA were Yale men who had, in fact, been teammates of Walter Camp.

The AAA had a natural rivalry with the Pittsburgh Athletic Club. The teams played for the first time on October 21, 1892, and the 6–6 tie didn't make anyone very happy. The PAC had an outstanding player named "Stayer," whom nobody had ever heard of before. It turned out that he was A. C. Read, the captain of the Penn State team.

It's likely that he was paid. The AAA certainly thought so, and said as much. In the meantime, the Chicago Athletic Club football team was touring the East. Among its players were Knowlton "Snake" Ames and Ben "Sport" Donnelly, both formerly of Princeton, and the legendary W. W. "Pudge" Heffelfinger, who had been a three-time All-American guard at Yale.

There was a newspaper story that the PAC was offering money to Heffelfinger and Ames to play in the November 12 rematch with the AAA. But, when the teams showed up, Heffelfinger and Donnelly were wearing AAA uniforms (Ames was nowhere in sight), while the PAC team had three players who belonged to other clubs.

Instead of a football game, spectators were treated to a long shouting match, as each club accused the other of professionalism. A game was finally played, but all bets were off, literally—and there were reports that as much as $10,000 was riding on the game.

The AAA won. Heffelfinger had the game's only score. He jarred the ball loose with a tackle, picked it up and ran 35 yards for a touchdown.

Now we come to a great (well, pretty interesting, anyway) unsolved mystery. In 1961 or 1962, someone walked into the office of Dan Rooney, the general manager of the Pittsburgh Steelers. He said his name was Nelson Ross and he handed Rooney a 49-page manuscript.

Rooney read the manuscript with great interest. It documented the long rivalry between the AAA and the PAC and, most important, it said that Pudge Heffelfinger had been paid $500 for that 1892 game and was therefore the first (or at least the first known) professional football player.

When Rooney finished reading, his visitor was gone. Football historians have been looking for Nelson Ross, if that was his real name, ever since. They haven't found him. Or, at least, they haven't found anyone named Nelson Ross who will admit to having written the manuscript.

Shortly after the Pro Football Hall of Fame opened in 1963, Ross was proven right. Rummaging through a large amount of material that had been donated, Dick McCann, the Hall of Fame's first director, found a page from the AAA's 1892 account book that recorded a payment to Heffelfinger of $500 in cash for playing in that November 12 game.

The page also revealed that Sport Donnelly had been paid $250 for the AAA's game against Washington and Jefferson College on November 19.

Also among the papers that McCann found was the first known professional football contract. Signed and witnessed on October 4, 1893, the contract said, "I hereby agree to participate in all regularly scheduled football games of the Pittsburg [the correct spelling at that time] Athletic Club for the full season of 1893. As an active player I agree to accept a salary of $50 per contest and also acknowledge that I will play for no other club during PAC games."

Unfortunately, the contract was torn and the signature was illegible, but it's generally believed to have been that of Grand Dibert, a graduate of Swarthmore College who had been playing for the PAC since 1890.

Whoever Nelson Ross was, wherever he got his information, whether or not Pudge Heffelfinger was really the first professional player, the AAA's hiring of Heffelfinger for one important game set the pattern for the early days of professional football.

In larger cities, football teams were usually organized by athletic clubs that also offered other sports. But, as football spread into Ohio, Indiana, Michigan, and Wisconsin, many smaller cities and towns that didn't have athletic clubs also began to organize teams during the 1890s and early 1900s.

These "town teams" were clubs in their own right, and they were usually run as cooperatives: Members paid dues or chipped in money to pay expenses and planned to share profits, if there were any. They may also have hoped to make some money by betting on games.

Just as the AAA and the PAC brought in an extra player or two or three for the big game, town teams often hired outsiders for an important game or two. Local rivalries, such as the one between Pittsburgh and Allegheny, could inspire major spending.

Canton and Massillon, in Ohio, were big-time rivals in the early part of the century. In 1906, the Canton Bulldogs hired four players away from

Massillon to assure victory. Massillon won anyway, 12–6, and Canton backers who lost money accused the team's manager, Blondy Wallace, of conspiring with some of his players to throw the game.

That killed football in Canton until 1911, when a new town team was organized. In 1912, a young man named Jack Cusack became the team's manager. Cusack, as much as anyone, deserves the title "father of professional football," and he's the main reason the Pro Football Hall of Fame is located in Canton.

Cusack realized the only way to keep a good team intact for an entire season was to pay salaries to the players instead of asking them to take a cut of gate receipts. He made offers to most of the previous year's college All-Americans in 1915, but pro football had a bad reputation then, and most of them were reluctant to play.

However, Jim Thorpe, the legendary halfback from Carlisle Indian Institute, was willing and Cusack signed him for $250 a game. Canton's attendance, which had averaged about 1,200 before that, leaped to 6,000 and 8,000 at fifty cents apiece for the next two games, with a twenty-five-cent premium for reserved seats.

By 1916, the Canton Bulldogs could no longer be called a town team. There were players from Colgate, Dartmouth, Georgetown, Harvard, Michigan State, Syracuse, and Wisconsin on the roster.

World War I slowed the growth of professional football, but it resumed immediately after the war. By 1919, there were a number of supposed town teams in Pennsylvania, Ohio, Indiana, Michigan, Wisconsin, and Minnesota, stocked with ex-collegians who were undoubtedly being paid.

Players were usually hired for just one game at a time, so a teammate one week might suddenly become an opponent the following week. One player of the era said that every time his team played a game during the 1919 season, Notre Dame Coach Knute Rockne, who was still in his prime as a player, was on the other side.

On September 17, 1920, a group of team owners and managers gathered in Ralph Hay's Hupmobile showroom in Canton. They established a league called the American Professional Football Association (APFA), with Jim Thorpe as president. Thorpe was really just a figurehead chosen because of his publicity value.

The APFA wasn't very well organized in its first year of operation. In fact, there's some doubt about which teams were actually in the league. Teams scheduled their own games and, because of travel expenses, they tended to choose opponents who weren't too far from home.

There were no formal standings, but the Akron Pros, who had an 8–0–3 record during the regular season, won a four-team playoff series for the championship. Interestingly, Akron had a black player-coach, Fritz Pollard, a former Brown University All-American. He was the only black coach of a professional team until Art Shell took over the Los Angeles Raiders in 1989.

The APFA made a major step in 1921 by replacing Thorpe with Joe Carr. An employee of the Pennsylvania Railroad Company's Panhandle Division in Columbus, Ohio, Carr had organized a company team, the Columbus Panhandles, in 1905 and served as team manager. He had also been a minor-league baseball executive at one time.

At the 1922 annual meeting, George Halas of the Chicago Bears suggested adopting the name "National Football League," and the other owners agreed. That was also a significant year because Carr ordered teams to stop using players who were still eligible to play college football.

Carr ruled the NFL until his death in 1939, with the cooperation of team owners and managers, who fully accepted his leadership. One of Carr's ploys during the early years was to have "road teams" that weren't particularly good. These teams played all of their games on the road. Their role was like that of the Washington Generals in their tours with the Harlem Globetrotters—to lose. A couple of easy, one-sided victories in home games helped the "real" NFL teams to draw fans and make them happy.

During his regime, the NFL became truly professional. Carr opened a full-time office in Columbus, drafted a constitution and bylaws, adopted a standard player's contract similar to that used in professional baseball, and issued official standings every Monday.

His long-term goal was to move out of the small towns that established the league and into major cities. In 1925, he persuaded bookmaker Tim Mara to start a team in New York. (Bookmaking was then legal.)

The franchise cost $500. Some of Mara's friends told him it was foolish to get involved with professional football, but he responded, "An exclusive franchise to anything in New York City is worth more than $500."

However, he must have wondered. Playing in the Polo Grounds, the Giants could draw only one-tenth the crowds that watched major-college teams on Saturday and Mara lost about $20,000 during his first season.

Shortly after the season ended, the great halfback Harold "Red" Grange, known as the "Galloping Ghost," played his last game for the University of Illinois and signed a personal services contract with promoter C. C. "Cash and Carry" Pyle, who in turn assigned the contract to the Chicago Bears.

The Bears went on a post-season barnstorming tour with Grange. His appearance against the Giants at the Polo Grounds drew 73,651 fans, wiping out Mara's losses and giving him a profit of about $20,000. The cross-country tour won much-needed publicity for the NFL, and Grange's signing also encouraged other college players to try pro football.

Pyle wanted an NFL franchise in New York for the 1926 season but he was turned down, so he formed the American Football League, with Grange playing for Pyle's team, the New York Yankees. Grange drew crowds but no one else did, and the league folded after one season. The Yankees then joined the NFL.

The 1919 Green Bay team lines up in the T formation for a photographer. This first Packer squad was organized and coached by Curly Lambeau, who's at right halfback in the picture. *Stiller Photo/Collection of Lee L. Lefebvre*

It's probably hard for a modern fan to see much appeal in pro football as it was played during the 1920s and into the 1930s. Shutouts were the norm and scoreless ties weren't unusual. Of 116 NFL games in 1926, for example, there were 86 shutouts and 10 scoreless ties.

The Green Bay Packers, who won three consecutive championships from 1929 through 1931, were considered a pass-happy team by the standards of the era. Yet, in compiling a 12–0–1 record in 1929, they scored just 196 points, an average of 15.1 a game, and they attempted a grand total of 227 passes, an average of 17.5 per game.

The Packers almost won a fourth championship in 1932, but they lost out because of a glitch in the way standings were kept. They had a 10–3–1 record, while the Chicago Bears were 6–1–6 and the Portsmouth Spartans were 6–1–4. At the time, ties didn't count at all, so Chicago and Portsmouth were tied with .857 percentages while the Packers were at .769.

That set up the historic championship game in Chicago Stadium. Today, a tie counts as half a win and half a loss. Under that system, the Packers would have won the title outright with a .750 winning percentage to .727 for the Spartans and .692 for the Bears.

Because of the publicity created by the 1932 playoff game between Chicago and Portsmouth, owners decided there should be a championship game each year. In 1933, the league was split into two divisions, the Eastern and Western, and the division champions met in a post-season game to determine the league champion.

That was a new idea in professional sports, since copied by every other major league, in baseball, basketball, and hockey. Another new idea was the draft of college players, adopted in 1936 at the suggestion of Bert Bell, then the owner of the Philadelphia Eagles and later the NFL's first commissioner. (Until Bell was appointed in 1946, the league was ruled by a president, Joe Carr's title.)

The 1932 season was the worst of all in terms of scoring. The champion Bears averaged only 11.4 points a game and three of the league's eight teams averaged less than 7 points a game.

The rules changes of 1933, along with the introduction of a slimmer ball that was easier to pass, brought a gradual increase in scoring. The New York Giants averaged 17.4 points a game in winning the championship that season and the Packers became the first NFL team to average more than 20 points when they won the 1936 title.

The big cities began to come aboard during the 1930s. The Dayton franchise moved to Brooklyn in 1930; the Boston Redskins entered the league in 1932; the Philadelphia Eagles and Pittsburgh Steelers (originally known as the Pirates) joined in 1933; the Portsmouth Spartans became the Detroit Lions in 1934; and the Cleveland Rams joined in 1937.

By 1939, when a sellout crowd of 32,729 fans watched the Green Bay Packers beat the New York Giants 27–0 for the championship, professional football was a genuinely major sport with its own following. The NFL received extensive coverage in major newspapers, games were broadcast live on radio, and Green Bay was (and still is) the only small city left in the league. The other franchises were in New York, Philadelphia, Pittsburgh, Washington, Cleveland, Detroit, and Chicago, which had two teams, the Bears and the Cardinals.

However, pro football still lagged far behind baseball in popularity for several reasons. With only eight teams in seven cities, geographical interest was obviously limited. Major-league baseball had sixteen teams in thirteen cities and there were also more than forty minor leagues across the country. Weather was another factor. Played in open stadiums in the North during the fall, pro football's attendance sometimes dropped from the thousands into the hundreds because of snow and cold.

That year, 1939, was important for a different reason, though no one could have foreseen it at the time. The Columbia-Princeton baseball game was televised in May of that year. It was the first televised sports event. Only a handful of people watched it, but a little more than a decade later television would cause an explosive growth in the popularity of pro football.

Before that happened, though, the NFL faced a new threat. The All-America Football Conference began operating in 1946, after the World War ended. The threat became a boon to the NFL in the long run. The AAFC had two teams on the West Coast, the Los Angeles Dons and the San Francisco 49ers and, because the new league had announced it would have a team in Cleveland, the NFL's Cleveland Rams moved to Los Angeles in 1946. For the first time, a major professional sport had franchises on the West Coast.

Also in 1946, black players reentered pro football for the first time since 1933. The Cleveland Browns signed fullback Marion Motley and guard Bill Willis while the Rams, in part to compete with the AAFC's Dons, signed two popular black players from UCLA, halfback Kenny Washington and end Woody Strode. (Interestingly, Washington had been a college roommate of Jackie Robinson, who was to integrate major-league baseball a year later.)

Perhaps most important, Paul Brown of the Cleveland Browns, the only coach ever to have a team named after him, brought a new level of professionalism to the sport. Brown hired the first full-time, year-round coaching staff. He made much more extensive use of scouting reports and game films than any coach had before him, and he was the first to use films of his own team in order to grade players on their performance in each game.

Brown left nothing to chance. His teams practiced recovering fumbles, catching tipped passes, and forming interference on an interception return as they would on a punt return. Classroom instruction was as important to Brown as practices and scrimmaging.

The Browns easily won all four AAFC championships. The team's success contributed to the demise of the AAFC, because there wasn't much fan interest in most other league cities. But, when the AAFC folded after the 1949 season, three of its teams—the Browns, the San Francisco 49ers, and the Baltimore Colts—entered the NFL.

A lot of people thought the Browns would be much less successful facing the stiffer opposition of the NFL. But they beat the defending champion Philadelphia Eagles 35–10 in their first regular-season game, and they went on to win the NFL title by defeating the Los Angeles Rams 30–28. In their first six NFL seasons, the Browns went to the championship game each year and won it three times.

Naturally, other coaches began copying Brown's techniques. In fact, the typical NFL team's day-by-day and hour-by-hour preparation for a game nowadays is very similar to what Brown began doing in 1946.

Television began in a small way in 1951, when the Dumont Network broadcast five regular-season NFL games and the championship game. Worried about the effect of television on attendance, Bert Bell instituted a policy of blacking out broadcasts in a team's home area, but a federal court ruled that such a policy was a violation of antitrust laws.

In 1954, Dumont telecast twelve games, one on each Sunday of the regular season. CBS did some games the following year, when NBC broadcast the championship, but in general teams controlled the rights to their own games during the 1950s and most telecasts were local.

The most important game in NFL history may have been the famous championship contest between the Baltimore Colts and the New York Giants on December 28, 1958. The score was tied 17–17 at the end of four periods and the television audience was growing as word spread that an exciting game was being played.

While 64,185 watched at Yankee Stadium, more than 50 million people were tuned in on their television sets when Baltimore fullback Alan Ameche scored on a 1-yard touchdown run at 8:17 of overtime to give the Colts a 23–17 victory. All of a sudden, pro football had millions of fans.

Television and pro football were made for each other. By the 1950s, the sport was much more exciting and more popular than it had been before World War II. A major reason was the modern T formation, which had been introduced by the Chicago Bears in 1940 after a lot of early experimentation.

Chicago's 73–0 victory over the Washington Redskins in the NFL championship game that year wasn't entirely due to the T formation, but it persuaded a lot of coaches that they should switch to it. By 1946, the Pittsburgh Steelers were the only professional team not using it, and the Steelers finally switched in 1952.

Free substitution, combined with the T formation, created the consummate football hero, the quarterback, the man who handles the ball on every play; who gets much of the praise or blame for his team's fortune or misfortune; and who is the center of the television picture at the beginning of every play.

Baltimore quarterback Johnny Unitas became something of a folk hero because of that overtime championship game, coolly completing all seven of his passes on the twelve-play drive that led to the winning touchdown. He was the first in a long line.

Football works much better than baseball on television because most of the action takes place in a much smaller area, not far from the line of scrimmage. The camera can easily show the entire offensive alignment and much of the defense, and it can move to follow the action, much as the spectator's eyes move to follow it. Covering baseball requires a whole sequence of cuts: From the batter swinging, to the fly ball in the air, to a closeup of the fielder catching, to a shot of a base runner tagging up at third, and so on. It's a completely different experience from watching a game at the ballpark and not nearly as satisfying.

While some NFL owners had their doubts about television, fearing it would cut into attendance, a rival league took full advantage of it and showed how important the medium and its money could be.

Oil millionaire Lamar Hunt wanted to buy a new NFL franchise for Dallas in 1959, but he was told the league wasn't interested in expanding. He then tried to work out a deal for the St. Louis Cardinals (originally the Chicago Cardinals), with the idea that he'd move the franchise, but that fell through.

However, Hunt learned that Max Winter of Minneapolis, Bob Howsam of Denver, and Bud Adams of Houston had also tried unsuccessfully to buy the Cardinals. He suggested forming a new league, and all three agreed.

Ironically, the announcement that a new league was in the works was made by NFL Commissioner Bell. He had come up with the idea of pooling television rights, but the league needed federal legislation to become exempt from antitrust laws. To bolster his contention that the NFL wasn't a monopoly, Bell told a congressional committee in July of 1959 that there would soon be another major professional football league.

When the American Football League opened for business in 1960, Minneapolis was replaced by Oakland because Max Winter had been awarded an NFL franchise. There were also teams in Boston, Buffalo, Los Angeles, and New York in addition to those in Dallas, Denver, and Houston.

Bert Bell, who had once owned the Philadelphia Eagles and had also been a part owner of the Pittsburgh Steelers, died of a heart attack in 1959 while attending a game between the two teams. His replacement as commissioner was a relative unknown named Alvin "Pete" Rozelle, who had entered pro football as the public relations director for the Los Angeles Rams, eventually becoming the team's general manager.

A lot of people thought Rozelle would be an interim commissioner while the NFL owners searched for someone else. But, because of his skills as a negotiator and lobbyist, he held the job for nearly thirty years.

Bell had run the NFL out of a back-room office in Bala Cynwyd, Pennsylvania. Rozelle moved the office to New York City and hired the first full-time staff. Even more than Bell, Rozelle realized how important television was going to be to the future of professional football. In his first year, the Chicago Cardinals were allowed to move to St. Louis. The main reason for the move was that, under the NFL's policy of blacking out broadcasts in a team's home area, games were never telecast in Chicago because one of the city's two teams was always at home.

The AFL, in the meantime, had landed a five-year television contract with ABC that virtually ensured the new league's survival for at least that period of time.

In 1961, Rozelle successfully lobbied Congress for passage of the Sports Antitrust Broadcast Act, which specifically allowed professional basketball, football, and hockey leagues to sell their television rights as a package. (Baseball wasn't included in the legislation because the sport had already won exemption from antitrust laws through a Supreme Court decision.)

At first, the policy of the NFL and its network, CBS, was to ignore the AFL completely. AFL scores weren't shown or mentioned during NFL telecasts. However, other media were so critical of the policy that it changed in 1962, after the NFL and CBS had agreed on a two-year, 4.65-million-a-year contract. Another two-year contract in 1964 raised the amount to $14 million. The same year, the AFL and NBC agreed on a five-year contract for $7.2 million a year, to begin in 1965.

Both leagues expanded in 1966, the NFL adding the Atlanta Falcons and the AFL adding the Miami Dolphins. Joe Foss, a former governor of South Dakota who had served as the AFL's commissioner from the beginning of the league, resigned early that year and was replaced by Al Davis, formerly coach and general manager of the Oakland Raiders.

Davis decided to launch an all-out attack on the NFL. He put together a war chest of money from all of his league's teams to sign NFL quarterbacks to future contracts. Within three months of his taking over, seven of them had agreed to sign.

However, peace talks between the leagues had begun without Davis' knowledge. On June 8, 1966, Pete Rozelle announced that an agreement to merge had been worked out. Although a complete merger couldn't take place until 1970, when the AFL's television contract expired, they agreed to a mutual draft of college players and, most important, to a post-season AFL-NFL championship game, which soon became known as the Super Bowl.

Davis was angered by the deal and by the fact that Rozelle was to be commissioner of the merged league. He immediately resigned and, within a short time, returned to the Raiders as managing general partner.

Rozelle again demonstrated his lobbying skills, getting Congress to pass another antitrust exemption to allow the merger. The two legislators most active in getting the bill passed were Senator Russell Long and Congressman Hale Boggs, both of Louisiana. Three weeks later, New Orleans was awarded an expansion franchise.

When the merger took place in 1970, the Baltimore Colts, Cleveland Browns, and Pittsburgh Steelers of the NFL joined the ten former AFL teams in the American Football Conference, while the remaining thirteen NFL teams formed the National Football Conference.

Each conference was aligned into three divisions, with the division champions and the two second-place teams with the best record—the so-called "wild card" teams—going into the playoffs to determine conference champions, who meet in the Super Bowl for the NFL title.

The Super Bowl quickly became the most watched American sports event and one of the most popular television events of any kind. In a list of the thirty-two top-rated television shows in history, the Super Bowl appears fourteen times.

The NFL's Green Bay Packers won the first two Super Bowls rather easily and the Baltimore Colts were big favorites to win Super Bowl III over the AFL's New York Jets. However, Jets' quarterback Joe Namath, who had brought the league its first major taste of publicity by signing a $400,000 contract in 1964, guaranteed victory and produced a 16–7 win. In Super Bowl IV, the last before the merger, the AFL's Kansas City Chiefs beat the Minnesota Vikings of the NFL 23–7.

From the time of the merger until 1994, CBS had television rights to NFC games, NBC telecast AFC games, and ABC had the immensely popular "Monday Night Football." As television revenue continued to grow through the 1970s and into the 1980s, the NFL Players' Association became more and more militant.

Players went on strike for part of the 1974 exhibition season and they struck again just before the 1975 regular season. That strike lasted only four days and no scheduled games were canceled or postponed.

A new collective bargaining agreement was reached in 1977. It expired in 1982, when the players staged their first regular season strike. The strike lasted fifty-seven days, with the players winning a higher minimum salary, severance pay, and a special fund of $50 million as a one-time bonus.

The season was extended into January, but the schedule still had to be shortened from sixteen games to nine. The NFL recouped much of its lost television money and most of its former public interest by having eight teams from each conference go into the playoffs.

George Halas said of the owners in a 1970 interview, "They thought in terms of the league, and that's one of the reasons why the league has been so successful—why the game has grown into the greatest sport in the country."

But "league think," as some critics derisively called it, was derailed in 1980, when Al Davis asked permission to move the Oakland Raiders to Los Angeles. NFL bylaws required a three-quarters vote of teams to allow a franchise to move and Davis was turned down.

Davis tried to move the team anyway, but was blocked by an injunction. He joined the Los Angeles Memorial Coliseum Commission in an antitrust suit against the league. In 1982, a federal jury found the NFL guilty of violating antitrust laws and the Raiders went to Los Angeles after all. That opened the way for the Baltimore Colts to move to Indianapolis without league approval in 1984.

Despite dissension among owners and on-and-off labor problems, the NFL continued to be a major success story through most of the 1980s. Television money grew to about $400 million a year in 1982, with all three major over-the-air networks involved, and to nearly $500 million a year in 1987, when the ESPN, and TNT cable networks also joined the mix.

There was some question about the television future, as the 1990s began with declining ratings and networks cutting back on their spending. But 1993 ended on an upbeat note for the NFL. In a surprise move, the Fox Network outbid CBS for the NFC games by agreeing to pay $395 million a year over a four-year period. Fox also hired the sport's most popular announcers, Pat Summerall and John Madden, away from CBS. With NBC, ABC, ESPN, and TNT all getting back into the act for four years, NFL television revenue increased by about 20 percent, to $1.1 billion a year. And the league announced that it would add two new franchises, the Jacksonville Jaguars (in the AFC's Central Division) and the Carolina Panthers (in the NFC's Western Division), in 1995.

A couple of dominant teams emerged in each decade, and it seemed that each successful team had its own formula for success. The Packers won five NFL championships during an eight-year period in the 1960s, along with the first two Super Bowls. Under Vince Lombardi, they built their victories by emphasizing execution of a relatively small number of plays.

Green Bay's powerful running attack, based on the power sweep, and the pinpoint passing of quarterback Bart Starr got most of the glory, but defense was an important element of the team's success.

In the early 1970s, the Miami Dolphins emerged as the league's best team. Like Lombardi, Miami's Don Shula emphasized the running game, but his attack was built primarily on running between the tackles with fullback Larry Csonka and halfback Jim Kiick. Mercury Morris occasionally relieved Kiick to add an outside running threat, and wide receiver Paul Warfield gave quarterback Bob Griese a deep passing threat to keep defenses honest.

In 1972, the Dolphins became the first team in NFL history to go undefeated through the regular season and the playoffs, winning all seventeen games, and they repeated as Super Bowl champions in 1973.

Then came the Pittsburgh Steelers. The "Steel Curtain" defense, led by tackle Joe Greene, linebackers Jack Lambert and Jack Ham, and defensive back Mel Blount, was the real strength of this dynasty, which also boasted the running of fullback Franco Harris and the strong arm of Terry Bradshaw, throwing to wide receivers Lynn Swann and John Stallworth. Chuck Noll's running offense featured trap plays and cutback running by the powerful Harris.

The Steelers were the first team to win four Super Bowls, after the 1974, 1975, 1978, and 1979 seasons, and they were acclaimed as the team of the decade.

The 1980s belonged to the San Francisco 49ers and the Washington Redskins. The 49ers, coached by Bill Walsh, used a ball-control passing attack that featured running back Roger Craig as a receiver. Quarterback Joe Montana ran the offense to near perfection as San Francisco won Super Bowls after the 1981, 1984, and 1988 seasons.

Walsh then retired and was replaced by George Seifert, who took the 49ers to a fourth Super Bowl victory after the 1989 season.

Joe Gibbs coached the Redskins to three Super Bowl wins using the one-back offense and an opportunistic defense. It's a tribute to the Gibbs system that Washington did it with three different starting quarterbacks.

The Redskins won Super Bowl XVII, after the 1982 season, behind Joe Theismann. Doug Williams, the first black quarterback to start in a Super Bowl, led them to victory after the 1987 season and Mark Rypien was the starter in their win after the 1991 season. Washington also went to Super Bowl XVIII, after the 1983 season, but lost to the Oakland Raiders.

A tremendous upheaval took place in Dallas when Jimmy Jones bought the Cowboys in 1989 and fired Tom Landry, who had coached the team through its first twenty-nine years of existence. Jimmy Johnson, a former teammate of Jones at the University of Arkansas, replaced Landry.

Emphasizing team speed, a swarming defense, the running of Emmitt Smith out of the I formation, and Troy Aikman's passes to wide receiver Michael Irvin, the Cowboys went from a 1–15 record in 1989 to Super Bowl victories after the 1992 and 1993 seasons.

Some observers predicted a Dallas dynasty, because the Cowboys had one of the youngest teams in the league. However, others doubted that there would ever be another genuine dynasty in the NFL because of extended free agency and the salary cap that went into effect before the 1994 season.

The Cowboys kept most of their front-line players, but they lost some important role players to free agency. They also lost Johnson, who quit because of an ongoing feud with Jones. He was replaced by Barry Switzer, the former University of Oklahoma coach who had left that school under fire in 1988, despite an excellent record, because of a number of scandals involving his players. Switzer guided the Cowboys to a 12–4 regular-season record, but they lost to the San Francisco 49ers in the NFC championship game. The 49ers went on to become the first team to win five Super Bowls, whipping the San Diego Chargers 49–26. Quarterback Steve Young, who had spent four seasons backing up Montana before taking over as the starter in 1991, finally emerged from Montana's long shadow. The NFL's player of the year in 1994, Young was also named Super Bowl MVP after throwing six touchdown passes to break Montana's record of five.

2 FS

The Rules of the Game

The impetus is not from a kick if a muff, bat, juggle, or illegal kick of any kicked ball (by a player of either team) creates a new momentum which sends it in touch.

That's the language that football rules are written in, a dialect of legalese that might be called "referese." Just as lawyer-legislators write laws in such a way as to create work for lawyers and judges, sports rules-makers write rules in such a way as to create work for officials and rules interpreters.

In this chapter, I intend to avoid "referese" and try to use relatively simple language to explain the essential rules of pro football.

THE FIELD

The football field is 120 yards long and 160 feet ($53\frac{1}{3}$ yards) wide, bounded by sidelines and end lines. There are goal lines marked 10 yards from each end of the field. The 10-yard area between a goal line and an end line is an end zone. Inbounds spots, better known as "hash marks," are located at 1-yard intervals, 70 feet, 9 inches from each side line. An area between the hash marks and the nearest side line is a side zone.

The field is marked by yard lines that extend all the way across it at 5-yard intervals.

27

THE COIN TOSS

Thirty minutes before kickoff, the team captains and the referee meet at the center of the field for the coin toss. The captain of the visiting team gets to call heads or tails. The winner of the toss has three options: Kick off, receive the kickoff, or choose which end of the field to defend. The loser is given the same options at the beginning of the second half.

Three minutes before the kickoff, the captains and referee meet again at the center of the field and the referee announces which team will kick off and which goal the receiving team will defend.

There's also a coin toss at the beginning of the sudden-death overtime period if the game ends in a tie.

THE CLOCKS

Each NFL stadium has a game clock that keeps official time. The line judge also keeps official time on a watch. If the stadium clock isn't correct—usually because the clock operator didn't stop it at the right time—the line judge tells the referee, who in turn tells the clock operator to reset the clock. If the clock doesn't work for some reason, the line judge takes over official timing.

Each of the four periods contains 15 minutes of playing time, with a 2-minute break between the first and second and the third and fourth quarters and a 12-minute intermission between halves.

There are two play clocks, one at each end of the field. The offense is usually given 40 seconds to put the ball in play. The play clock begins counting down when the referee marks the ball and blows his whistle.

The play clock is set at 25 seconds after a time out, change of possession, measurement, or any other unusual delay. If the offense doesn't snap the ball within the 40/25 second period, the infraction is delay of game.

STOPPING THE CLOCK

The game clock stops when:

1. The ball goes out of bounds
2. A team or an official calls time out
3. A forward pass is incomplete
4. The ball is dead in or beyond an end zone
5. The play comes to an end after a foul or infraction has occurred

6. A player makes a fair catch

7. A player is injured; in the case of an injury time-out, the player must leave the game for at least one play

THAT SPECIAL TWO MINUTES

When two minutes remain in a half, the referee calls time-out and gives the "two-minute warning" to both benches and to the spectators. The clock may actually run to a little under two minutes, since it can't be stopped while a play is in progress.

On a kickoff during the last two minutes, the clock doesn't start until the ball is touched by a player while it's inbounds. (Normally, it starts when the ball is kicked.)

At any other time in the game, a time-out isn't charged to a team when a player is injured. During the last two minutes, however, an injury time-out is a charged time-out. Each team is allowed three time-outs in each half. If a team has used all of its time-outs, one injury time-out is allowed. Each subsequent injury time-out is an infraction calling for a 5-yard penalty.

FREE KICKS

There are three types of free kicks. The kickoff is a special type, and by far the most common, but it has to be a place kick. (A drop kick is still allowed in the rules, but no one's done that since the 1940s.) A punt can be used on other types of free kicks.

The kickoff is used to put the ball in play from the kicking team's 30-yard line at the beginning of each half, after a field goal, and after a conversion attempt.

All the players on the kicking team must be behind the ball when it's kicked, and all the players on the receiving team must be at least 10 yards away. There's one exception: A soccer style kicker can plant his non-kicking foot in front of the ball before kicking.

Once the kick has gone 10 yards, it's a free ball and can be recovered by either team. The kicking team can't advance the ball after recovering.

If the kick doesn't go 10 yards, it's an infraction calling for a 5-yard penalty, unless a player on the receiving team touches it. If it goes out of bounds before reaching the goal line, the receivers have the option of taking over at their own 40-yard line or at the spot where it went out.

After a safety has been scored against a team, that team puts the ball in play with a free kick from its own 20-yard line. A punt is almost always used in that case. It's rarely seen, but a team can also make a free kick immediately after one of its players has made a fair catch, and it's possible to score a field goal in that situation.

If either of these free kicks goes out of bounds, the receiving team can take the ball at the spot where it went out or at a spot 30 yards beyond the kicking point.

THE SCRIMMAGE

Except on a free kick, the ball is always put in play with a center snap from scrimmage. The offensive team must have at least seven players on the line of scrimmage and any player, except the quarterback, who isn't on the line has to be at least 1 yard behind it. The infraction is *illegal formation.*

The neutral zone is an area, the length of the ball, between the offensive and defensive lines. If a defensive player enters the neutral zone and makes contact with an offensive player before the snap, he is guilty of *encroachment.* If a player is in the neutral zone when the ball is snapped, he is *offside.* An exception is made for the center (called the "snapper" in the official rules), who is allowed to be over his own line, represented by the back tip of the ball, as long as he's not over the defense's line, represented by the front tip.

One offensive player can be in motion at the snap, provided he's at least 1 yard behind the line and is moving laterally or away from the line of scrimmage. Forward movement by such a player, or movement by two or more players, at the snap is *illegal motion.*

FALSE START

This has to be a section by itself, because it covers a multitude of sins by the offense.

First, a personal note: I hate the way this infraction is handled. A false start is a so-called dead ball foul. Even if the ball is snapped and action takes place, the legal falsehood is that *absolutely nothing happened* after an official (usually the head linesman) called the infraction.

I've seen a number of situations where the defense was, in effect, penalized for the offense's infraction, because quite often the players don't hear the whistle. For example: Third down and short yardage, the offense runs a play into the line, it gets stuffed for no gain, and the team will have to punt.

But wait: There was a false start. The play didn't count—*it never happened*—and the offense is penalized 5 yards. Some penalty. On third and six, a pass is completed for a first down, and the offense keeps the ball.

Anyway, I feel strongly that a false start should be treated exactly like illegal motion or offside. Let the play go on and then give the defensive team the option of accepting or declining the penalty.

End of long personal note. Back to complete objectivity and neutrality.

The general rule is that no player on the offensive team can make a movement that "simulates the start of a play" before the ball is snapped. It used to be that a false start was almost always called on an offensive lineman who lurched forward before the snap. Because of today's ferocious pass rushes, it's now more often called on a lineman who flinches or rocks back from his stance to get into pass protection.

A false start can also be called on the quarterback if he jerks his head, pulls away from center, or barks a "Hut" more loudly than normal in an attempt to pull the defense offside. For that matter, the punter and the holder on a place kick can be called for the infraction. Once the punter holds out his hands to receive the ball, for example, he can't pull them back as if he's catching the ball if it hasn't yet been snapped.

Occasionally, a false start is called on the center. He has to snap the ball with a quick, continuous motion; any kind of hitch in his delivery is a false start. He's also not allowed to move his feet abruptly until the ball has left his hands.

Once an offensive interior lineman has taken his stance—called the "set position"—he can no longer move until the snap. Backs and wide receivers are allowed to shift to new positions, but they have to be set for at least one second before the snap takes place.

FIRST DOWN

When a team takes over possession, it has four downs on which to gain 10 yards or score. If the team fails on fourth down, the ball is awarded to the other team. This is known as "losing the ball on downs."

The first down markers are two rods connected by a 10-yard length of chain. One marker is set at the point where the series began and the other marks the "necessary line" that the team has to reach to get another first down and another series of downs. A third rod, the down marker, marks the present line of scrimmage and shows what down it is.

Assistant officials called "rod men" handle the first down markers and the "box man" handles the down marker and first down box. They're supervised by the head linesman.

If the offense appears to be close to first-down yardage, the referee calls an official time-out for a measurement. The linesman picks up a link of chain that's exactly on a yard line and brings it out to where the ball is, accompanied by the rod men. He then puts the link on the yard line at that point and the chain is stretched out to determine whether the team made a first down. Since the spot of the ball is its very front tip, it's a first down if that tip so much as touches the marker.

OUT OF BOUNDS

The out-of-bounds rule is really quite simple: A runner is out of bounds if he is touching a sideline or endline, or if he touches anything, other than another player, that is on or outside the line. The ball is out of bounds under the same circumstances and when it's in the possession of a runner who is out of bounds.

About the only time controversy arises over the out-of-bounds rule is when a receiver catches the ball near a sideline. He has to have clear possession of the ball with both feet inbounds. It sometimes appears that a receiver has made a good catch but the pass is ruled incomplete because he was juggling the ball as he went out of bounds.

SPOTTING THE BALL

The common misconception is that a ball carrier is down only when his knee touches the ground, but the rulebook says he's down when any part of his body except his hands or feet touch the ground after he has made contact with a defensive player.

He's also down if he falls and makes no effort to get up and advance the ball, if he goes out of bounds, if his forward progress is stopped by defending players, or if he slides feet first as a signal declaring himself down. (That, of course, is a maneuver by the quarterback to avoid injury.)

The ball is usually spotted at the point it reached when the runner was declared down. That is, if he's tackled and his knee touches at the 50-yard line, the ball may be spotted a half yard farther downfield. The position of the ball, not the runner's knee, determines the spot.

This is true even if the runner goes out of bounds. For example, if a runner falls down and his foot touches the sideline at his own 20-yard line, the ball may be spotted a yard or so beyond the 20 because that's where *it* was located at the time.

A few words about forward progress: When the ball carrier is absolutely stopped by defenders and obviously can't go any farther, even if he hasn't gone down, the ball is dead at that point and pushing him back has no effect on the spot. However, if he loses ground on his own to evade a tackler and is eventually brought down behind the point of his farthest advance, he gets no credit for forward progress.

If a loose ball goes out of bounds, it's usually spotted at the point where it crossed the sideline. But if the ball is fumbled forward and goes out of bounds, the spot is at the point of the fumble.

When a loose ball stops and no player tries to recover it within an instant or two, a whistle blows and the ball is dead at that spot. This usually happens on a punt; in that case, the ball goes to the receiving team. On any other kind of play, it goes to the team that was last in possession.

BLOCKING, TACKLING, AND HOLDING

The runner is allowed to use his hands and arms to try to fend off tacklers, but no other offensive player can push an opponent, grab him, or encircle part of his body with an arm. The infraction is *offensive holding*.

A block below the knees is usually legal, if the blocker is in front of the blockee. But there is an *illegal chop block*, which most often occurs on or near the line of scrimmage. If one offensive player is blocking a defender, a second offensive player cannot use a chop block on that defender.

There's also the *illegal crack back block*. The usual scenario: A wide receiver starts down the field as if he's on a pass route. But the play is a sweep, and a linebacker moves laterally to stop it. The wide receiver comes back and hits him with a block below the waist. Coaches were very fond of this trick—at least, offensive coordinators were—because it was about the only way a 180-pounder could effectively block a 240-pounder, but it caused so many injuries that it was outlawed. The rule applies only within 5 yards of the line of scrimmage.

Blocking from behind and below the waist is usually *clipping*. However, it's allowed in "close line play," which means in the area from offensive tackle to offensive tackle and within three yards of the line of scrimmage.

When the ball changes hands on a kick, interception, or fumble, blocks below the waist are prohibited.

A defensive player is obviously allowed to tackle the runner, and he may also tackle a potential runner who has pretended to take a hand-off and is running into the line. He can't tackle anyone else, but he is allowed to use his hands and arms to ward off someone who's trying to block him.

"Ward off" is a key phrase. It doesn't include aggression against an offensive player, such as using a slap to the head or a blow with the forearm. Those infractions and many others are lumped together as "personal fouls."

Defenders are allowed to block offensive players. It usually happens on a sweep or other type of play to the outside, when a defensive player simply wants to take a blocker out of the play so someone else can make the tackle. However, a receiver who's stationed more than 2 yards outside the offensive tackle can't be blocked below the waist.

Defensive holding is most commonly called when a defensive player grabs a receiver to keep him from breaking away. However, it can also be called when a defender grabs a blocker and throws him aside, or if he tackles a back when there was no fake hand-off.

FORWARD PASSES

A forward pass can be thrown only on a play from scrimmage, and it must be thrown from behind the line of scrimmage. The crucial factor is where the passer's hand is when he releases the ball. That is, he might have a foot over the line, but if the point of release is behind the line, it's a legal pass.

Only one forward pass can be thrown on a play. In a 1993 playoff game, Phil Simms of the New York Giants had a pass batted back to him. He caught the ball and threw it again. That was an *illegal forward pass*.

To qualify as an eligible receiver, an offensive player has to be stationed on one end of the line of scrimmage or in the backfield. The quarterback isn't an eligible receiver if he takes a hand-to-hand snap from center, but he is eligible if he's positioned more than 1 yard behind the line, as in the shotgun formation. The pass has to be touched first by an eligible receiver or a defender. Once a defender touches the ball, any offensive player can touch or catch it.

Ineligible receivers cannot be downfield when the ball leaves the passer's hand. There is a loophole here: If an offensive lineman is blocking a defender, he can push him downfield and cross the line in the process, but as soon as he loses contact, he has to retreat behind the line again.

In the early days of the "bump and run," defensive backs were allowed to make repeated contact with receivers, all over the field. Now, however, a defender is allowed to contact a receiver only once, within 5 yards of the line of scrimmage. Doing it more than once, or after the receiver is more than 5 yards downfield, is *illegal contact*.

One of the most controversial calls in football is interference, because a lot is left to the official's judgment. The rule explicitly says that both the receiver and the defender have a right to the ball. If they're both legitimately trying to make the catch, a great deal of incidental contact is allowed.

Interference can be called only after the ball has left the passer's hand. If a defender tackles a receiver before he's touched the ball, it's *defensive pass interference*. It's also interference if he deliberately gets in the receiver's path to the ball. In man-to-man coverage, defensive backs are taught to look at the receiver, not the passer. As a result, a defender is sometimes caught with his back to the passer when the ball is thrown. In that situation, he's not allowed to hold up his hands to block the receiver's vision.

In general, the same rules apply to the receiver. *Offensive pass interference* is most commonly called when he uses his hands to "push off" on a defender in order to make a cut to the ball.

Interference isn't supposed to be called if the pass is "clearly uncatchable." Once the pass has been touched by an eligible receiver or a defender, there can be no pass interference.

If the passer, while in the pocket, deliberately throws the ball away to avoid a sack, it's *intentional grounding*. He is allowed to throw it away, though, if he's out of the pocket. "Out of the pocket" means beyond the original position of the tight end or the offensive tackle, if there is no tight end on that side of the field. The pass, however, has to land near or across the line of scrimmage; the passer can't simply throw the ball into the ground in front of him.

The one time he *can* throw the ball into the ground is when his team wants to stop the clock without calling a time-out. Immediately after taking the snap from center, he has to throw it forward and down to accomplish that.

Once the passer has thrown the ball, he is essentially protected from defenders. A defensive player can run into him if his charge began before the ball was released and, in the judgment of the referee, he was unable to stop because of his momentum. Even then, however, the contact must be minimal. He can't, for example, grab the quarterback and throw him violently to the ground; that's *roughing the passer*.

A defender is also not allowed to deliberately roll into the passer's legs or to tackle him from the knees down unless it's absolutely necessary. If, for example, the defender has fallen or been blocked to the ground, he can grab the quarterback's lower legs in an attempt to tackle him.

The passer is also protected from having defenders gang up on him before he throws the ball. If one defensive player has the quarterback securely in his grasp, so that he could bring him down if he wanted to, the referee blows his whistle to stop the play. The "grasp and control" rule, as it's called, is more strictly interpreted now than it used to be. When it was originally put into the rule book, referees at times blew the whistle a little too fast, just as the passer was breaking away or throwing a complete pass.

BACKWARD (LATERAL) PASSES AND FUMBLES

As far as the NFL rulebook is considered, any pass that doesn't go forward is a backward pass, even if it goes sideways. But the average fan calls such a pass a "lateral," meaning sideways, even if it goes backwards. Any number of backward passes, or laterals, can be thrown by any number of players on any play.

A lateral is usually part of a designed play. Every team has running plays on which the quarterback tosses or pitches the ball to another back rather than handing it off. There are also a couple of fairly standard trick plays involving laterals. For example, the quarterback straightens up from center and throws the ball overhand to a wide receiver who has retreated 3 or 4 yards behind the line of scrimmage. Since that pass is a lateral, the wide receiver can now throw a forward pass.

If a lateral isn't caught, it's treated exactly as a fumble. The ball is live and can be recovered and advanced by either team. As with a fumble, if it goes out of bounds, the ball belongs to the team that last had possession.

When a player fumbles on a fourth-down play from scrimmage, he's the only offensive player who can advance the ball after recovering it. If the fumble goes forward and one of his teammates recovers it, the ball comes back to the spot where the fumble occurred.

Those rules were put in to prevent a player from deliberately fumbling, after failing to pick up a first down, in the hope that a teammate would recover it or pick it up and advance it to first-down yardage.

If a fumble goes out of bounds, the ball belongs to the team that last had possession, *not* the team that last touched it. For example: A Packer running back fumbles and a Bear linebacker, in an attempt to recover, knocks it out of bounds. The ball belongs to the Packers, because the Bears never actually had possession.

PUNTING

Teams often used to punt on third down and sometimes even on second down when they were deep in their own territory. Now, of course, a punt is always a fourth-down play, because offenses have progressed to the point that teams are reluctant to give up the ball unless they absolutely have to.

Only the two end men on the punting team can go beyond the line of scrimmage before the ball is kicked. An end man is the player who's farthest from the center on his side of the field. He can be a lineman, the equivalent of a split end, or a back, the equivalent of a flanker. If any other player crosses the line before the kick, he's an *ineligible downfield*.

If a punt is blocked, it's a loose ball and either team can recover and advance the ball. However, the kicking team still has to gain its first-down yardage to retain possession. If a member of the kicking team recovers the ball behind the line of scrimmage, the receiving team takes over on downs.

Once the kick crosses the line of scrimmage, it's considered a punt, even if it's been partially blocked. The kicking team technically cannot recover the ball, or even touch it, before it's been touched by a player on the receiving team. The penalty for an *illegal touch*, however, is minor: The ball is dead at the spot of touching and possession goes to the receiving team.

If a player on the receiving team is the first to touch the ball without actually gaining possession, it becomes a free ball and can be recovered by either team. The receiving team can advance the ball, but the kicking team can't. This is technically a "muff." It most often comes up when a receiver tries to catch the ball and it goes through his hands. If he actually catches the ball and loses possession later, it's a fumble and either team can recover and advance.

Like the passer, the punter is protected from defensive contact after the ball leaves his possession. If a defender accidentally makes relatively minor contact with him, the infraction is *running into the kicker*. Violent contact is *roughing the kicker*.

There's no infraction if the defender is blocked into the kicker or if he touches the kicked ball before making contact.

FAIR CATCH

A kick receiver can signal a fair catch by raising a hand over his head and waving it from side to side. Players on the punting team are not allowed to touch him (although minor accidental contact may be ignored) and he's not allowed to run with the ball after catching it. However, he can run with it after it touches the ground or if it hits a member of the kicking team while still in flight.

Even if the receiver doesn't signal a fair catch, he has to be given a chance to catch the ball. If he's hit before he has that chance or if he's hit after signaling a fair catch, the infraction is *interfering with a fair catch*.

Although most commonly seen on punts, a fair catch can also be called on a kickoff or other free kick. That usually happens on a high, short kick that's going to be fielded by a lineman who has no intention of running it back, for fear of fumbling.

Several special rules apply here. The receiver has to make a distinct signal. If, for example, he simply sticks his right arm into the air and then lowers it, the call is *invalid fair catch signal*. After signaling, even if the signal is invalid, the receiver cannot advance the ball, although he's allowed to take one step in order to keep his balance. Any attempt to run back the kick is *delay of game*.

A receiver who has signaled for a fair catch isn't allowed to block an opponent until after the ball has been touched by someone. Before that rule was put into effect, it was common for a receiver to make the fair catch signal on a punt landing near his goal line and then make a block to keep the ball from being touched before it reached the end zone.

When a fair catch is made, the receiving team has the option to try a free kick rather than running a play from scrimmage. If the free kick is a place kick, a field goal can be scored.

TOUCHBACK

The key word in defining the difference between a touchback and a safety is "impetus." If the ball is dead in or beyond the end zone of the team in possession, it's a touchback if the other team provided the impetus that put it there.

The touchback is seen most often on a punt or kickoff. A kickoff, however, is a free ball and a receiver actually has to have possession of the ball in the end zone to get a touchback. If a player from the kicking team recovers in the end zone, it's a touchdown.

An interception behind the goal line also results in a touchback, even if the player who intercepted tries to run the ball back and is tackled in the end zone. If a player fumbles into the opponents' end zone and the ball either goes out of the end zone or is recovered by the opposition, it's a touchback.

After a touchback, the ball is put in play on the offense's 20-yard line.

TOUCHDOWN

Football's most exciting play is rather simple to describe. If a player carries the ball, catches a pass, or recovers a loose ball while inbounds across the opposition's goal line, it's a touchdown.

There are two types of controversy that can arise. The goal line has a mythical extension above the field, the "plane of the goal line," and if the ball touches or crosses that plane while in possession of a player, it's immediately dead and a touchdown is awarded. Sometimes there's debate about whether the ball actually did break the plane, and viewers are treated to quite a few slow-motion replays.

Since the end line, as well as the sideline, is out of bounds, a receiver who catches the ball deep in the end zone has to have both feet inside the end line when he takes possession in order for it to be a legal catch and a touchdown.

A touchdown, of course, is worth 6 points, but it's often considered to be worth 7 points because the extra point, or conversion, is almost automatic. NFL teams made 98.2% of their extra point attempts in 1993.

FIELD GOAL

Most of the rules that apply to a punt also apply to a field goal. In fact, both are covered under the same heading, "Scrimmage Kick," in the official rule book. But, because a field goal is an attempt to score, the same rules rarely come into play.

A place kick or drop kick has to be used on a field goal attempt, and no kicking tee is allowed. To be successful, the kick has to pass over the crossbar and between the outer edges of the goal posts. As with the goal line, the goal posts are considered to extend indefinitely above the playing field, though they're only 30 feet high. The crossbar is 10 feet above the field and is 18 feet, 6 inches wide.

There are some restrictions on how the defending team can attempt to block a kick. Defenders who line up within 1 yard of the line of scrimmage can leap, but a player who lines up farther back than that is not allowed to take a running start and leap. Players are also not allowed to jump or stand on one another, and a defender cannot leap up to deflect the ball just as it's about to pass over the crossbar.

Both the holder and the kicker are protected from defensive contact, as the punter is, after the kick.

It rarely happens, but a short field goal can be run back, just like a punt, and a player can call a fair catch, as on a punt.

CONVERSION

This term goes back to the very, very early days of football, when it was still basically Rugby and a touchdown didn't count for anything; it simply gave the team a free kick at goal. If the free kick was successful, the touchdown had been converted into a score—hence "conversion."

Then a touchdown became worth 1 point, a successful conversion 4 points. As time went on, the value of the touchdown gradually increased and the value of the conversion decreased until it became the "extra point." The term had almost died out when the 2-point conversion was introduced into college football in 1958. Then the word "conversion" came back strong, because no one wanted to call it a "2-point extra point" or, perhaps even worse, "the extra 2 points." The 2-point conversion, scored by running or passing from the 3-yard line, is still part of college football. It was adopted by the American Football League in 1960 but dropped with the AFL-NFL merger in 1970. Over twenty years later, NFL owners voted 23–4 to adopt the 2-point conversion rules for the 1994 season.

In pro football, the conversion, or point after touchdown, is a special kind of field goal, worth 1 point. The ball is put in play from the opposition's 2-yard line, unless there has been a penalty on a previous attempt.

Once the attempt has clearly failed, the ball is dead in pro football and it's time for a kickoff. In college football, however, it remains alive and the defensive team can score. If, for example, the extra point kick is blocked, the defensive team can run it back for 1 point. If there's an interception or fumble recovery on a 2-point conversion attempt, the defensive team can run it back for 2 points.

Although a kick is almost always intended in pro football, two points can be scored on a run or a pass. If the holder fumbles the ball, or if the kick is blocked, any player on the kicking team can recover and advance it into the end zone to score the points. All the rules that apply on any play from scrimmage also apply on the two-point attempt.

SAFETY

The key word, "impetus," has already been discussed under the touchback. If the ball is dead in or beyond a team's end zone while in that team's possession, it's a safety if that team provided the impetus that put it there.

A safety most commonly occurs when a passer or ball carrier is tackled or goes out of bounds in his own end zone. It's also a safety if a player fumbles and the ball goes out of bounds in the end zone. (And remember that the end line, as well as the sideline, is out of bounds.)

Certain infractions committed in the end zone also result in a safety. For example, a player intercepts a pass in the end zone and attempts to lateral to a teammate, but the ball goes forward. It's an *illegal forward pass* and a safety. Or an offensive lineman, retreating into the end zone to protect the passer, is guilty of holding—that's also a safety.

PERSONAL FOULS

Many of the infractions already discussed, such as roughing the passer, fall under the general category of personal fouls. The phrase includes a variety of potentially harmful acts, also classified as unnecessary roughness, such as piling on top of the runner, kicking, tripping, using the helmet as a weapon, grabbing and pulling on the face mask, or making unnecessary contact with a player who is clearly out of bounds.

UNSPORTSMAN-LIKE CONDUCT

Unsportsman-like conduct is the general phrase for a number of infractions, among them using abusive language or gestures toward officials or other players; baiting or taunting an opponent; prolonged, excessive, and premeditated celebration; any act or sound by the defense intended to make it difficult for offensive players to hear the snap count; hiding the ball under clothing or equipment; and aiming a punch or kick at another player, even if no contact results.

ODDS AND ENDS

There are a few infractions that don't fit comfortably under any of the above headings. A player isn't allowed to enter the game while play is in progress and a player leaving the game must go to his own bench. He can't leave the field on the opponents' side or through either end zone.

Of course, a team can't have more than eleven players on the field while play is in progress. It also used to be against the rules to have fewer than eleven, but that's no longer the case.

No player is allowed to bat or punch a loose ball (except a forward pass in flight) toward the opposition's end zone while it's in the field of play or in any direction if it's in an end zone. Deliberately kicking a loose ball is also not allowed.

PALPABLY UNFAIR ACT

Since rules can't cover every possibility, the "palpably unfair act" is written into the book to allow officials to deal with strange things that might come up. In the 1954 Cotton Bowl, for example, Dickie Moegle of Rice was running down the sideline with a clear field to the end zone when Tommy Lewis of Alabama came off the bench and tackled him.

It was ruled a palpably unfair act, Rice was awarded a touchdown, and Lewis was thrown out of the game. After consulting with other officials, the referee can impose any penalty that he considers equitable.

PENALTIES

Announcers often say, "There's a penalty on the play," but that's not technically correct. A foul or infraction has been committed, and a penalty may result, but the team that was offended against usually has the option to accept or decline the penalty.

Sometimes a foul is committed without even being noticed by the announcers and most fans. For example, if a member of the kicking team is the first player to touch a punt after it has crossed the line of scrimmage, the foul is illegal touching and the penalty is that the ball goes to the receiving team at the spot where it was touched.

Usually, though, a penalty is loss of yardage for the offending team. Most penalties are assessed from the "previous spot," meaning the spot at which the ball was last put into play. In the case of a dead ball foul after the play, the penalty is assessed from the "succeeding spot," meaning the spot at which the play ended.

Flagrant unsportsman-like conduct and roughness fouls can result in the offender being disqualified from the game, in addition to the yardage penalty.

The only time a team can be penalized more than half the distance to its goal line is when defensive pass interference is called. In other cases, the team is penalized half the distance. For example, if the Patriots are guilty of a false start when the ball is on their 6-yard line, they're penalized back to the 3-yard line.

If both teams commit a foul on the same play, the penalties offset one another if they're equivalent and the down is replayed. However, if one foul calls for a 15-yard penalty and the other calls for a 5-yard penalty, the 15-yard penalty is assessed.

A summary of infractions and their penalties:

Defensive holding	5 yards and first down
Defensive pass interference in end zone	ball is awarded to offense at defense's 1-yard line
Defensive pass interference in field of play	ball is awarded to offense at spot of foul
Delay of game	5 yards
Disqualified player returning to game	15 yards
Encroachment	5 yards
Extra injury time-out	5 yards
Falling or piling on	15 yards

False start	5 yards
Forward pass from beyond line of scrimmage	5 yards and loss of down
Head slap	15 yards
Illegal advance after a fair catch	5 yards
Illegal blocking below the waist	15 yards
Illegal chop block	15 yards
Illegal contact to the face or head	15 yards
Illegal crack back block	15 yards
Illegal formation	5 yards
Illegal kicking of loose ball	10 yards
Illegal motion	5 yards
Illegal substitution	5 yards
Illegal touching of free kick	5 yards
Illegally assisting runner	10 yards
Illegal batting or punching of ball	10 yards
Incidental grasp of face mask	5 yards
Ineligible receiver downfield on pass or kick	5 yards
Ineligible receiver touching pass	10 yards
Interfering with fair catch	15 yards
Invalid fair catch signal	5 yards
Making second forward pass	loss of down
Offensive holding	10 yards
Offensive pass interference	10 yards

Offside at snap	5 yards
Prolonged, excessive, premeditated celebration	5 yards
Roughing the kicker	15 yards
Roughing the passer	15 yards
Running into the kicker	5 yards
Striking, kneeing, or kicking	15 yards
Too many men on the field	5 yards
Unnecessary roughness	15 yards
Unsportsman-like conduct	15 yards

THE OFFICIALS

There are seven officials at an NFL game: The referee, umpire, head lines-man, line judge, back judge, side judge, and field judge. They're some-times referred to as "zebras" because they wear black-and-white striped shirts. The referee wears a white cap and the other officials wear black caps with black visors.

Each official has a whistle and a weighted gold penalty flag. When an official is certain the ball is dead, he blows his whistle to signal the referee, and if he detects a foul, he drops or throws his penalty flag. Any official can call any foul on any play, but each also has his own assigned duties and areas to cover.

The officials arrive the day before the game, usually on a Saturday, and review film of their previous game. They meet at least two hours and fifteen minutes before game time in their dressing room and they have to appear on the field ten minutes before the game begins.

The referee is the chief official. He conducts the coin toss before the game and he's responsible for marking the ball ready for play, for announc-ing and enforcing penalties after infractions, and for determining whether a team has gained the necessary yardage for a first down when a measure-ment is required.

Before the snap, the referee positions himself in the offensive backfield, deeper than any back and usually slightly to the right of the center. His chief responsibility during a passing play is to watch the quarterback. The referee is usually the official who calls roughing the passer. If the ball comes free from the quarterback's hand, the referee usually determines whether it's a forward pass or a fumble. He may also sometimes call offensive holding when it occurs relatively near or behind the quarterback.

The umpire is positioned behind the defensive line and linebackers, in a location from which he has a clear view of most linemen. He determines whether the offense has the required seven men on the line of scrimmage, and he's generally responsible for the conduct of players on or near the line when a play is in progress. He is often the official who calls offensive holding.

In addition, the umpire keeps track of the number of time-outs charged to each team, works with the head linesmen to determine whether an ineligible receiver was illegally downfield on a pass play, and works with the referee to determine possession when a fumble occurs near the line of scrimmage.

The head linesman and the chain crew are positioned on one side of the field, chosen by the referee, during the first half and on the other side during the second half. He stands near the side line, right at the line of scrimmage, and is chiefly responsible for calling illegal motion, offside, encroachment, and false start infractions.

He also supervises the chain crew, works with the line judge on illegal motions and shifts, and with the umpire on offensive or defensive holding on his side of the line. The head linesmen also makes sure that the offense has only eleven players on each play.

Directly opposite the head linesman, on the other side of the field, is the line judge. He's responsible for timing the game on a stop watch, for ensuring that the official game clock is correct, and for telling the referee when to give the two-minute warning. If the game clock malfunctions, the line judge takes over official timing. When a period ends, he fires a pistol into the air as a signal to the referee.

During play, the line judge has the same responsibilities, on his side of the field, as the head linesman.

The back judge works on the same side of the field as the line judge, about 20 yards downfield. His primary responsibilities arise on passes thrown into his area. In that area, he has to determine whether or not a ball was trapped and whether a receiver caught the ball inbounds. He also makes most interference calls in that area.

In addition, he is supposed to cover the runner from his area of the field to the end line. On long runs or passes, the back judge determines when the ball is down and works with the referee to determine possession after a loose ball.

The side judge is directly across the field from the back judge and has basically the same responsibilities in his general area and further downfield.

The field judge is stationed in the middle of the field, about 25 yards beyond the line of scrimmage. He counts the number of defensive players on the field before each snap, and he's also responsible for operation of the play clock, for timing time-outs, and for timing the intermissions between periods. If the play clock malfunctions, the field judge takes over timing.

He has the same responsibilities as the back judge and side judge in his area of the field and he's mainly responsible for covering the ball on punts and field goal attempts. The field judge also has two odd little chores: Before each kickoff, he has to tell the kicker that a place kick or drop kick, not a punt, has to be made, and he inspects the kicking tee to make sure that it's legal.

On field goal attempts, the back judge stands under the upright on his side of the field and the field judge stands under the opposite upright. They have joint responsibility for signaling to the referee whether or not the kick clears the crossbar between the outer edges of the uprights.

Pro Football Terms

A The weak-side running back, as a receiver.

ace The one-back formation.

across A pass route for the tight end in which he cuts sharply over the middle after running straight downfield for about five yards.

active list A list of up to forty-five players who are eligible to play in a given game. If the *emergency quarterback* is used, there are actually forty-six eligible players.

acute in A pass route on which the receiver goes downfield 15 to 20 yards and then cuts back toward the quarterback at about a 120-degree angle.

acute out A pass route on which the receiver goes downfield 15 to 20 yards and then cuts back and toward the sideline at about a 120-degree angle.

against the flow See *flow*.

against the grain Same as "against the flow." See *flow*.

air it out To throw a long pass.

all curl A pass pattern on which all receivers run *curl* routes; usually used on relatively short-yardage passing situations.

all-out blitz   A blitz on which all the linebackers, and often a defensive back or two, are coming after the quarterback.

alley oop   A pass thrown deliberately high in the air, in the belief (or hope) that the receiver can out-jump his defender to catch the ball.

alley   The area between the sideline and the *hash marks*.

angle block   A block from the side, rather than head-on, meant to drive the defender in a specific direction away from the play.

area blocking   See *zone blocking*.

audible   A signal used by the quarterback to change the play at the line of scrimmage. There are three ways of doing this. Most teams use a number code: If the first number is the snap count, the quarterback is changing the play. For example, if the ball is to be snapped on "2," the audible "2–43" means the team is now going to run play 43. If the quarterback shouts "1–43," it's a *dummy audible*. Other teams use a color code, with the "live" color usually changing each quarter. The third method is with an audible that's inaudible, believe it or not. With a very noisy crowd, the quarterback uses hand signals to alert his wide receivers to a change in the pass pattern.

automatic   See *audible*.

B   The strong-side running back, as a receiver.

backer   See *linebacker*.

backs divide   A maneuver, on a passing play, in which each running back sets up to block a blitzing linebacker on his side of the formation and then gets into the pass pattern if there's no one to block.

balanced line   An offensive formation in which the same number of linemen are deployed on each side of the center. This usually means there are two tight ends but, in the *run and shoot*, the line is balanced because there are no tight ends.

ball control   The strategy of consuming as much time as possible on offense, usually by running and using short, safe passes, to keep the ball out of the hands of the opposing team.

belly   A maneuver on which a running back first moves away from the line of scrimmage before starting upfield. The opening move on a *flare pass* and often on a *toss* or *pitch*.

bird cage   A face mask.

blast   A blocking scheme, commonly used in short yardage or goal-line situations, in which offensive linemen simply try to move defensive linemen off the line of scrimmage.

blind side   Surprise! It's the side where a player isn't looking. Frequently used of the quarterback; when a right-handed quarterback turns to throw the ball, his blind side is to his left, but that's to the defense's right, which is why a team's best pass rusher is usually the right defensive end or right outside linebacker. Also used as a verb; a player who is hit from the blind side is said to have been "blind-sided."

blitz   A defensive maneuver on which a linebacker or defensive back rushes the passer. When used alone, it most often refers to a linebacker blitz. See also *corner blitz*; *safety blitz*.

blocking scheme   The entire pattern of blocking assignments and other offensive maneuvers designed for a specific play against a specific defense. On most teams, the center, after sizing up the defense, calls out a code that tells the offensive linemen what blocking scheme is to be used.

blown coverage   A missed assignment, usually by a defensive back, that allows a receiver to get wide open, often leading to a touchdown or, at least, a long gain.

blue   An offensive formation in which the fullback is stationed behind the quarterback and the halfback is behind the weak-side tackle.

bomb   A long pass.

bomb squad   See *suicide squad*.

bootleg   A play on which the ball carrier, most likely the quarterback, fakes a hand-off to a teammate and runs in the other direction. So called because, in the original version of the play, the ball was held against the side of the leg away from the defense to conceal it, though that's not often done now. See also *naked bootleg*.

bounce it outside   To go wide on a running play that was supposed to go between tackles, usually because there was no *hole* inside. See also *veer*.

bread-and-butter play   An offensive team's most effective play; a staple of the offense.

break off   A deliberate failure to carry out the planned pass route. When a receiver sees that the route he's supposed to run isn't likely to be successful against the defense being used, he will break off his route to get into an open area of the field. A receiver may also break off his route when he sees that the quarterback is scrambling.

broken play   A play on which an offensive player doesn't carry out the right assignment. Most often it's a running back who runs the wrong way, for example to the quarterback's left rather than his right. The same problem arises if the quarterback turns the wrong way after receiving the snap. The best thing he can do in either situation is to follow the running back into the hole.

brown   An offensive formation in which the fullback is stationed behind the quarterback and the halfback is behind the strong-side tackle.

brush block   A very brief block by an offensive player, meant to momentarily slow or distract a defender, usually followed by another maneuver. The tight end will sometimes make a brush block as a delaying tactic before getting into the pass pattern. An offensive lineman is often called upon to make a brush block before carrying out his primary blocking assignment.

buck   Obsolete term for a run into the line between the offensive tackles.

bullet pass   A pass thrown very hard and straight toward its target.

bump and run   A type of pass coverage in which a defender, usually a cornerback, makes contact with the receiver at or near the line of scrimmage to slow him down and then attempts to run with him on his pass route. See also *chuck*.

busted play   See *broken play*.

buttonhook   The original name for the *hook* or *curl* pass route.

caught in a vise   Said of a defensive player who is pinned between two blockers.

chain   The 10-yard chain, fastened to two markers, that's used to determine whether the offensive team gained the yardage necessary for a first down.

chain gang   The crew of three assistant officials, under the jurisdiction of the head linesman, who handle the first-down yardage equipment. The two rod men are responsible for the chain and its poles, while the box man handles the pole marking the present spot of the ball and changing the marker to indicate what down it is.

chalk talk   A meeting at which coaches discuss plays, tactics, strategy, etc., with the players, often drawing or writing on a blackboard.

check off   1. To call an audible. 2. When said of a running back, to look for a blitzer who has to be blocked before running a pass route.

chicken fight   A battle between an offensive and defensive lineman on a pass play. Also sometimes used as a verb.

chuck   Contact made with a receiver, usually by a linebacker or defensive back, at or near the line of scrimmage to slow him down in his effort to get into a pass pattern.

circle   A pass route on which a running back runs a curved route, outside the offensive tackle or tight end, and then toward the middle of the field. It should be called a semicircle, since if he actually ran a circle, he'd end up right back where he started from. See also *double circle*.

circus catch   Originally from baseball, this term is now also used to describe a spectacular catch by a receiver or, occasionally, a defender.

clear   1. To move a defender out of a given area by running through it. For example, a wide receiver goes downfield, taking a cornerback with him; the area formerly occupied by the cornerback has been cleared. 2. To get past or free of. Against a zone defense, for example, the quarterback may want to throw to a receiver after he has cleared a linebacker and before he has reached a defensive back.

cleats   The blunt protrusions attached to the soles of football shoes, allowing players to get better traction. Also, by extension, the shoes themselves.

closed end   A tight end who is even tighter than usual, 1½ yards or less from the tackle.

closed formation   An offensive alignment used in short-yardage situations, in which most of the players are packed tightly together.

clothesline   An illegal maneuver in which a player, usually a linebacker or defensive back, holds his arm out so an opposing player will run into it.

coffin corner   The area near the intersection of the goal line and the sideline. Punters often aim at the area, hoping the kick will go out of bounds near the goal line; the result is a coffin corner kick.

combination block   A blocking scheme in which two or more offensive linemen coordinate their actions. For example, a *cross block*.

combo defense   A type of pass defense that combines man-to-man and zone coverage.

come off the ball   To charge aggressively the instant the ball is snapped; commonly used in praise: "He really comes off the ball."

comeback   A route on which the receiver runs down the field, then turns and comes back toward the quarterback.

contain   On a running play, one defensive player on each side of the field is assigned to keep the runner from *making the corner*. He doesn't necessarily have to make the tackle, but he does have to contain the play and make the runner turn inside, where other defenders can do it. On a passing play, especially against a mobile quarterback, defenders are similarly assigned to keep the passer from scrambling to the outside and possibly gaining a lot of yardage on a run.

corner   A pass route on which the receiver starts downfield, then angles toward the *coffin corner*.

corner backer   An outside linebacker; not often used now.

corner blitz   A blitz by a cornerback.

cornerback   A defensive back who plays an outside position; usually responsible for a wide receiver when man-to-man coverage is used.

cough up the ball   To lose a fumble.

count   See *snap count*.

counter   A play that appears to be going in one direction but ends up going in the other.

counter trey   So called because it's a counter play on which three linemen pull out to lead interference. This was the trademark running play of the Washington Redskins under Coach Joe Gibbs and has since been adapted by most other NFL teams.

coverage sack   A *sack* that's caused by good coverage in the secondary rather than a good pass rush.

crash   A quick rush across the line of scrimmage and toward the center of the field. Usually used by a defensive end or outside linebacker.

crease   On a running play, a small opening that can be exploited by the ball carrier. On a passing play, an area between zones. See also *seam*.

criss-cross   Outmoded term for *crossing pattern*.

cross block   A type of blocking scheme on which two offensive linemen switch their normal assignments. For example, a tackle blocks in on the defensive tackle and the guard steps behind him to block out on the defensive end.

cross body block   A block on which the blocker uses his torso, often below the opponent's waist.

cross buck   Type of old single-wing and early T-formation play. One example: The right halfback heads toward the left side of the line, passing close to the quarterback, and the left halfback then heads toward the right side of the line. The quarterback hands the ball to one of the backs, faking a hand-off to the other. Some professional teams are again using "cross buck action," most often with the fullback and the halfback.

crossing pattern   A pass pattern on which the routes of two or more pass receivers cross one another.

crossing route   A pass route on which a receiver crosses the field.

cup   See *pocket*.

curl   A pass route on which a receiver goes downfield, then turns in and comes back toward the passer.

cut   1. A sharp change in direction. 2. A block below the knees, intended to bring a defender to the ground. Also used as a verb in both senses.

cut back   A type of run on which the ball carrier starts outside, then cuts toward the center of the field. This is sometimes planned and sometimes simply a maneuver by a runner who is looking for *daylight*.

daylight   An opening for a running back.

deke   From "decoy," a fake by a running back, who often then cuts in the opposite direction.

delay   A type of pass route on which the receiver waits for a count or two, often making a *brush block*. Also, a *draw* play.

deuce   A formation with two running backs.

diagonal   A pass route on which the receiver, usually a tight end, goes just a few yards downfield and then slants to the inside at a 45-degree angle.

dime   A defensive formation with six backs. See also *nickel*.

dime back   A sixth defensive back.

dive   A play on which the running back goes straight into the line of scrimmage.

do dad   See *combination block*.

dog   Short for *red dog*.

double circle   A maneuver on which both running backs run circle routes. Effective when there's a single middle linebacker, because he usually has to choose which one to cover, and the quarterback can then throw to the other.

double motion   1. Motion by two offensive players at the same time. 2. A type of motion on which the motion man starts in one direction and then reverses it.

double out   A pass route on which the receiver cuts outside, starts to run downfield, and then cuts outside again.

double slot   An offensive formation in which there are two *slot* men.

double team   1. A blocking scheme on which two offensive players block the same defender. 2. A type of defense that has two defenders covering the same receiver.

double wing   An offensive formation in which there are two *wingbacks*.

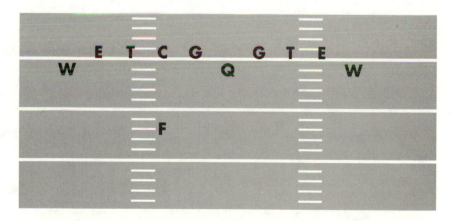

DOUBLE WING
Another Warner invention, the double wing emphasized speed and deception rather than power. Ernie Nevers starred as the formation's triple-threat
fullback at Stanford and in the NFL.

double zone   A type of *zone defense* meant primarily to protect the sidelines late in a half, when the offense is likely to throw sideline passes so the receiver can get out of bounds to stop the clock. The cornerback covers a relatively short zone on his side of the field, while the safety man covers the deep zone. The result is something like *up-and-under* coverage on each wide receiver.

down and in   A pass route on which the receiver starts downfield and then cuts in at a right angle.

down and out   A pass route on which the receiver starts downfield and cuts toward the sideline at a right angle.

downfield block   A block made three or more yards past the line of scrimmage.

drag   A pass route on which one receiver runs through an area to clear it and another receiver then enters the area.

draw   A running play that looks like a pass but turns into a run. So called because the intent is to draw the defensive lineman into the backfield and then have the ball carrier run past them.

drive block   A hard shoulder block by an offensive lineman to move a defender off the line of scrimmage or out of the ball carrier's path.

drop   Movement by the quarterback away from the line of scrimmage to set up for a pass; also, the distance he retreats, as in a "three-step drop."

dummy audible   A signal called by the quarterback at the line of scrimmage that sounds like an *audible*, but isn't.

dump off   A short pass to a back, usually an *outlet receiver*, when other receivers are covered.

Eagle defense   Originally a 5–2 defense with four defensive backs, used by the Philadelphia Eagles in the 1950s, in which one or both defensive ends might drop back into pass coverage, effectively turning it into a *4–3* or *3–4*. More recently, it has been used, inaccurately, to describe the *46 defense* developed by Buddy Ryan with the Chicago Bears.

eat the ball   To be tackled for a loss rather than throwing a pass that might be intercepted.

emergency quarterback   An NFL team is allowed to activate forty-five players for a game. A forty-sixth may be designated as the emergency quarterback. If the other quarterbacks are injured, the emergency quarterback can be used, but the injured quarterbacks are now ineligible to reenter the game.

end around   A running play on which an end or flanker is given the ball on a *reverse* to run around the other end.

even defense   Any defensive alignment in which there is no player stationed opposite the center; the standard *4–3 defense*, for example. Against an even defense, the center is free to block on a linebacker, to help *double-team* a tackle, or to make a *fill block* on a tackle while a guard pulls to lead interference.

fade back   The action of the quarterback when he takes his *drop*.

false shake   A pass route on which the receiver makes a sharp cut to the outside, fakes inside, and then continues toward the *corner*.

fan   A pass route for a running back on which he starts downfield and then cuts to the outside.

fill block   When an offensive lineman pulls to lead interference, one of his teammates often has to make a fill block on a defender in the area that was vacated.

first sound   To catch the defense unaware, the offensive team will sometimes run a play before anyone even seems to be ready. On such a play, the ball is snapped on the first sound the quarterback makes, probably something that sounds like the beginning of an audible rather than the usual "Hut."

flag   A *corner* pass route; also, a *penalty flag*.

flanker   A wide receiver who lines up about 2 yards behind the line of scrimmage and 6 to 12 yards from the nearest offensive lineman, usually the tight end.

flare   A maneuver on which a running back runs parallel to the line of scrimmage and then turns upfield after clearing the tight end or offensive tackle. Also, a pass thrown to a back who is flaring. Similar to a *swing*, but quicker because the receiver doesn't *belly* back.

flea flicker   A play on which a running back takes a hand-off, stops just short of the line of scrimmage, and tosses a lateral back to the quarterback, who then throws a forward pass.

flex defense   A defense developed by the Dallas Cowboys under Tom Landry in which a defensive tackle and the defensive end on the other side play somewhat off the line of scrimmage, allowing them to *read and react* to the play.

flood   To send two or more receivers into the same zone.

flow   The general direction of an offensive play. A running back who suddenly cuts in the other direction is said to "go against the flow."

fly   A pass route on which the receiver runs as fast as he can straight down the field, often after faking another route. Also called a "go route." See also *hitch and go*; *sideline and go*; *square out and go*; *turn and go*.

force   On a running play to the outside, a defensive player, most often a cornerback, is responsible for forcing the play to the inside. To make the force, he has to come up hard and take on the outside blocker. His main job is not to make the tackle, but to keep the runner from *making the corner*.

forearm shiver   An illegal maneuver on which a player hits an opponent in the head with a stiffened forearm.

forty-six defense   A defense developed by Buddy Ryan when he was defensive coordinator for Mike Ditka with the Chicago Bears. All the defensive backs except the free safety are positioned near the line of scrimmage, and they usually all blitz, along with the linebackers. Although thought of as a defense against the pass, the 46 also disrupts blocking schemes on a running play. It requires very strong, mobile players who can penetrate fast, since it's obviously vulnerable to any kind of long pass. See also *Eagle defense*.

four-down territory   An area of the field where a team will be willing to go for the first down on fourth down. The score and time remaining are vital factors, of course. If a team is losing by a touchdown or more with less than two minutes to play, any area is four-down territory.

4–3 defense   A defensive alignment with four down linemen and three linebackers.

free agent   A player who is not under contract to any team.

free ball   Said of the ball when it doesn't technically belong to either team and can be recovered by any player. For example, a fumble, a muffed punt, or a kickoff that has traveled more than 10 yards even if it hasn't been touched by anyone. See also *loose ball*.

free safety   Usually the safety man opposite the weak side of the offensive formation; so called because, in standard man-to-man coverage, he doesn't have to cover a specific pass receiver and is therefore free to roam, either to help another defender or to try for an interception. Also known as the weak safety.

frequency chart   A breakdown, based on scouting reports and films, showing what the opposition is most likely to do, offensively and defensively, in certain situations.

Frisco defense   A 4–3 defense in which the strong-side tackle moves opposite the offensive center rather than the guard.

front four   In the 4–3 defense, the tackles and ends.

full house backfield   The original version of the T formation, with a fullback lined up directly behind the quarterback and the halfbacks positioned behind the offensive tackles, or between the guards and tackles. All three running backs are 4 to 6 yards behind the line of scrimmage. Teams rarely run from it nowadays, but they sometimes line up in the formation and then shift into another alignment.

fundamentals   The basic skills required for football, especially blocking and tackling.

games   Unusual maneuvers by defensive linemen, such as *stunts* and *loops*.

gang tackling   Two or more defenders ganging up on the ball carrier.

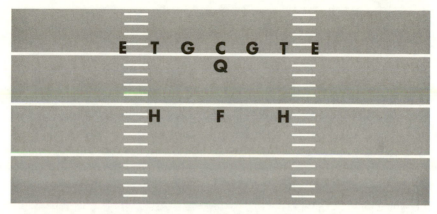

ORIGINAL T (FULL HOUSE BACKFIELD)
The original T formation, developed by Walter Camp in 1882, was generally considered obsolete by 1912. However, the Chicago Bears used it, with modifications, throughout the 1920s and 1930s.

gap defense   See one-gap.

gap   The space between two linemen on the same team.

go for it   To attempt to make a first down or score a touchdown on fourth down rather than kicking.

go   See *fly*.

goal line defense   A defensive alignment that has more linemen and fewer backs than the standard defense. Similar to *short yardage defense*.

goal line stand   A successful attempt by the defense to prevent a touchdown when backed up to its own goal line.

goal posts   The posts that rise from the ends of the crossbar to aid officials in deciding whether a place kick is successful. Also known as "uprights."

goal to go   When a team gets a first down inside the other team's 10-yard line, it can't get another first down without scoring a touchdown. Therefore, it's "first down and goal to go." Sometimes abbreviated to "first down and goal." Of course, all succeeding downs will also be "goal to go."

grind it out   To move the ball slowly but surely down the field, usually on running plays.

H back   In the *one-back formation*, a player who is used sometimes as a second tight end and sometimes as a *motion man*, often becoming the *lead blocker* on a running play.

Hail Mary   A last-second pass, usually thrown toward several receivers in an area near or across the goal line in the hope (and with a prayer) that one of them will catch it.

halfback blitz   A *corner blitz*.

halfback option   A play, usually based on the *sweep*, on which the halfback has the option of passing the ball or running with it.

handkerchief   A *penalty flag*.

hang time   The amount of time a punt or kickoff spends in the air.

hash marks   Marks, at 1-yard intervals, 70 feet and 9 inches from each sideline. Officially called "inbound spots," they show where the ball will be put back in play after having gone out of bounds or after the previous play ended between the hash marks and the sideline.

head hunter   A player with a reputation for trying to injure opponents.

hear footsteps   When a receiver drops the ball because he's anticipating contact from a defender behind him, an announcer will often say something like, "He didn't catch that pass because he heard footsteps."

high cuts   Football shoes that come up above the ankle, offering more protection and stability.

hip   See *peel*.

hitch   A pass route on which the receiver runs a short distance downfield, then stops and faces the quarterback to receive a quick pass.

hitch and go   A pass route on which the receiver runs a hitch and then speeds downfield again.

hole   The area through which the runner is supposed to carry the ball, in the hope that there will actually be an opening. See also *numbering scheme*.

hook   A pass route that's similar to the *hitch*, except that the receiver moves back toward the quarterback after turning. Similar to a *curl*.

hook and go   A pass route that begins as a hook, but the receiver then runs downfield again.

hook and ladder   A play on which a receiver catches a *hook* pass and quickly laterals it to a teammate who's running at top speed.

hook block   A type of block on which the offensive lineman makes a quick move to the side, as if he's going to *pull* or *cross block*, in order to get an *angle block* on a defender to move him out of the *hole*.

hurry-up offense   Originally the *two-minute offense*, used in the last two minutes of the first half of the game, in an attempt to score by running as many plays as possible. More recently, the Cincinnati Bengals and Buffalo Bills have used it throughout most of the game, and a couple of other teams have used it from time to time when they aren't in the two-minute situation. Two or more plays may be called in the original huddle, or the quarterback may call audibles after his offense lines up and he has a chance to survey the defense.

I back   The deepest back in the *I formation*.

I formation   An offensive alignment in which there's a fullback 4 to 5 yards behind the quarterback, with another running back 7 to 8 yards deep. Running plays out of the I often use *zone blocking* and the deep back runs to *daylight*.

in   A quick pass route on which the receiver starts downfield and then makes a very sharp cut toward the middle.

in and out   A type of *double coverage* on which a receiver has one defender on his inside and another on his outside. See also *up and under*.

inbound spots   See *hash marks*.

influence   A move by an offensive player that is meant to pull a defender out of position. For example, a guard pulls to the left, which usually means the play is going in that direction, making the middle linebacker move with him. Instead, the play goes through the very area that the guard vacated, or in the other direction.

inside hand-off   A hand-off on which the ball is exchanged when the running back is between the quarterback and the line of scrimmage.

inside help   1. When a defensive back is responsible for covering a zone to the outside of the field, he gets help from another defender if a receiver moves from that zone to a zone nearer the center of the field. 2. When *in and out* coverage is used, the defender with outside responsibility gets "inside help" from the other.

inside linebacker   Most often one of the two interior linebackers in the *3–4 defense*, but occasionally used to mean the *middle linebacker* in the *4–3 defense*.

inside reverse   An unorthodox kind of *reverse* on which the ball carrier runs between the tackles rather than going wide.

inside slip   A synonym for the *slant* route.

inside split   A pass route on which a running back goes downfield in the *seam* between the safeties while wide receivers are diverting them. If a long pass is thrown to a running back, it's usually on this route or the *outside split*.

interior line   The offensive linemen, from tackle to tackle. The offensive equivalent of the *front four*, except that there are five of them.

isolation block   See *isolation play*.

isolation play   An offensive play that's designed to make one defensive player, often an inside linebacker, solely responsible for making the tackle before a gain is made. The poor defender is then usually confronting a blocker and a running back. The blocker will try to take him in either direction and the runner will cut the other way.

jot step   Not often used now. See *stutter step*.

juke   See *deke*.

jump ball   A pass thrown with a high arc that's likely to be caught by the player with the longest reach. From basketball, of course. See also *alley oop*.

jump pass   A pass thrown as the passer jumps from the ground to see and throw over defenders. Unusual now, but once fairly common.

kamikaze squad   See *suicide squad*.

keeper   A play on which the quarterback, usually after a fake hand-off, keeps the ball. He will most often *roll out* and run, though there may be an option pass involved.

key   Usually something a defensive player looks at that will help him figure out where the offensive play is going. For example, an inside linebacker may watch a guard to see which way he's moving. The guard is his key. The quarterback looks for a key, often one of the safety men, to tell him what kind of pass coverage is being used. Also used as a verb: The linebacker keys on the guard, the quarterback keys on the free safety.

kick-out   A block on a defender, usually a linebacker or defensive back, to move him to the outside so the ball carrier can run inside.

kicking tee   See *tee*.

kill the clock   1. To use as much time as possible to run out the clock and preserve a victory. 2. To stop the clock for exactly the opposite reason.

lateral   A pass thrown backward or sideways—just throw it any which way but forward. On a designed play, it's almost always a *pitch* or *toss*. A lateral may also be spontaneous. On a kick return, for example, a player who's not very good at runbacks may lateral the ball to someone who's a better runner. And after an interception, a linebacker might lateral to a faster cornerback or safety.

lead blocker   A blocker, often the fullback, who goes into the hole ahead of the ball carrier to clear it out for him.

lead draw   A type of draw play on which the ball carrier has a *lead blocker*.

lead   To throw a pass to the spot where a receiver will be when the ball arrives.

left   A special kind of *down and out* or *down and in* route on which the receiver goes downfield to the first-down marker and cuts sharply to his left.

leg whip   An illegal maneuver in which a player, on the ground, hits an opponent with his leg or legs.

long gainer   A play that gains a lot of yardage.

long side   1. The side of the offense that has the player who is farthest from the center. 2. The side of the field where the offense has the most room to operate. If the ball is on the right *hash mark*, for example, the left side of the field is the long side.

long trap   A type of *trap* play on which the blocker travels a relatively long distance. For example, the right guard *pulls* to the left and traps the defensive right end.

look-in   A very quick pass route on which a receiver, usually the tight end, slants toward the middle of the field and the quarterback throws to him immediately after receiving the snap.

look off   Said of the quarterback when he looks to one side of the field before throwing a pass to the other side. His intention is to keep defensive backs, particularly safeties, from knowing where the ball is going. A television announcer or commentator will often say something like, "He looked off the free safety."

look out block   A block, most often in pass protection, that isn't made. So called because the offending offender should shout "look out" to the quarterback or running back after missing the block.

loop   A maneuver on which one defensive lineman *stunts* and an adjacent lineman loops behind him. Usually, but not always, used in passing situations. The object is to have the first lineman occupy two blockers, while the second isn't blocked at all.

loose ball   Said of the ball when it is not in anyone's possession and either team can recover it. See also *free ball*.

low cuts   Football shoes that are cut below the ankle, often worn by running backs and receivers because they allow greater speed.

make the corner   When a running back gets outside the defender who is nearest the sideline, he is said to have "made the corner"; he's now free to turn downfield and probably gain considerable yardage.

man in motion   See *motion man*.

man over   A defensive alignment in which a lineman is shifted one position to his right or left. For example, if the nose guard lines up opposite the offensive right guard rather than the center, he is said to be "a man over" to the left.

man-to-man   A defense in which each defensive back and linebacker is assigned to cover a specific pass receiver. In the standard man-to-man, each cornerback covers the wide receiver on his side of the field, the strong safety covers the tight end, and linebackers are responsible for running backs.

middle guard   The player stationed opposite the center in a five-man defensive line; rarely used now, because the five-man line is rarely used. See also *nose guard*; *nose tackle*.

middle linebacker   Generally, the inside linebacker in a *4–3* defense, but occasionally used to mean one of the *inside linebackers* in a 3–4.

mid-field stripe   The 50-yard line.

misdirection   Any offensive maneuver that's meant to make the defense think a play is going in one direction when it's actually going in the other.

motion man   An offensive player who is in motion before and/or at the snap of the ball.

mouse-trap   See *trap*.

muff   To touch the ball without catching it. This is a technical term when applied to a punt. If a player on the receiving team muffs a punt, it's a *loose ball* that can be recovered by the kicking team, but it can't be advanced. If the returner catches the ball and then fumbles it, however, the kicking team can advance it.

naked bootleg   A play on which the quarterback fakes the ball to a back going in one direction, then hides it and runs in the other direction. It's not always a designed play. Sometimes the quarterback will call a play, say a sweep, in the huddle, and simply not hand the ball off as he's supposed to. It often works best that way, because even the offense is fooled. Called "naked" (or "nekkid" by some coaches and commentators) because the quarterback is on his own, with no blockers.

naked I   A version of the I formation in which there is no fullback, just a single running back stationed 7 to 8 yards behind the quarterback. It differs from the standard *one-back formation* in that the running back is deeper.

near back   The running back nearest the side to which the play is designed to go.

necessary line   The yard line that the offensive team must reach in order to get a first down.

neutral zone   An area the length of the ball between the offensive and defensive lines that can't be entered by any player except the center until the ball is snapped.

nickel back   A fifth defensive back who enters the game in a likely passing situation.

nickel defense   A defense with five defensive backs.

north and south   A complimentary adjective applied to a runner who always heads toward the other team's goal line, with little or no lateral movement.

nose guard   Most commonly the *middle guard* in a five-man line, but sometimes applied to a defensive linemen who is opposite the offensive center in a four-man line. See also *nose tackle*.

nose tackle   The lineman stationed opposite the offensive center in a three-man defensive line; occasionally, a lineman opposite the center in a four-man line.

numbering scheme   A method by which running plays are given numbers. The most common is to assign each back a number, with the quarterback as 1, the right halfback 2, the fullback 3, and the left halfback 4. *Holes* are usually given odd numbers on the left side, even numbers on the right, with lower numbers closer to the center. The hole between the center and right guard is the 2 hole, the hole between the right guard and right tackle is the 4 hole, and so on. The digits for the back and hole are then combined into a two-digit number to call the play. For example, "24" means that the right halfback is supposed to run into the hole between the right guard and right tackle; "31" means the fullback is to run into the hole between the center and the left guard.

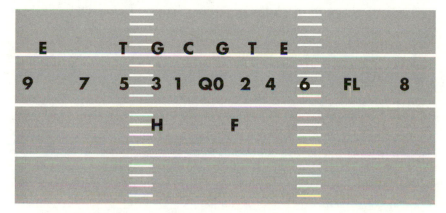

HOLE NUMBERING SCHEME
This hole numbering scheme is used by many NFL teams. Even numbers are to the right, odd numbers to the left.

odd defense   Any defense in which there's a lineman opposite the offensive center. Even though four is an even number, a four-man line is said to be an odd defense if there's a *nose tackle* or *nose guard* in the alignment. Blocking schemes are entirely different for an odd defense because the center is not free to block on a linebacker or to help on a double-team block.

off guard   The guard on the side of the line opposite the direction the offensive play is designed to go. If the play is going to the right, the left guard is the off guard.

off side   The side of the offensive formation opposite the direction the play is designed to go.

off tackle   1. The tackle on the side of the line opposite the direction the play is designed to go. 2. A type of running play designed to go over the tackle's spot, or through the gap between a guard and a tackle.

on side   The side of the offensive formation where the play is designed to go.

on the ground   A *loose ball* is said to be on the ground. When a player fumbles, sportscasters often say something like, "He put the ball on the ground."

on the numbers   Said of a perfectly thrown pass, as in, "He hit him right on the numbers."

one-back formation   An offensive alignment in which there's only one running back, usually positioned directly behind the quarterback and 4 to 5 yards deep.

one-gap   A type of defense in which defenders are positioned in the gaps, or splits, between offensive lineman. The usual goal is for each defender to charge through the gap as quickly as possible. Often used in goal-line or short-yardage situations. See also *two-gap*.

one-on-one   1. Pass coverage in which a defender is solely responsible for a receiver, as in a *man-to-man* defense. 2. A block on which an offensive player is solely responsible for a specific defensive player.

onside kick   A kickoff that, by design, travels only a short distance to give the kicking team a chance of recovering it. If it travels more than 10 yards, it becomes a *free ball*.

open end   The tight end, when he is split out 4 or more yards from the offensive tackle. Formerly the *split end*, but now obsolete in that sense.

opposite   A running back's position when he's in the *slot* on the opposite side of the line from the *flanker*.

option   Any play on which a player has a choice of what to do. Most often it means an option to run or pass, as on the *halfback option*, but it may also refer to a choice of run or pass routes. On a sweep, a running back has the option to *cut back* if he can't *make the corner*. Against a zone defense, a receiver may have the option to *break off* his route.

option block   A blocking assignment on which the blocker targets no specific defender. For example, a pulling guard on a sweep may be assigned to block the first open defender he sees to the inside, who might be an end, a linebacker, or even a safety.

out   1. A pass route on which the receiver goes downfield and then cuts toward the sideline at a 90-degree angle. 2. The position of a running back who's in the *slot* on the same side of the formation as the *flanker*.

outlet receiver   Most often a running back who is available for a *dump-off* pass if the quarterback can't find any other receiver.

outside help   1. When a defensive back is responsible for covering a zone toward the center of the field, he gets help from another defender if a receiver moves from that zone to a zone toward the outside. 2. When *in* *and out* coverage is used, the defender with inside responsibility gets "outside help" from the other.

outside linebacker One of the two exterior linebackers in the *3–4 defense* or *4–3 defense*. The left outside linebacker is usually the bigger of the two, since he's often lined up opposite the tight end, while the right outside linebacker is likely to be faster, because he is more often used on *blitzes*.

outside split A pass route on which a running back goes downfield between a safety and a cornerback.

over the top Said of a long pass, usually one that goes farther than the deepest defender.

overload An offensive or defensive alignment in which a large number of players are concentrated on one side or in one area. For example, if the offense has a *slot* man between the tight end and the flanker, the formation is overloaded to that side. The defense may create an overload by having two linebackers and a defensive back blitz from the same side.

overshift Any offensive or defensive alignment in which a player or players are not in their usual positions. In the *Frisco defense*, for example, the strong-side tackle is overshifted to the weak side.

P. A. T. Point after touchdown. See also *conversion*.

pads Protective equipment.

pancake A devastating block on which the blocker flattens the defender to the ground. Also a verb: "He really pancaked his man."

pass pattern A particular combination of *pass routes* being run by all receivers. Because it can take a great deal of time to call all of the pass routes in the huddle, teams have standard patterns that can be called by name or number. Often but erroneously used to mean "pass route."

pass protection It's actually the passer, not the pass, that's being protected. The phrase refers to the type of blocking that's normally used, with offensive lineman retreating to form a semicircular *pocket* from which the quarterback can operate.

pass route The maneuver a receiver is supposed to make on a pass play.

pass rush Defensive charge whose chief goal is to *sack* the quarterback.

passing down A down on which the offense is likely to throw the ball, because of the amount of yardage to be gained for a first down or because the team has to score points quickly.

passing situation Same as *passing down*.

pattern See *pass pattern*.

peel Movement by a running back or wide receiver away from the center before the snap.

penalty flag A yellow marker dropped by an official to indicate that an infraction has taken place.

pick An illegal maneuver on which a receiver deliberately impedes a defensive player to keep him from covering another receiver. The actual infraction is offensive pass interference.

pick off 1. An interception. 2. A block, most often by a running back, on a blitzer.

picket line A line of blockers that sets up on a kick return. The object is to keep defenders from getting to the sideline area so the runner has a clear path.

pinch A *double-team* block by the tight end and tackle.

pirate Outmoded now. See *nickel back*.

pitch A lateral pass, usually to a back to initiate a running play. Often a *shovel pass*, it's thrown rather hard and fast, unlike a *toss*.

pitchout See *pitch*.

pivot A pass route on which the receiver first runs a *hook* and then pivots and runs toward the sideline.

play action pass A pass play that begins with a fake running play.

play loose To stay some distance from the receiver being covered, in most cases to prevent a long pass.

play tight To stay very close to the receiver being covered.

playbook A notebook that contains everything a player needs to know in order to play for his team: Not only play diagrams, but terminology, formations, etc. When a player leaves the team, he's required to turn in his playbook, and there's a sizable fine for losing it.

plunge A straight-ahead run into the line.

pocket The area in which the quarterback stands while looking for a receiver. Ideally, offensive linemen form a semicircle to protect the passer and keep the pocket free of defenders. Also sometimes called "the cup."

point of attack The area where a running play is designed to go. The offense's general goal is to get at least as many blockers as there are defenders at the point of attack.

pop A pass route on which a running back crosses the line of scrimmage between the tackles and settles into an open area.

possession play A play designed to gain a first down so that the offense can keep possession of the ball.

post A pass route on which the receiver starts downfield, then cuts inside, toward the nearest goal post.

power block A block on which the offensive lineman simply drives into a defender to knock him off the line of scrimmage.

power I   A version of the I formation in which there are two block-ing backs in front of the deep back, one of them positioned directly behind the quarterback and the other 2 to 5 yards to one side of him.

power play   A running play that relies on brute force blocking at the *point of attack*, rather than any sort of finesse. Most often used in short-yardage situations.

power sweep   A type of *sweep* on which two or more linemen *pull* to lead interference. Although it seems as if the play is designed to *make the corner*, the back's best route is most often to cut between the pulling linemen, since one of them will usually block to the inside while the other blocks to the outside.

prevent   A defense that has extra defensive backs, all of whom *play loose*. Usually used near the end of the first half of the game when the defending team has a sizable lead.

primary receiver   The first receiver the passer looks at in a specific *pass pattern*. The primary receiver is often different against different defenses.

pro set   The "standard" offensive alignment with a tight end, split end, flanker, and two running backs; not so standard anymore.

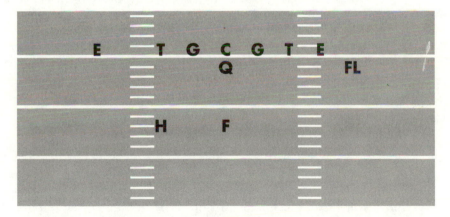

PRO SET WITH FLANKER
Still the basic offensive formation for most NFL teams, the pro set was devel-oped by Clark Shaughnessy with the Los Angeles Rams in 1949. Crazylegs Hirsch, the original flanker, averaged 47.8 yards on his 17 touchdown receptions in 1951.

pull   The action of an offensive lineman who runs laterally behind the line of scrimmage before carrying out his blocking assignment. After pulling, he may make a *trap* block or lead interference on a play such as the *power sweep*.

pump   A fake pass by the quarterback, often used on a route such as a *hitch and go*. The intent is to make a defender move toward the receiver, who can then run past him.

pursuit angle   The angle at which a defensive player should run in order to intercept the ball carrier. Taking the correct pursuit angle is much like leading the receiver when throwing a pass. The goal is to arrive at a given point in the ball carrier's path at the same time the ball carrier gets there.

quarterback draw   A designed play on which the quarterback drops back as if to pass and then runs with the ball.

quarterback keep   See *keeper*.

quarterback sneak   A short-yardage play on which the quarterback simply plunges into the line after taking the snap.

quick count   A surprise tactic in which the ball is snapped before the defense expects it, often before offensive linemen have come to a *set position*. See also *first sound*.

quick draw   A *draw* play on which the running back delays for just a beat or two before moving forward to take the hand-off.

quick kick   An unexpected punt, most often before fourth down. Not seen often nowadays, but quarterback Randall Cunningham of the Philadelphia Eagles has quick-kicked effectively several times from the *shotgun* formation.

quick opener   A play on which the running back hits the hole quickly.

quick release   Said of a quarterback who gets rid of the ball quickly. Dan Marino of the Miami Dolphins is rarely sacked because of his quick release.

quick trap   A *trap* play, usually right up the middle, that happens fast. In most cases, one guard will trap the defensive tackle on the other side of the line while the center makes a *fill block* and the other guard blocks either the *nose tackle* or an *inside linebacker*.

ram   A block on which a guard steps back as if he's going to *pull*, then crosses the line of scrimmage to block an inside linebacker.

read and react   A defensive philosophy that requires most players to read certain *keys* to determine what the offense is doing.

ready list   The list of plays that a team has practiced during the week. The ready list changes from week to week because it contains some plays specifically designed to be effective against the opposition's defense.

red   An offensive formation in which the two running backs line up behind the tackles or just inside them. Also called "split backs."

red dog   The original name for the blitz. Now outmoded.

red gun   The Atlanta Falcons' version of the run and shoot offense.

red zone   The area from the opposition's 20-yard line to the goal line. The effectiveness of an offense is often measured in terms of how often it scores when it gets inside the red zone.

release   1. To free oneself from a defender in order to get downfield. Most commonly said of the *tight end*, especially when he makes a *brush block* before getting into the pass pattern. 2. When a receiver leaves one pass defense zone and enters another, the defender responsible for the first zone is said to release him to the second defender. 3. The action of the quarterback as the ball leaves his hand on a pass attempt. See also *quick release*.

remaining back   A running back who doesn't carry the ball on a specific play.

reverse   1. A running play that seems to be going wide in one direction and turns out to be going wide in the other direction. 2. The type of hand-off commonly made on such a play: A ball carrier running across the field hands the ball off to a player running in the other direction. See also *inside reverse*.

reverse field   To change direction completely. For example, the ball carrier is running a sweep to his right, finds his way blocked, and turns to run back to the left. He has reversed his field.

reverse hand-off   A type of hand-off on which the quarterback turns away from the center in one direction and hands the ball off in the other.

reverse pivot   When the quarterback turns away from center in the direction opposite that to which the play is going. For example, he receives the snap, pivots to his right, then makes a hand-off or pitches the ball to the left.

ride in   A block on which the tight end tries to move or keep a linebacker to the inside.

ride out   A block on which the tight end tries to move or keep a linebacker to the outside.

right   A pass route that's the opposite of a left route. See *left*.

roll out   Describes the quarterback's movement when he moves to one side of the field or the other as he drops back. Normally a means of getting away from the pass rush, but the roll out may also lead to a run or a pass-run option.

rotate   When setting up a zone defense, players have to move in various ways to get into the correct positions, and this movement is usually described as rotation. For example, the right cornerback rotates up to cover the short right zone, the free safety rotates right to cover the deep right zone, the strong safety rotates right to cover the deep middle zone, the left cornerback rotates back to cover the deep left zone, and the outside left linebacker rotates left to cover the short left zone.

route   See *pass route*.

rover   A defensive player who has no specific assignment and is therefore free to follow the play to wherever it's going. Since the strong safety is usually the biggest defensive back and the best tackler in the secondary, he's often used as a rover against running plays. When a team is in man-to-man pass coverage, the free safety is a rover.

run and shoot   An offense, originally devised by Mouse Davis at little Cleveland State College, that uses four wide receivers, one running back, and no tight end. Rather than using predesigned pass patterns, the run and shoot usually requires the receivers and quarterback to read the defense and react accordingly. For example, if the defense is in a deep zone, each outside receiver will run a *sideline* route, hoping to occupy defenders on that side of the field, while the slot receivers run *slants*. The main object of the run and shoot is to get the ball quickly to a receiver with room to run after he catches it.

run blitz   A blitz that's designed to stop the run rather than put pressure on the passer. On a run blitz, defensive linemen usually play a *two-gap* defense while linebackers and possibly some defensive backs rush into the gaps between the offensive lineman.

run out the clock   To use time-consuming plays that aren't likely to stop the clock. Commonly done by the team with a lead near the end of the game.

sack   A tackle of the quarterback before he can throw the ball. Oddly, the word comes from fox hunting, where the fox is put into a sack after being caught.

safety   A defensive back generally stationed near the middle of the field. See *free safety*; *strong safety*.

safety blitz   A blitz by a safety man.

safety valve   See *outlet receiver*.

scatback   A running back noted for speed and elusiveness. Not often used now.

scramble   Improvised, often frantic movement by the quarterback to evade the pass rush.

screen block   See *shield block*.

screen pass   A short pass thrown to a running back who is behind a screen of blockers. The effect is much like that of a running play on which a back follows two or more blockers who are leading interference.

seal   A block meant to keep a defender from getting to the ball carrier's path, rather than moving him out of it. For example, on a sweep to the right, the tight end might be called on to seal the left inside line-backer.

seam   The area between two pass defense zones. Against a zone defense, a receiver is often supposed to alter his route somewhat to find a seam.

second effort   An extra push or thrust by a ball carrier after being hit that enables him to gain extra yardage.

secondary receiver   The receiver the quarterback looks for if the *primary receiver* is covered.

secondary   The defensive backs, collectively.

sequence   A series of plays designed to look very much alike. For example, on the first play of a sequence, the quarterback hands off to the fullback and fakes a pitch to the halfback. On the second play, he fakes the hand-off and throws the pitch. On the third play, he fakes both the hand-off and the pitch and throws a forward pass.

series   A single continuous possession by one team. A series begins with the team's first play from scrimmage and ends when it scores or loses possession of the ball.

set back   A running back who is aligned behind the quarterback, in normal running position, as opposed to a *flanker* or *slot* back.

set position   The position taken by an offensive lineman, usually a *three-point stance*, in preparation for the beginning of a play. Once a lineman is set, he can't move until the ball is snapped.

set up   The action by an offensive lineman of straightening up somewhat and beginning to retreat into *pass protection*.

shake   A pass route on which the receiver goes downfield, makes a sharp cut toward the sideline, then cuts back to the inside.

shank   A poor punt caused by the punter not making contact correctly. Named for a golf shot that's hit off the shank of the clubhead. Also used as a verb: "He really shanked that kick."

shield block   A block, often used downfield by receivers, on which the blocker simply tries to get his body between the opponent and the ball carrier to impede the defender's progress.

shift   The movement by one or more players from one position to another. For example, a player lines up in the backfield, then shifts into a *slot*. A defensive lineman will sometimes shift shortly before the snap to confuse the blocking scheme.

shoestring catch   A catch made by a receiver down around his feet or ankles, just before the ball hits the ground.

shoot   A route on which a running back goes a few yards downfield and cuts to the sideline at a 90-degree angle.

shoot the gap   Said of a defender, commonly a linebacker, who charges through a *gap* into the offensive backfield.

short side   1. The side of the offense opposite the *long side*. 2. The side of the field on which the ball is closest to the sideline. If the ball is on the right *hash mark*, the right side of the field is the short side.

short trap   A type of *trap* play on which the blocker travels only a short distance. For example, the right guard *pulls* to the right and traps the defensive left end.

short-yardage defense   A type of defense that typically has more linemen and fewer backs and/or linebackers than usual in an attempt to prevent the offense from gaining a small amount of yardage for a first down. See also *goal line defense*.

shotgun   A formation in which the quarterback is positioned 4 to 5 yards deep, behind the center. Used by the San Francisco 49ers as a standard offensive formation under Red Hickey in the early 1960s, it fell into disfavor but was revived by Tom Landry of the Dallas Cowboys for use in passing situations. Many teams now use the shotgun in such situations, though a few coaches dislike it because of the possibility of a poor snap from center.

shovel (or shuffle) pass   A pass thrown underhanded, sometimes with both hands. Often but not necessarily a lateral. So called because the arm action is much the same as that used in shoveling.

sideline and go   A route on which the receiver cuts sharply toward the sideline, then dashes straight downfield.

sideline route   A pass route on which the receiver drives downfield and cuts sharply to the sideline.

sideline takeoff   A route on which the receiver fakes a sideline route and then cuts downfield. Similar to the *sideline and go*, except that the pass is likely to be thrown much sooner.

silver stretch   The Detroit Lions' version of the run and shoot offense.

situational substitution   The use of substitute players based on the down and yardage situation. For example, on third down and long, the offense brings in more pass receivers and the defense counters with more defensive backs.

skinny post   A type of post route, usually used when the offense is near the goal line, on which the receiver is running almost straight down the field toward the goal post.

slam   Similar to a *brush block*, but with much harder contact. The intent is actually to move the defender before releasing to carry out another assignment.

slant   1. A play on which the running back, by design, follows a slanted route until he reaches the line of scrimmage. 2. A route on which the receiver goes downfield a few yards before cutting to the inside at a 30-degree angle.

slot   The area between the split end and the tackle, or between the flanker and tight end. An offensive player stationed in this area is called a "slot man" or "slot receiver."

snake in   A type of *curl* route on which the receiver is looking for first-down yardage. He runs a couple of yards beyond the first-down marker and then curls to the inside, back to the marker.

snake out   Similar to the *snake in*, but with an outside curl.

snap count   The number on which the ball is to be snapped. The quarterback used to call numbers in sequence, "1–2–3," but since about 1950 the word "hut" (if that's a word) has been used. If the snap count is 2, the ball will be snapped the second time the quarterback says "hut."

snap   The exchange of the ball from the center to a back that starts an offensive play.

sneak receiver   A receiver who delays for a couple of counts, possibly making a *brush block*, before sneaking out into the pass pattern. Most often the tight end or a running back.

spearing   Illegal maneuver in which the helmet is used as a weapon, often against the back of an opponent.

split backs   See *red*.

split end   An end who is stationed 4 or more yards from the offensive tackle.

spot pass   A route on which the receiver runs to a predetermined spot on the field and the quarterback throws the ball to that spot. See also *timing route*.

spread end   Now obsolete term for the *split end*.

sprint out   A maneuver on which the quarterback, after taking the snap, runs to one side or the other, also retreating somewhat. It's much faster than the *rollout*, and the quarterback doesn't get as deep. Often the prelude to a quick pass.

spy   A defensive player whose chief responsibility is to watch the quarterback to keep him from gaining yardage on a run when he can't find a receiver. A spy is used only against a very mobile quarterback, such as Randall Cunningham of the Philadelphia Eagles or Steve Young of the San Francisco 49ers. Also used as a verb: "The middle linebacker is spying on the quarterback."

square in   A route on which the receiver goes a short distance downfield, then cuts in at a 90-degree angle.

square out   A route on which the receiver goes a short distance downfield and cuts toward the sideline at a 90-degree angle.

square out and go   A route on which the receiver first runs a square out, then sprints downfield.

squeeze   A *double-team block* by the offensive guard and tackle.

stack defense   An alignment in which linebackers are positioned directly behind defensive linemen, rather than in the gaps between or outside them. Rarely used now, but featured by the Kansas City Chiefs under Hank Stram in the late 1960s.

stickum   Now illegal substance formerly used by some receivers and defensive backs to help the ball literally stick to their hands. Fred Biletnikoff of the Oakland Raiders was known for carrying huge gobs of the stuff on his socks.

stiff arm   To extend the arm in order to ward off a tackler. Also a noun: "You don't often see a running back with a good stiff arm nowadays."

stop and go   See *hitch and go*.

straight arm   See *stiff arm*.

streak   Same as *fly*.

string it out   To force a running back and his blockers toward the sideline before he can reach the line of scrimmage. While the defender who has *force* responsibility is usually supposed to try to keep a play to the inside, he should push it to the outside if it's obviously designed to go inside.

strong safety   The safety opposite the *strong side* of the offensive formation. Also known as the "tight safety" because, in a standard *man-to-man* defense, he covers the tight end.

strong side   The side of the offensive formation where the tight end is lined up.

stunt   A charge at an angle by a defensive lineman. Stunts are usually coordinated by two or more defenders and often by all of them. On an inside stunt, the linemen to the right of the ball charge to the left, and linemen to the left of the ball charge right. An outside stunt is just the opposite. There are also left stunts and right stunts. The basic idea is to confuse the offense's blocking scheme by turning a *two-gap* defense into a *one-gap* defense. A stunt is often coordinated with a *loop*.

stutter step   A short, choppy step used as a delay or misdirection tactic. On a *counter* play, for example, a running back will take one or more stutter steps in one direction to *influence* the defense before going in the other direction.

submarine   A maneuver on which a defender charges very low to get underneath his blocker. Often used by all defensive linemen in *short-yardage* situations. The intent is to confront the running back with a pile of players, both offensive and defensive.

suicide squad   The special team used on a kickoff or punt.

sweep   A play on which the running back goes wide, usually behind one or more pulling linemen. See also *power sweep*.

swing   A route on which a running back *bellies* back and then turns downfield outside the tight end or tackle. The ball will usually be thrown to him immediately after he turns, while he's still behind the line of scrimmage, so he can catch it while running at full speed. See also *flare*.

swing divide   A pass pattern on which the tight end angles to the middle of the field and the *near back* runs a swing route to the same side.

swirl   A route on which a receiver looks as if he's going to run a *crossing route*, then makes a sharp cut to the sideline.

tackle eligible   If there's no end stationed outside a tackle, he becomes an eligible receiver. The tackle eligible play used to be a surprise maneuver, but he's now required to tell an official that he'll be an eligible receiver on the play and the defense is notified.

tailback   A running back who's positioned directly behind the quarterback, 4 to 8 yards deep, with no other back behind him. Most commonly said of the deep back in the *I formation*.

taxi squad   NFL teams used to be allowed to have some players under contract who were not on the official roster. They practiced with the team and were sometimes activated as replacements for injured players. The phrase originated because Mickey McBride, the original owner of the Cleveland Browns, owned a taxicab company and hired spare players as cab drivers.

tee   A support used to hold the ball on kickoffs, but not allowed on field goal or conversion attempts.

3–4 defense   A defensive alignment with three linemen and four linebackers.

three-point stance   The most common position taken by a down lineman or running back, with one hand touching the ground, the knees at the same width as the shoulders, and the weight balanced.

tight end   An end usually stationed 2 to 4 yards from the offensive tackle, most often on the same side of the center as the *flanker*, which is the *strong side* of the formation. He functions both as a blocking lineman on running plays and as a pass receiver.

tight safety   See *strong safety*.

tight T   See *full house backfield*.

tip   Any small movement or change of position by a player that tells an opponent what his team is about to do. For example, if a cornerback is lined up slightly closer to the line of scrimmage than normal, it may tell the quarterback that the defense is going to use a zone. If a running back points his foot slightly in one direction or the other when he's in his stance, it may tell a defender that the offensive play is going in that direction.

toss   A lateral, usually to a running back, that's thrown rather softly so that he can catch it while running at top speed.

touch pass   A pass that's not thrown particularly hard but in the perfect location for a receiver to catch it. Often said of a throw that has to be lofted somewhat to get over a defender and into the receiver's hands.

trap   1. A type of play on which a defender is allowed to penetrate and is then blocked from the side so the running back can go through the area he vacated. Originally "mouse trap." 2. The type of block executed on a trap play.

trenches   The area on and near the line of scrimmage where offensive and defensive linemen collide when a play begins. Many coaches and commentators like to say, "This game will be won in the trenches."

triple flanker   An offensive alignment that has three pass receivers on one side, usually the split end, a flanker, and a *slot* man.

trips   Shorthand for the *triple flanker* formation, as in "trips right," meaning the three receivers are on the right side.

turn and go   A pass route, most commonly for the tight end, on which he cuts at a 90-degree angle toward the near sideline, moves back a couple of yards toward the center of the field, and then sprints downfield.

turn block   A block on which a lineman lets his defender get almost past him and then blocks him from the side to change his course. The effect is similar to that of a *trap* block.

turn in   A route on which a receiver drives downfield, turns in at a 90-degree angle, and comes back toward the quarterback.

turn out   A route on which a receiver goes downfield, cuts at a 90-degree angle toward the sideline, and comes back toward the quarterback.

turn out and in   A route on which the receiver seems to be running a *turn out*, but then comes back across the field at a 90-degree angle.

turn the corner   After a runner *makes the corner*, he turns it; that is, he turns downfield and runs along the sideline.

two-deep zone   A zone defense in which the cornerbacks and safeties cover the deep areas, while the linebackers cover the short areas.

two-gap   A defense in which each lineman is positioned directly opposite an offensive lineman. His goal is usually to charge straight ahead and try to control his blocker. So called because, if he succeeds, the defensive lineman controls the gaps on each side of the blocker.

two-minute drill   Technically, a practice session at which a team practices its *two-minute offense*, but often used to mean the offense itself, as in, "The Saints are going into their two-minute drill now."

two-minute offense   The type of offense used by a team trying to drive in the last two minutes of a half. Such an offense generally uses more passes than the team usually would, especially outside routes that allow a receiver to stop the clock by running out of bounds. See also *hurry-up offense*.

two-point stance   A stance on which the player doesn't have a hand on the ground. Commonly used by wide receivers and the tailback in the I formation. See also *three-point stance*.

U-back   See *H-back*.

up   A pass route, usually for the tight end, on which he begins straight downfield, fakes to the outside, and continues downfield at full speed.

up and under   A type of *double coverage* on which a receiver has one defender in front of him ("under") and another behind him ("up").

uprights   See *goal posts*.

V out   A pass route on which the receiver goes downfield, cuts in at about a 30-degree angle, then cuts back to the outside at about a 45-degree angle.

veer   A play on which, by design, the running back appears to be going into the line but then cuts outside the tackle or tight end. Sometimes a back will perform the same maneuver, not by design, but simply because there's no *hole* inside. See also *bounce it outside*.

victory defense   Outmoded term for *prevent defense*.

waffle   See *pancake*.

weak safety   See *free safety*.

weak side   The side of the offensive formation opposite the tight end.

wedge   1. A short-yardage running play on which the linemen usually use *power blocks* and the back simply tries to find a *crease* that he can force himself through. 2. The group of players, usually four or five, who are stationed in front of the kickoff returner to run interference.

wedge breaker   A player on the kickoff team whose assignment is to smash into the *wedge* in an attempt to break it up.

wide out   See *wide receiver*.

wide receiver   A flanker or split end; in general, any receiver who lines up 4 or more yards from the tight end or offensive tackle.

wide side   See *long side*

wingback   A back who lines up, most often, just outside the tight end but occasionally just outside the weak-side tackle.

wrap-around draw   A *draw* on which the quarterback retreats behind the running back, then reaches around him to make the hand-off.

X   The left end. Usually the split end, but the tight end if the left side is the strong side.

Y stretch   An offensive alignment on which the flanker is on the line of scrimmage, becoming an end, while the tight end lines up outside him and then goes in motion back toward the center of the field, often to become the *lead* blocker.

Y   The right end. Usually the tight end, but the split end if the left side is the strong side.

Z   The flanker.

zig in   A pass route on which the receiver goes down the field, fakes to the inside, cuts outside for a short distance, then cuts back to the inside and runs toward the post.

zig out   A pass route on which the receiver goes down the field, fakes to the outside, cuts inside for a short distance, and finally cuts outside again to run toward the corner.

zone blocking   A blocking scheme in which offensive players are assigned to block anyone in a specific area, rather than a specific defender.

zone defense   A type of pass defense in which defenders cover specific areas of the field, rather than specific receivers.

The Offense

I haven't seen a new football play since I was in high school. You have just so many holes in a line and you have eleven men playing, and there's only so many ways you can go through those holes, and those ways have been used for forty, fifty years.

—Red Grange, quoted in Myron Cope, *The Game That Was*

Grange was probably right, in a sense. Having a guard pull to lead interference was developed at Yale in 1888. In fact, the first pulling guard was the now familiar Pudge Heffelfinger. The famous power sweep that helped the Green Bay Packers establish a dynasty under Vince Lombardi in the 1960s was simply a T formation version of the single-wing cutback play devised by Pop Warner about 1912. The "flea flicker" was created by Grange's college coach, Bob Zuppke, in 1906. Two years later, Zuppke invented the screen pass.

Yet there's no question that football is much more sophisticated today than it was when Grange played in the late 1920 and early 1930s. For one thing, in Grange's era there were fewer than twenty players on the roster, the eleven starters were expected to stay in the game for all sixty minutes unless they got hurt, and a team usually had one player who did most of the passing and kicking.

Today, of course, there are forty-seven players on an NFL squad for any given game, and all of them are specialists in one way or another. The two-platoon system, which replaced the one-platoon system when free substitution was adopted, has in turn been replaced by a multi-platoon system.

The typical NFL team has not only a punter and a place-kicker, but a long snapper, a receiver who's used only in passing situations, a running back who comes in only on third-down situations, a second tight end for short-yardage plays, a backup offensive linemen who's used as a third tight end in ultra short-yardage situations, a couple of defensive backs for the nickel and dime defenses, and probably a defensive lineman or two who are pass rushing specialists.

As in medicine, specialization means that players can intensively practice the things that they're called upon to do. Today's salaries also allow them to be full-time professionals. Until about 1960, most players had off-season jobs. Now most of them spend a good part of the off-season staying in shape and building strength. They go to "mini-camps" in the spring to sharpen their skills and report to full-scale training camps in July.

And yet—yes, Grange was basically right. To look at the development of offensive and defensive strategy and tactics as an evolution isn't quite the right perspective. It's been more cyclical than evolutionary. The pro offenses of the 1960s greatly resembled the single-wing offenses of the 1920s, and the "newest" of formations, the run and shoot, is very much like the spread formation developed by Dutch Meyer at Texas Christian University in the mid-1930s.

The goal of the offense is rather simple: Get more players at the point of attack, wherever it is, than the defense has. There are two basic ways of doing it. The first is to mass your own players there to overwhelm the

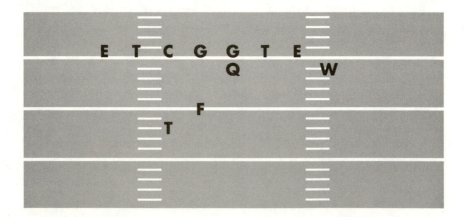

SINGLE WING
Devised in 1912 by Pop Warner at the Carlisle Indian Institute, the single wing was the most commonly used offensive formation until well into the 1940s, and the Pittsburgh Steelers used it until they switched to the T formation in 1952.

defenders. The second is to use deception to move defenders away from the point of attack.

Any team uses both methods, or a combination of the two, at one time or another, but each team prefers one to the other because each coach has his preferences.

The modern "pro set" was developed by Clark Shaughnessy, coach of the Los Angeles Rams, in 1949. At that time, pro teams usually lined up in the straight T formation, often with one end split wide, and then sent a halfback in motion. Shaughnessy had Tom Fears as his split end and, instead of using a man in motion, he positioned halfback Elroy Hirsch as a flanker on the other side. With quarterbacks Bob Waterfield and Norm Van Brocklin throwing, the Rams developed an outstanding passing attack.

By 1954, all NFL teams were using the formation, though there were some variations. Running plays out of the pro set originally emphasized finesse. Offensive linemen were split somewhat, creating holes in the defense, and blocking schemes generally used simple one-on-one blocks to keep those holes open for quick plays.

Vince Lombardi changed that after joining the New York Giants as an assistant coach in 1954. A single-wing guard in his college days, Lombardi built a running attack based on single-wing principles, with double-teaming, cross-blocking, and pulling guards. His success with the Giants and later as head coach during the Green Bay Packer dynasty years led many teams to adopt the same type of attack.

The Lombardi philosophy was to use the run to set up the pass, and that became the philosophy of most NFL coaches during the 1960s and well into the 1970s. Meanwhile, Bill Walsh, a young assistant coach with the Cincinnati Bengals in 1968, began building an offense with the opposite philosophy: Use the pass to set up the run.

Walsh became head coach of the San Francisco 49ers in 1979 and took the team to three Super Bowl victories during the 1980s. Using the same system, the 49ers won a fourth Super Bowl after Walsh temporarily left coaching. Again, success bred imitation. In 1993, four former Walsh assistants were NFL head coaches and four others were offensive coordinators.

The Walsh system usually uses split backs, often sending one in motion, and it features a short, quick drop by the quarterback and a quick release to avoid sacks. Two or three receivers often enter the same zone, and the pass frequently goes to the shallower receiver, since zone defenses are basically designed to prevent longer passes.

Running backs are often used as receivers and the pass becomes what announcers like to call a "long hand-off," designed to give the receiver a chance to run for considerably more yardage after catching the ball. Once the short pass has been established, a pump fake to a shallow receiver can often allow a deeper receiver to break away from his defender for a long gain.

The other very successful offense of the 1980s, though less imitated, was the one-back formation. Like Lombardi and Walsh, Joe Gibbs originally developed the formation as an assistant coach, with the San Diego Chargers. Gibbs took over the Washington Redskins in 1981. He took them to four Super Bowls and won three of them during the next twelve seasons.

The one-back offense is so called because there's only one running back behind the quarterback. There are usually two tight ends and two wide receivers. One reason Gibbs designed the offense is that so many defensive teams were putting fast linebackers on the weak side to blitz the passer. With two tight ends, there is no weak side and each outside linebacker is confronted by a blocker.

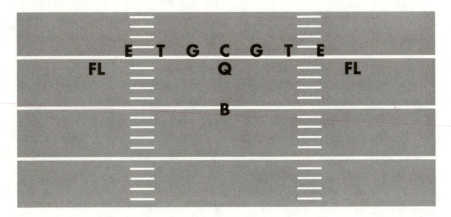

ONE-BACK FORMATION

As an assistant coach with the San Diego Chargers in 1979 and 1980, Joe Gibbs helped create the one-back formation. He then became head coach of the Washington Redskins and guided them to three Super Bowl victories using the formation.

Many coaches don't like the idea of the one-back formation for two reasons: There's less deception, since only one back can carry the ball, and there's no fullback to act as a lead blocker. However, the Gibbs system often puts a tight end in motion, as a so-called "H back," either to get into a pass pattern or to turn into the line and make a lead block. The one-back system works best when that one running back is a strong, powerful runner, since most plays go between the tight ends.

· Another formation that gained some popularity in the late 1980s and early 1990s was the "run and shoot," which uses four wide receivers, one running back, and no tight ends. The Houston Oilers were the first NFL team to try it, under Jerry Glanville in 1985, and they've continued using it since Jack Pardee took over in 1990. Glanville, meanwhile, installed a similar system, called the "Red Gun," with the Atlanta Falcons. The Detroit Lions began using the "Silver Stretch," another version of the run and shoot, in 1989.

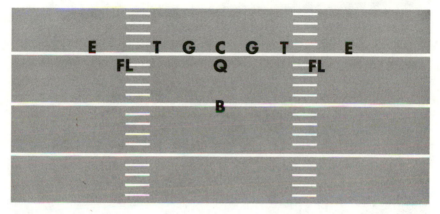

RUN AND SHOOT
The Houston Oilers began using the run and shoot in 1985 and it was later adapted as "the red gun" by the Atlanta Falcons and as the "silver stretch" by the Detroit Lions. However, all three teams have now abandoned it, primarily because it's not a good scoring formation when the offense is close to the goal line.

With a good passer like Houston's Warren Moon and three or four good receivers, the run and shoot can eat up yardage quickly. Its biggest drawback is that it becomes less effective as the team gets closer to scoring. When there's less field to work with, the four wide receivers can't spread out the defensive backs as they can when they're farther from the goal line, and the lack of a tight end makes it difficult for a run and shoot team to punch the ball in on the ground from close range.

One other relatively recent approach should be mentioned. The "hurry-up" or "no-huddle" offense, originally developed by Sam Wyche when he was with the Cincinnati Bengals, isn't a formation. As the name suggests, it speeds up the game by having the quarterback call plays without huddling up his team. Its chief advantage is that it keeps the defense from making the situational substitutions so common in pro football today.

Of course, the offense can't make situational substitutions, either. The Buffalo Bills have done well with the no-huddle approach because their running back, Thurman Thomas, is an excellent receiver as well as a fine runner. He can stay in the game to catch the ball on third-down situations when other teams would bring in another running back for that purpose.

Whatever type of offense a team uses, it all starts with the quarterback, literally. Although the play is sent in from the sidelines, except in the no-huddle offense, the quarterback has to call it in the huddle. In a kind of code, he tells his teammates the formation, the play, and the snap count.

For example, he may say something like, "Red right 24 trap on two." "Red" is a commonly used code word for the formation also known as split backs. "Right" is the strong-side of the formation, where the tight end will line up.

Running plays are usually given numbers. Numbering systems vary from team to team, but quite often the quarterback is 1, the right halfback 2, the fullback 3, and the left halfback 4, based on the backfield positions of the original T formation.

Holes are also numbered. Most teams use even numbers for holes on the right side of the line, odd numbers for holes on the left side. With this system, a running play called "24" sends the right halfback through the hole between the right guard and right tackle.

However, there are different ways of getting a back to and through a particular hole. On this particular play, "24 trap," the left guard is going to pull to make a trap block on the left defensive end. In order to give the guard time to make his block, the halfback will delay by taking a quick step to his right before heading forward to take the hand-off.

Meanwhile, the other back bellies to the right, because later on there will be another play in the same sequence, "46 pitch," on which the quarterback fakes the hand-off to the first back and throws a pitchout to the second back going outside the tight end.

Teams often have some commonly used plays that are identified by names rather than numbers. For example, when Franco Harris was the fullback for the Pittsburgh Steelers during their Super Bowl years, he gained a lot of yardage on an off-tackle play that was simply called "Franco."

Receivers are identified by letters. "A" is the weak-side running back, "B" the strong-side running back, "X" the left end (usually the split end), "Y" the right end (usually the tight end), and "Z" the flanker. In the split backs formation, the 4 back is "A" and the 2 back is "B." If either of them moved into the fullback spot, directly behind the quarterback, he would become the 3 back on a running play, but his designation as a receiver would remain the same.

Pass routes have names, but most teams now use a numbering system to call patterns. The call for a pass play might sound something like this: "Red right, A flare, X fly, Y out, Z post, on two." Since it can take a lot of time to tell four or five receivers their pass routes, the numbering system is utilized to give the quarterback a three digit number telling the ends and flanker what to do. For example, "294" tells the X receiver to run his 2 route, the Y receiver to run his 9 route, and the Z receiver to run his 4 route. The sequence is always X, Y, Z.

AT THE LINE

After calling the play, the quarterback brings his team to the line of scrimmage and quickly sizes up the defense. The original play was almost certainly sent in from the sideline, but the quarterback has to make the final decision on whether it's the right play against the defense he's going to face.

The quarterback looks for unusual changes in alignment, sometimes quite small and sometimes glaring. A safety man may be cheating slightly in one direction or the other so he can get into his zone coverage quickly. Or all the linebackers may be somewhat closer to the line of scrimmage than usual, indicating that they're going to blitz.

If such a "tip" tells the quarterback that he should run another play, he can call an automatic, or audible. At this point, he says something like "Green, 42—Hut—Hut—." If green is the "live" color, he has just changed the play to 42. If it's not the live color, it's a dummy audible meant only to mislead the defense. Some teams change the live color each quarter and others change it from one series to the next.

The audible is not nearly as common as it used to be, largely because defenses now do so much faking of their own. Defenders, for example, often fake a blitz to try to get the quarterback to call an audible, then drop out of it when he begins the snap count.

When Lombardi's style of offense was in fashion during the 1960s, fans were often told to watch the guards. If the guards both pulled, it meant the "power sweep." If only one of them pulled, it meant a trap play in that direction. If they both charged forward, it usually meant a run inside the tackles, though a play-action pass might be coming up. And if they both retreated, it was a pass play or a draw.

The trouble was, the defense could read the same keys fans were told to read. Offenses had to become less readable by changing their blocking schemes. They developed "sucker" plays, in which a guard pulls only to mislead the defense, and they also began pulling tackles and even, on occasion, the center. Under Joe Gibbs, the Washington Redskins had a play on which a guard and tackle pulled in one direction to influence the defense, while the other guard pulled in the opposite direction to lead the play.

There are still things to look for, keys that the fan and the defense can both read. First is the formation. The red, or split backs, formation is often used in passing situations, but a team can run outside quickly on pitches or tosses out of the alignment. It's also a good formation for quick traps and draw plays.

The blue formation, which was the original version of the pro set, with the strong-side running back lined up between the guard and tackle, can send the fullback quickly up the middle as a runner or lead blocker. The power sweep is often run out of this formation, with a fake to the fullback and a hand-off to the sweeping back.

The brown formation, which is the opposite of the blue, offers the same possibilities to the weak side, but the power sweep won't be nearly as powerful because there's no tight end to help with the blocking there. Since three receivers—the tight end, flanker, and strong-side running back— are in a position to get into a pattern quickly, the brown formation can be effective with several combination patterns. For example, a drag pattern, in which one of the receivers moves through a zone to clear it of defenders and the back then enters the cleared area, could work well.

In any of these sets, if one of the backs is positioned somewhat closer to the line of scrimmage than the other, it's likely that he will be a lead blocker on a running play.

The I formation, in which two running backs line up behind the quarterback, one about 4 to 5 yards deep and the other about 7 to 8 yards deep, is a well-balanced running formation. The deep back, who is usually the ball carrier, gets the hand-off far enough behind the line of scrimmage to allow him to react to the defense and choose a hole. A common play out of the I is a quick toss sending him wide in one direction or the other, but he'll often cut back against the grain if the defense over-pursues to the outside. The I can also be a good passing formation, since the quarterback is already in passing position after faking the deep hand-off.

Motion before the snap is used for several reasons. As already noted, one of the tight ends in the one-back formation often comes in motion toward the center of the field in order to become a lead blocker. He turns into the line of scrimmage as soon as the ball is snapped and the running back will soon follow. Some teams use the single tight end in a similar way. Of course, if he goes in motion, the flanker has to be positioned on the line of scrimmage, not behind it, or the offense will be penalized for an illegal formation.

When a wide receiver goes in motion, he often comes all the way across the formation; that is, from one side of the field to the other. The motion makes it more difficult for a defender to slow him up and it also gives the receiver some momentum. The 49ers and other teams that use a form of Bill Walsh's offense like to have this receiver cross the line of scrimmage at an angle toward the outside and then cut sharply to the sideline to take advantage of that momentum.

If a defensive back comes running across the defensive formation with the receiver, he's going to have man-to-man coverage. Sometimes motion is used primarily to find out whether the defense will be man-to-man or zone.

In a passing situation, many teams like to go to the split backs formation and send one of the backs in motion. When this happens, there's likely to be some kind of combination pattern on that side of the field. For example, the tight end and flanker may run a crossing pattern, while the back runs a route right through the spot where they crossed.

Immediately after the snap on a passing play, the quarterback and receivers have to read the defense. As will be seen in the next chapter, there are several types of zone defense, and pass routes will vary accordingly. While man-to-man coverage is more straightforward, there are some possible variations. And some defenses combine man-to-man and zone principles.

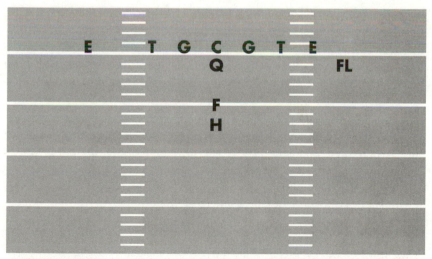

I FORMATION
Originally developed on the college level, the I formation has sometimes been used by professional teams to feature an outstanding running back, such as Eric Dickerson, Earl Campbell, or O. J. Simpson.

The quarterback and his receivers have to read the same thing, or the result is likely to be an interception. Suppose the split end is supposed to run a post pattern and he has man-to-man coverage. Although the cornerback will be covering him one-on-one, there will be inside help from the free safety if the ball is thrown in his direction.

A post pattern would normally take the receiver right into the area of the free safety. He has to change his route to a "skinny post," on which he goes straighter downfield than usual, to avoid the safety, and the quarterback has to throw the ball quickly and without too much loft to give the safety little time to help on coverage. But if the receiver runs a skinny post and the quarterback throws the regular post, the free safety has a virtually certain interception.

Most route adjustments are made against zone coverage. Generally, any time a receiver sees that his planned route is going to take him into the strength of a zone, he should alter or break off his route to get into a seam or dead area between zones.

Adjustments also have to be made against blitzes. Most teams have pre-determined pass patterns against particular blitzes. Since man-to-man coverage is assured, deep routes can be effective, especially if a receiver has the speed to outsprint his defender.

A blitz adjustment pattern will often have the team's fastest receiver running a fly or post, with a second receiver running a quick slant and perhaps a third simply getting into the shallow middle area vacated by the blitzing linebackers. The quarterback will have to throw the ball quickly, but he can still complete a deep pass if the receiver can get there quickly enough. Because of the lack of defenders in the secondary, even a short pass can gain a lot of yardage because the receiver may well have plenty of room in which to run.

DOWN-AND-YARDAGE

Offensive coordinators think in terms of down-and-yardage situations. What they plan to do depends in large part on the type of defensive unit they'll be facing for a particular game, but some generalizations are possible.

First-and-ten Any coach or television commentator will tell you this is the most important down of all. If a team consistently gains good yardage on first down, it can keep the defense guessing about what it will do on subsequent downs. But an incomplete pass or a running play that gains little or no yardage sets up the dreaded second-and-long situation. The offense would like to gain at least 4 yards.

The worst thing that can happen on first down is a sack. Young quarterbacks are sacked too often on first down. Veteran quarterbacks are more likely to throw the ball away, if it's at all possible. The next worst thing is a holding penalty. The loss of 10 yards obviously hurts, but at least there's no loss of down as there is with a sack.

Early in the game, you'll see the teams' "bread-and-butter" plays. A running team will generally use the running plays it has most confidence in. A passing team will throw the passes that should be most successful against this particular defense.

A certain amount of probing goes on here, especially on a team's first few series of downs. The coaches in the press box will be watching closely to see how the defense reacts. If a play that should have worked, in theory, is stopped because the defense did something unexpected, it may set up another play that takes advantage of that defensive reaction.

Against a strong running attack, for example, the defense may mass eight men near the line of scrimmage to stop it, and the offense should switch to play-action passes to loosen up the defense and make the running game effective.

First and long This can come up, of course, only if there's an offensive penalty on first down. It's a similar situation to second and long. The offense would like to gain a pretty good chunk of yardage, but not necessarily a first down. Look for a medium-range pass, a short pass to a back after other receivers have gone deep to lure defenders away, a screen pass, or a draw play.

Second and long The key phrase for the offense is "Don't get greedy" in this situation. Unless a receiver unexpectedly comes open deep, the goal should be to gain at least half the yardage required for the first down. If it's, say, second and eighteen after a sack, the offense wants a minimum 9 or 10 yards.

As with first and long, a pass to a back or another type of quick pass, such as a slant, that gives the receiver a chance to run for additional yardage, is a good possibility. Draws and screen passes are most often run on second and long.

Second and medium With 3 to 6 yards to go on second down, the possibilities are almost endless, which is why a good gain on first down is so important. The one thing the offense doesn't want to do is lose yardage, so slow-developing plays, such as draws and screens, are unlikely, as are long passes, since there's the risk of a sack. Otherwise, almost anything goes.

Second and short There are two ways of playing this situation: Pretend it's third and short and go for the first down, or try for a long gainer, quite likely on a play-action pass. If it's incomplete, there's still a good chance of picking up first-down yardage on the next play. If the offense does throw the ball, the quarterback absolutely has to avoid being sacked or intercepted. If he's rushed hard, or if he can't find a receiver, he's got to throw the ball safely away.

Third and long Desperation time. A pass is almost a certainty. A few teams will occasionally run a draw play in this situation, but most coaches don't like to do it because a draw is a gamble and, if it fails, they don't have another down on which to pick up the first down.

The general philosophy here should be to throw the ball at least far enough downfield to get the first. That's more difficult than it sounds. During the last several seasons, there have been many third and long plays on which a pass was thrown a yard or two short of first-down yardage and the receiver was immediately tackled.

Why does that happen? Because defenses are perfectly aware of where the first-down marker is. In this situation, the defensive team is likely to play a very tight zone that, in effect, sets up a picket line of three or four defenders across the field at that point. Since a receiver is trained to break off his route against a zone defense, he tends to do it even in this situation and comes up short of the first down.

There are pass routes and patterns designed specifically to gain first downs. The "all curl" pattern, for example, calls for all receivers to go down the field past the first-down marker and then come back toward the quarterback. But against a good, all-out pass rush, there probably won't be time to throw the ball if there's too much yardage to be gained.

On third and long, some teams will deliberately throw the ball short to a receiver on the move in the hope that he'll be able to run for the first down. The San Francisco 49ers have used Jerry Rice and the Green Bay Packers have used Sterling Sharpe on that kind of route with a great deal of success. But it takes a special kind of receiver to make it work. There aren't many Jerry Rices or Sterling Sharpes around.

This is the one situation where a sack isn't so terrible, unless the team is deep in its own territory. Even at the risk of being sacked, the quarterback should be willing to wait just a little longer than usual for a receiver to get free.

Third and short Notice that there is no third and medium. That's because the offense has to get the first down right now or kick the ball, so even third and three or four is considered third and long, from a strategic standpoint. In fact, a surprising number of teams go into the shotgun formation on third down and less than three. That mystifies me, because it eliminates not only the threat of the run, but the play-action pass.

Only teams with great confidence in the running game go to the run on third and short, unless it's very short yardage. The defense will be massed at the line of scrimmage, so a quick pass off a play fake can be very effective here. Other types of quick passes, from a short drop, are also possibilities: A look-in to the tight end, for example, or a quick slant by a wide receiver.

Occasionally, you might see a swing or flare pass to a back, but most coaches don't like that play in this situation, again on the principle that the ball should be thrown far enough downfield to get the first down.

The two-minute offense A team that has the ball at or near the two-minute mark in a half will usually go to a hurry-up offense, unless it has the lead late in the game. When the clock is stopped, two or more plays will be called in the huddle; when it's running, the quarterback will use audibles at the line of scrimmage.

You can expect a pass on almost every play unless it's a very short yardage situation, when the offense will sacrifice some time with a run to get a new series of downs.

Field position, the score of the game, and the number of time-outs available have much more to do with play calling during the two-minute drill than down and yardage situations. A team that needs only a field goal and has all three time-outs left will be much more likely to run a draw play or something like a quick trap than a team that needs a touchdown and has only one time-out.

During the two-minute drill, it's almost as if every down is second and long. The defense will be trying to stop the long pass, so the offense will probably have more success with medium range throws. Outside routes that allow the receiver to get out of bounds to stop the clock after catching the ball are more likely than routes over the middle. However, if the team has the luxury of being able to call a time-out or two, a pass into the middle of the field might be very productive, because the defense will be protecting the sideline areas.

There are situations in which a team is quite willing to settle for a field goal. If the score is tied or the opposition leads by just 1 or 2 points with time running out in the game, a field goal will obviously provide the winning points. The offense will try to save a time-out to make it easier to get the field goal unit into the game.

Clock management is vitally important in such a situation. Within relatively easy field goal range, the offense wants to use time rather than conserving it so the opposition won't be able to mount a scoring drive after the kick. If the ball is on a hash mark, a simple run might be used to get it closer to the middle of the field. And the kick may well be attempted before fourth down; if it's blocked, or if the snap is mishandled, there will be another chance.

POSITIONS

To this point, we've looked at the offense as a unit. Now let's take a quick look at the qualities a player needs to excel at each of the offensive positions.

Center

Center may well be the most difficult position to play, after quarterback. In the 1940s and early 1950s, when defenses used a five-man line, the center was one of the biggest offensive linemen because he had to cope with a large middle guard every week. Then the four-man defensive line came in and centers shrank, since they were called upon primarily to block middle linebackers.

Today, some teams use three-man fronts and others use four-man fronts, so the center's role changes from one week to the next. In addition, the center is often given the responsibility of calling the blocking scheme for a play, depending on how the defense sets up. So modern centers need to be big, fast, *and* intelligent.

The average starting center in the NFL is 6-foot-3 and weighs somewhere between 270 and 280 pounds. However, Bruce Matthews of the Houston Oilers, perhaps the best in the game right now, is bigger than most at 6-foot-5 and 291 pounds.

Linemen

Offensive linemen in general have become much bigger in the last twenty years. During the early 1970s, most offensive tackles were 6-foot-4 to 6-foot-5 and weighed 245 to 255 pounds. Guards were somewhat smaller, at about 6-foot-3 and 240 to 250 pounds. Their roles were considerably different: Guards had to do a lot of pulling, while tackles were basically stationary.

There's less difference between the positions now. The average guard or tackle of the 1990s is about 6-foot-4 and ranges from 280 to 300 pounds, though there are quite a few over 300. Tackles, too, are frequently called on to pull out to lead interference and guards spend a lot of time helping the center handle the nose tackle when facing the 3–4 defense.

Good run blocking requires speed, power, and aggressiveness. Good pass blocking is essentially passive. On pocket passes, an offensive lineman is taught to retreat gradually, absorbing blows from the defender and using agile footwork to keep his body between the defender and the quarterback at all times. Fast reaction time is also a requirement. Defensive rushers use all sorts of moves to try to fly past blockers. When a defensive end takes a strong outside rush, the best thing the offensive tackle can do is to keep him outside until he's gone well past the quarterback, but that's much easier said than done.

Only the very best NFL linemen are exceptionally good at both run blocking and pass blocking, because such different traits are required. In general, a team's left tackle is usually the best pass blocker, because he usually has to handle the defense's best rusher, while the right tackle is probably a better run blocker. The left guard is likely to be the best of the linemen at pulling because he'll do a lot of the leading and trapping on the strong-side, and the right guard will more often be called on to drive block a defensive tackle or help the center with the nose tackle against the 3–4.

Tight End

The ideal tight end is rare. He would have the size and power to block a defensive end one-on-one, the speed to get into a pass pattern quickly, and great hands. Because that's an unusual combination of qualities, many teams now use one tight end in running situations and another in passing situations.

Of course, a team that emphasizes the running game will choose a tight end for his ability to block, while a passing team will want a skilled receiver. As a result, there's a tremendous variation in size among professional tight ends. At one extreme is the 6-foot-5, 284-pound Eric Green of the Pittsburgh Steelers. At the other is Brent Jones of the pass-oriented San Francisco 49ers, who is 6-foot-4 and 230 pounds.

Perhaps the best all-around tight end in the NFL right now is Keith Jackson of the Miami Dolphins. At 6-foot-2 and 249 pounds, Jackson is a devastating blocker, but he's also a sure-handed receiver with surprising speed. Although he was used almost entirely as a blocker during his college career at the University of Oklahoma, Jackson caught 81 passes in his rookie season, 1988, when he was with the Philadelphia Eagles.

Wide Receivers

Wide receivers also come in a variety of sizes, but for a different reason. A team that uses the standard pro set most of the time would ideally like to have a speed receiver and a possession receiver in the starting lineup.

Although it's not a hard and fast rule, pure speed receivers tend to be rather small, by pro football standards. A few years ago, there were quite a lot of small receivers in the league, collectively referred to as "Smurfs." Among the best was the 5-foot-9, 181-pound Mark Clayton, who caught 81 touchdown passes in ten seasons as a starter with the Miami Dolphins.

Possession receivers tend to be taller and stronger. They're often called upon to go over the middle to catch relatively short passes for first-down yardage, and they frequently need to out-jump or out-fight defenders for the ball. Among the best of that type is Haywood Jeffires (pronounced "Jeffries") of the Houston Oilers. The 6-foot-2, 201-pounder led the NFL with 100 receptions in 1991, averaging just 11.8 yards a catch and scoring only 7 touchdowns. Clayton caught 30 fewer passes that season but scored 5 more touchdowns.

The very best, of course, can function as speed receivers or possession receivers. They're big, strong, and fast, able to break tackles and elude defenders to turn short passes into long gains. The three best all-around wide receivers in the NFL right now are probably Jerry Rice of San Francisco, Sterling Sharpe of Green Bay, and Michael Irvin of Dallas. They're similar in size. Rice and Irvin are both 6-foot-2 and 200 pounds, while Sharpe is an inch shorter and five pounds heavier. None of them is a real speedster, but all three have above average speed and they all have the moves to throw defenders off balance so they can get free deep. They're also very good at running with the ball after the catch.

Running Backs

Running backs come in several different packages. But the best runners of today are about the same size as those of twenty years ago. In 1973, the top fifteen rushers in the NFL averaged out at 6 feet tall and 211 pounds. In 1993, the average was 5-foot-11¾ and 215 pounds.

The best pure runner of them all, Detroit's Barry Sanders, is only 5-foot-8, but he weighs 203 pounds. The two best all-around running backs, excellent receivers and runners, are Thurman Thomas of Buffalo and Emmitt Smith of Dallas. Thomas is 5-foot-10 and 198 pounds, while Smith is 5-foot-9 and 209 pounds.

The type of offense a team uses dictates the type of running backs it looks for. Both Buffalo and Dallas like to use a back as a lead blocker, often out of the I formation, so they both have big fullbacks who don't often carry the ball. Daryl "Moose" Johnston of Dallas is a 238-pounder and Buffalo's Carwell Gardner weighs 244 pounds.

If a team usually uses the standard pro set, with backs lined up at the same depth, there is no genuine fullback. However, such a team may have a bigger back who's usually aligned behind the quarterback to act as lead blocker, with a smaller, faster back who does most of the actual running.

The one-back offense works best with a big, powerful, and durable runner, since he's called upon to carry the ball often between the tackles without having a lead blocker. The Washington Redskins had their most success with the offense when the 6-foot-4, 235-pound John Riggins played the position.

Many teams now have a back who's used primarily as a receiver on third-down situations. These are players who have a knack for catching the ball in an open area of a zone defense and running for additional yardage. A couple of the best during recent years have been Ronnie Harmon of the Buffalo Bills and San Diego Chargers and Todd McNair of the Kansas City Chiefs.

Other teams have a kind of change-of-pace back, usually a smaller, speedier runner who's brought in from time to time to give the offense options it wouldn't have with its starter. The 5-foot-7, 180-pound Dave Meggett plays that role for the New York Giants. A speedy, darting runner, Meggett frequently catches short passes that give him a chance to use his elusiveness in the open field, and he sometimes runs the ball on draw plays out of the shotgun formation. Eric Metcalf is a similar kind of role player for the Cleveland Browns.

Quarterback

The ideal quarterback is often described in physical terms: Height, weight, arm strength, and so forth. But the two most important qualities for a winning quarterback are confidence and leadership. Given those qualities, he can overcome most physical deficiencies.

Yes, height helps the quarterback see downfield. But, with pass rushers in the 6-foot-3 to 6-foot-8 range, no NFL quarterback is tall enough to "see over the defensive linemen," as some commentators insist he must. Yes, a solid physique helps a quarterback stand up to the punishment he takes. And, yes, a strong arm is also a valuable attribute.

But Joe Montana, whom some consider the greatest quarterback of all time, isn't exactly an imposing physical specimen at 6-foot-2 and only 195 pounds, and he can't throw the ball nearly as far down the field as, say, John Elway. Montana wasn't even a full-time starter in his college days at Notre Dame, and the San Francisco 49ers didn't choose him until the third round of the 1979 NFL draft.

However, Montana quickly established himself as a superb professional quarterback because of the two qualities mentioned above: Confidence and leadership. The two go hand in hand. If a quarterback is a leader, he communicates his confidence to his teammates and they become better players as a result.

Joe Theismann is another example. Only 6 feet tall and 190 pounds, he was projected as a kick returner or defensive back by most NFL teams and he spent three years in the Canadian Football League because he wanted to play quarterback. After joining the Washington Redskins in 1974, he was used primarily as a punt returner for two seasons. But he finally became the team's starting quarterback and led the Redskins to victory in Super Bowl XVII after the 1982 season.

Whatever scouts and coaches may have thought of him, the fiery, combative Theismann never doubted his own abilities and neither did his teammates.

A quarterback whom many scouts considered a "can't-miss" prospect because of his size and skills, Vinnie Testaverde is 6-foot-5 and 215 pounds and he has one of the strongest arms ever seen on a football field. Testaverde is a prime example of what happens to many promising young quarterbacks. The first player chosen in the 1987 draft, by the Tampa Bay Buccaneers, he was consigned to a poor team that offered little support and his confidence was destroyed.

Testaverde was traded to the Cleveland Browns in 1993 and became the team's starting quarterback midway through the season. With a better supporting cast, he showed signs of living up to his potential that season and restored confidence may yet make him a top quarterback.

That's what happened to Jim Plunkett, under similar circumstances. Another sure-fire prospect, Plunkett won the Heisman Trophy at Stanford and was the rookie of the year with the New England Patriots in 1971. However, he took a beating behind an inferior line for five years and was traded to the San Francisco 49ers, who released him after the 1977 season.

Picked up by the Oakland Raiders in 1978, Plunkett was a backup until the 1980 season, when he had to take over after starter Dan Pastorini suffered a broken leg. All he did was guide them to six straight regular season victories and an NFL championship. He completed 13 of 21 passes for 261 yards and 3 touchdowns to be named most valuable player in Oakland's Super Bowl victory over the Philadelphia Eagles. Again, it was new-found confidence that made the difference in his career.

Intangibles are important at any position and many players have succeeded in pro football despite a lack of sheer physical ability. But those intangibles, the things that can't be measured by scales or rulers or stopwatches, are most important at the quarterback position.

The prototype of the pro quarterback who had intangibles in abundance was Bobby Layne. Teammates kidded him about his awkward walk, his potbelly, and some of the "dying quail" passes he threw, but Layne led the Detroit Lions to NFL championships in 1952 and 1953.

The Lions took over on their own 20-yard line, losing 16–10 to the Cleveland Browns with time running out in the 1953 championship game. A Texan, Layne told his teammates in the huddle, "Y'all just block and ol' Bobby'll pass you right to the championship. Ol' Bobby will get you six big ones."

During the next sixty seconds of play, he completed five of seven passes for 80 yards and the tying touchdown—the "six big ones." The extra point won the title for Detroit.

If Layne were entering the pros out of college today, he probably wouldn't be rated highly by scouts. He wasn't, even in his own time; he began his NFL career as a third-string quarterback for the Chicago Bears. Like Johnny Unitas, Bart Starr, and a number of other Hall of Fame quarterbacks, Layne was not appreciated until he finally got the chance to show how he could lead a team. And that's what being a quarterback is all about.

CHAPTER 5

The Defense

Until 1933, when the forward pass became a much bigger part of pro football than it had been, defenses were rather simple. Teams almost always used a seven-man line. The standard defense in a running situation was the seven-box, with two linebackers and two defensive halfbacks. In a passing situation, the defense would usually shift into the seven-diamond, with one linebacker, two defensive backs, and a safety man.

As the game began to open up somewhat, the 6–2–2–1 became the standard defense. With two linebackers, two backs, and a safety man, there was now someone behind the defensive line to cover each of the five potential receivers. In this defense, the ends were responsible for protecting the outside, while the two linebackers had inside responsibility.

When the modern T formation arrived in 1940, the defense faced a new set of problems. At that time, the running game out of the T emphasized quick-hitting plays. A halfback went in motion on virtually every play and had to be followed by a linebacker. With the linebacker out of position, a quick opener into the area he'd vacated could spring a running back immediately into the secondary.

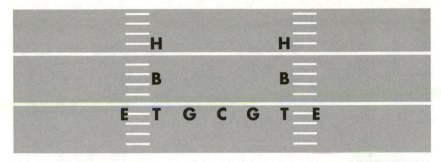

7 BOX DEFENSE
The 7-box defense was standard in running situations until the early 1930s . . .

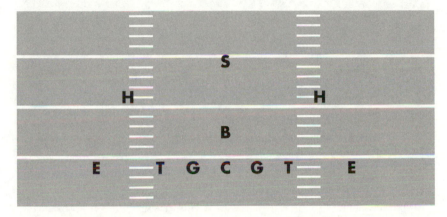

7 DIAMOND DEFENSE
. . . and the 7-diamond was generally used in passing situations.

The defensive answer was the 5–3–3. On running plays, the outside linebackers in this defense had outside responsibility, while the ends usually crashed to the inside. The man in motion no longer took the linebacker away from the area he was supposed to protect on runs. In passing situations, each defensive halfback covered an offensive end, each outside linebacker covered a running back, and there was a safety man who functioned much as today's free safety does in a man-to-man defense.

During the late 1940s and early 1950s, passing attacks became more sophisticated. The Cleveland Browns and Los Angeles Rams, in particular, were great passing teams. The Rams pioneered what is now known as the "pro set," with a split end on one side of the formation and a flanker on the other. The Browns often used two wingbacks, an early version of today's one-back formation.

Now there were three or four speedy receivers who could get quickly into a pass pattern. The linebacker assigned to cover the running back on his side of the formation was overmatched against a flanker or a wingback.

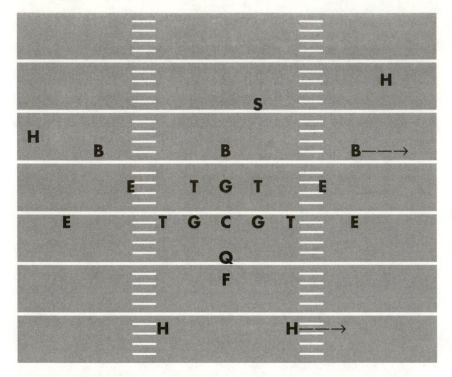

5–3–3 DEFENSE
The 5–3–3 was the defensive response to the modern T formation with one man in motion. The outside linebackers were given outside responsibility, while the ends and middle linebacker protected against inside runs.

Two coaches known for their defensive innovations came up with similar, but somewhat different, responses. Greasy Neale developed the "Eagle defense" in Philadelphia. This defense was a 5–2–4, but it had seven men on the line of scrimmage. The ends played very wide so they could crash quickly into the backfield, while the two linebackers were aligned opposite the offensive ends. Their first job was to hold the ends at the line for a moment while reading the play and reacting to it.

Using that defense, the Eagles won the 1949 NFL championship. They lost only one game that year, 38–24 to the Chicago Bears. They gave up only 96 points in their eleven regular season victories and they beat the Rams 14–0 in the championship game.

Steve Owen of the New York Giants devised the "umbrella defense" specifically to stop the Cleveland passing attack. The umbrella also had four defensive backs, with a six-man line and a single linebacker. However, in a passing situation the ends usually dropped into coverage.

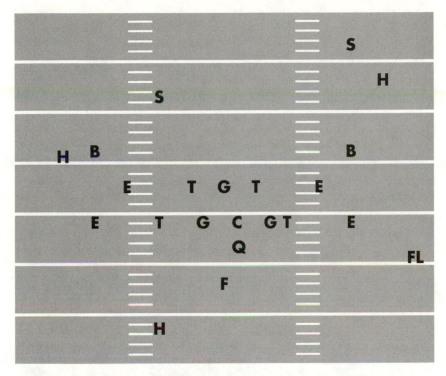

EAGLE DEFENSE VS. PRO SET
The first effective response to the pro set was the Eagle defense, devised by
Greasy Neale of the Philadelphia Eagles. Using this defense, the Eagles shut
out the high-scoring Los Angeles Rams 14–0 in the 1949 NFL championship
game.

This alignment was similar to the modern two-deep zone. The four
backs covered the deep areas while the ends and linebacker covered the
shallow areas. The result: The Browns scored 297 points in their ten games
against other teams in 1950, but they managed a total of only 21 points in
three games against the Giants, including an 8–0 victory in the Eastern
Conference championship contest.

Within a couple of years, the ends became linebackers and the
umbrella defense turned into the 4–3, which was pretty much standard in
the NFL for nearly two decades. The 4–3 defense actually looks like a 5–2,
since the strong-side linebacker is on the line of scrimmage opposite the
tight end. However, he stands up rather than getting into the lineman's
three-point stance.

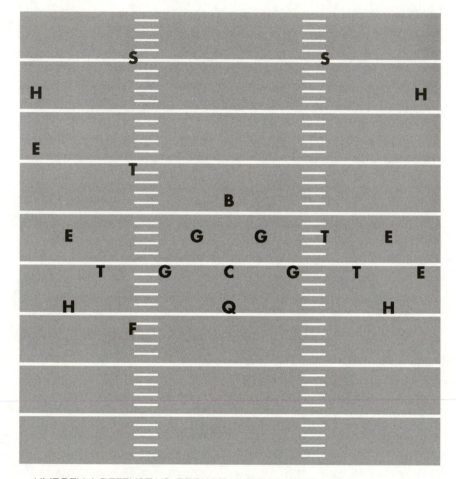

UMBRELLA DEFENSE VS. BROWNS' DOUBLE WING
Steve Owen of the New York Giants created the umbrella defense specifically
to stop Cleveland's double wing. On passing situations, the ends usually
dropped back to defend against short passes, rather than rushing the passer.

In the normal 4–3, the defensive ends are opposite the offensive tackles and the defensive tackles are opposite the offensive guards. Some teams like to move a tackle over the center, however, and others put a tackle in the gap between the center and a guard.

The 3–4 defense was originated by the Oakland Raiders of the American Football League in 1962. On passing downs, they moved a defensive end to an outside linebacker spot, usually to blitz. In 1971, the Miami Dolphins began using the 3–4 consistently on passing downs and three years later the New England Patriots and Houston Oilers went to the alignment on every down.

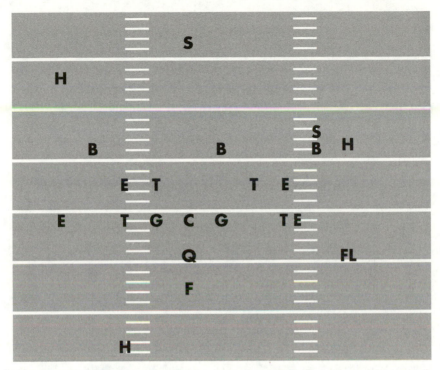

4–3 DEFENSE VS. PRO SET
The 4–3 developed out of the umbrella and Eagle defenses to become standard in the NFL from the early 1950s right up to the present day.

During the 1980s, the 3–4 became the predominant defense in the NFL. Lately, however, more and more teams have been going back to the 4–3. The decision is often based on personnel: If a couple of defensive linemen are out with injury, a team might use the 3–4, while a lack of linebackers might dictate use of the 4–3 defense.

Against the run and shoot offense, most NFL teams use a modern version of the umbrella defense, with five or even six backs. The four-man line is generally favored, because it offers a quicker pass rush.

Of course, the way the defense lines up is only the starting point. Linemen and linebackers can play all sorts of games, and what looks like a 3–4 can suddenly become a 5–2 or even a seven-man line just before the ball is snapped.

Among NFL coaches and their defensive coordinators, there are two totally different philosophies about what a defense should do. The traditional approach is to read and react. The more daring approach, which is becoming more and more common, is to attack and disrupt the offense.

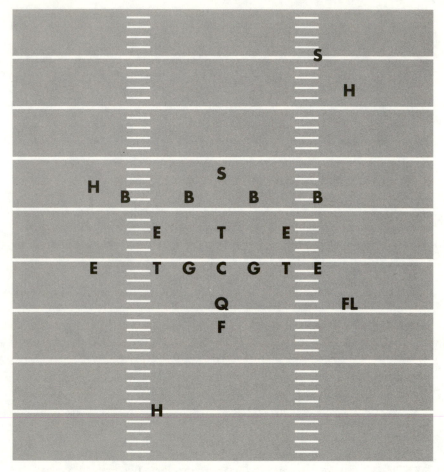

3–4 DEFENSE VS. PRO SET
Hailed as the defense of the future during the 1980s, the 3–4 has now been dropped by many NFL teams in favor of the older 4–3.

Read and react defenses don't normally do anything very fancy. Linemen and linebackers are expected to take on their blockers, control them, fight against pressure, and move toward the point of attack. Some defenders are assigned keys to read. In a 4–3 defense, for example, the middle linebacker often keys on the guards. If he sees a guard pull, he heads in the same direction.

Although it's not a hard and fast rule, coaches who like a read and react type of defense tend to prefer zone pass coverage. You won't see such a team use an all-out blitz on passing situations very often, since that forces man-to-man coverage in the secondary. However, a blitz by the weak-side linebacker, or by both outside linebackers from the 3–4, wouldn't be unusual.

The run blitz, on the other hand, is often used by read and react teams. It's not nearly as aggressive as the pass blitz. Defensive linemen generally try to control their blockers while linebackers and perhaps a defensive back shoot the gaps between linemen. Rather than charging hard in an attempt to reach the quarterback, they simply want to penetrate into the offensive backfield in order to stop any sort of run as soon as it gets started.

Because of the controlled charge, the run blitz is usually effective against draw plays and screen passes. Defenders aren't likely to go past the runner on a draw, and they're in good position to react quickly to the outside against a screen. However, the run blitz is vulnerable to a quick draw or trap and to a quick pass over the middle.

The ultimate read and react defense was the "flex" developed by Tom Landry with the Dallas Cowboys. Landry had his right defensive tackle and left defensive end playing slightly off the line of scrimmage, giving them a split second to size up what the offense was trying to do before they encountered blockers. They often functioned almost as linebackers. On a sweep to the right, for example, the tackle and end would both pursue in that direction, rather than attacking the line of scrimmage.

The general philosophy of the flex, as with read and react defenses in general, is to "bend but not break," as coaches like to say. It's relatively easy to gain a couple of yards against the flex, but it's hard to make significant gains. The major goal of the flex is to stop the first down running play in order to set up a second and long situation.

Dallas usually had good defenses during the long Landry reign, but no one else ever adopted the flex. Other coaches felt the Cowboy defense owed its success to personnel rather than the formation itself. There was some truth in that idea. The Cowboys had great left defensive tackles in Bob Lilly and then Randy White through most of those years, and they also had outstanding defensive ends, such as Harvey Martin and Ed "Too Tall" Jones, and fine linebackers, such as Lee Roy Jordan, Chuck Howley, and Steve Kiner. Players of that caliber could undoubtedly make any kind of defense work pretty well.

The flex's chief problem was its vulnerability to the pass, since it couldn't develop much of a rush. As other teams began to throw on first down against the Cowboys, the defense became less effective and Dallas was forced to use other alignments more often, even in apparent running situations.

Another Landry innovation *was* widely copied. In the standard 4–3, the left linebacker is usually on the line of scrimmage, opposite the tight end. His first job is to attack the tight end, to keep him from getting quickly into a pass pattern and to prevent him from releasing to make a block on another defender. The right linebacker is generally lighter and faster, as he is responsible for covering a running back on passing plays.

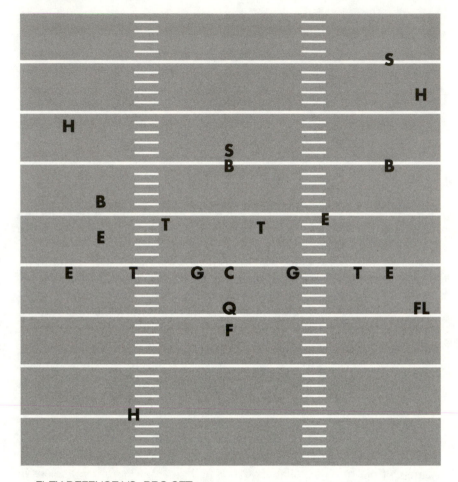

FLEX DEFENSE VS. PRO SET
The ultimate "read and react" defense was the flex, used by the Dallas
Cowboys under Tom Landry. The left defensive tackle and right defensive
end played slightly off the line of scrimmage so they could size up the play
before attacking

This worked fine as long as the offense put the tight end on the right,
as was almost always done during the 1960s. But some teams began to line
up strong to the left on occasion to put the tight end on that smaller right
linebacker.

Landry's response was to "flip flop" his backers. Instead of right and
left outside linebackers, he had a strong-side linebacker and a weak-side
linebacker. They didn't take their positions until the tight end went to one
side or the other of the offensive formation.

In the 4–3, a read and react defense features the middle linebacker. A chief goal of the defense is to keep blockers away from him so he can get in on the play. Its heyday was also the heyday of great middle linebackers such as Bill George, Chuck Bednarik, Sam Huff, Ray Nitschke, Willie Lanier, Joe Schmidt, and Lee Roy Jordan.

The outside linebackers are usually the featured run defenders in the 3–4. The growing popularity of that defense during the late 1970s and through the 1980s brought a different type of linebacker into the NFL— big, fast, and agile, equally effective at rushing the passer from the outside, crashing into the backfield to break up running plays, or dropping back into coverage.

The prototype was Ted Hendricks, known as the "Mad Stork" because of his 6-foot-7, 220-pound frame and his style of play. Hendricks was not only a great linebacker but an outstanding kick blocker. He joined the Baltimore Colts in 1969 and had his best years from 1974 through 1983 with the Oakland Raiders, who used the 3–4 primarily to take advantage of his skills.

His successors have generally been shorter and heavier, but just as mobile. Perhaps the greatest of all was Lawrence Taylor of the New York Giants, at 6-foot-3 and 240 pounds. Others in that mold have included Tim Harris of the Packers and 49ers, Pat Swilling of the Saints and Lions, Andre Tippett of the Patriots, and Derrick Thomas of the Chiefs. Attacking defenses are often built around such a player.

The idea of attacking the offense instead of simply reacting to it began in the late 1940s and early 1950s, when the 4–3 defense replaced the 5–3. It's often difficult to generate a pass rush out of the 4–3, since the blockers outnumber the defensive linemen and the best defender can usually be double-teamed.

The solution to that problem was the blitz, originally known as the "red dog." The blitz was often used in combination with stunts and loops by defensive linemen, designed to confuse blocking assignments and create an opening for a linebacker to rush through.

At first, the blitzer was usually the middle linebacker, but teams soon began sending other backers as well, sometimes two or three at a time. In 1961, the St. Louis Cardinals came up with the safety blitz, using future Hall of Famer Larry Wilson, who twice sacked New York Giants' quarterback Charlie Conerly in the game in which the maneuver was unveiled.

But the blitz is just an occasional thing, used only in obvious passing situations. The strategy of attacking the offense on every play was developed by the Pittsburgh Steelers, the "Team of the Seventies" under

Chuck Noll. Defensive tackle "Mean Joe" Greene was the key player. Greene lined up at an angle in the gap between an offensive guard and the center, with middle linebacker Jack Lambert directly behind him. Because of his fast, aggressive charge, Greene usually tied up two blockers, leaving Lambert unoccupied. If he wasn't double-teamed, Greene could penetrate into the backfield and entirely disrupt the offense.

The Steelers won Super Bowl IX, after the 1974 season, holding the Minnesota Vikings to only 17 yards in a 16–6 victory, and they went on to win three more Super Bowls during the decade. Their success inspired some other teams to go to an attacking defense.

With speedy outside linebackers, the 3–4 can be played very aggressively. The Oakland Raiders often send their inside linebackers against the offensive guards. The result is virtually a 5–2. Every interior lineman is occupied at the line of scrimmage, allowing the outside linebackers to blitz virtually unopposed on a passing play or to clean up against a run.

But 3–4 defenses have more often used their outside linebackers as the chief attackers. The New Orleans Saints were particularly successful because of Pat Swilling and Rickey Jackson, who combined for 51½ sacks during the 1991 and 1992 seasons. Swilling and Jackson usually lined up well to the outside and were sent flying into the offensive backfield at the snap. In addition to their ability to get to the quarterback, both are fast enough to catch running plays from behind, often for losses.

The ultimate attacking defense was created by Buddy Ryan, when he was defensive coordinator for the Chicago Bears from 1978 through 1985. Known as "the 46," it was a 4–3 with both cornerbacks and the strong safety stationed much closer to the line of scrimmage than usual.

Primarily designed to stop the run, the 46 can also be very effective against the pass because it offers so many possible blitzing combinations. Ryan often sends one or more of his defensive backs as blitzers, while dropping a defensive end or even a tackle into pass coverage, which thoroughly confused blockers. He also installed the defense as head coach of the Philadelphia Eagles and as defensive coordinator of the Houston Oilers.

It might be said that the philosophy of an attacking defense is to "break but not bend." The goals are to force the offense into long-yardage situations and, above all, to create turnovers. In 1985, when the Bears were NFC champions using the 46, they led the league in fewest points allowed, rushing defense, overall defense, interceptions, and takeaway-giveaway ratio. They recovered three fumbles, intercepted two passes, and racked up a safety in their 46–10 Super Bowl victory over the New England Patriots.

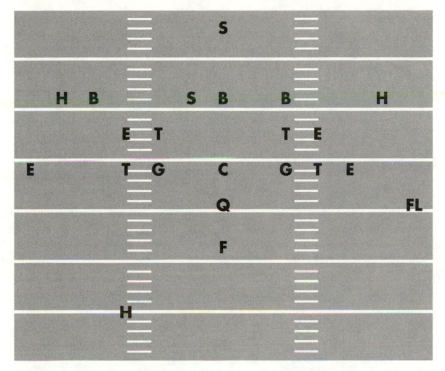

46 DEFENSE VS. PRO SET
As defensive coordinator for the Chicago Bears, Buddy Ryan developed
the ultimate attacking defense, the 46. The Bears gave up only 198
points in 1985 and went on to beat the New England Patriots 46–10 in
Super Bowl XX.

Any attacking defense, and particularly the 46, can be vulnerable to
the long pass. But it has to be thrown quickly, and that can be difficult,
because cornerbacks are either blitzing or holding up wide receivers at the
line of scrimmage to keep from getting into their pass routes.

The basic defense to be used on a given play is usually signaled in from the
sideline, and a middle linebacker is generally responsible for passing it on
to his teammates. Like the quarterback, he can call an audible if he sees an
unexpected offensive formation.

The middle linebacker's audible will not usually change the formation, but he can call for a certain kind of line charge, including stunts and
loops, and he may on occasion audible to a blitz.

Modern offenses often force the defense to make adjustments right
up to the instant the ball is snapped. If a running back moves into a slot, or
any offensive player goes in motion, it usually forces a change in the

defense. You'll see linebackers and defensive backs yelling and signaling to one another as they move around in response.

The type of pass coverage to be used in the secondary is often dictated by what the front seven will be doing. In an attacking type of defense, the secondary is often forced into man-to-man coverage. And the man-to-man is also dictated any time two or more defenders blitz.

However, the man-to-man is not nearly as conventional as it used to be. Defenses often use some sort of combination, or "combo," coverage. For example, when both outside linebackers blitz out of the 3–4, the inside backers may play a kind of zone in the middle of the field, getting into the most likely passing lanes in order to deflect or intercept the ball. while the cornerbacks and strong safety are in single coverage and the free safety acts a "centerfielder," reading the quarterback's eyes and reacting to the ball as soon as it's released.

Against an exceptionally dangerous wide receiver, such as Jerry Rice of the 49ers, a team will usually go to double coverage even out of the man-to-man. There are two basic types of double coverage. "Up-and-under" coverage, most often used against speed receivers, has one defender, usually a cornerback, between the receiver and the ball and another defender, usually the free safety, staying behind the receiver. "In-and-out" coverage, commonly used against good possession receivers, gives one defender inside responsibility and the other outside responsibility.

A major innovation in man-to-man coverage was developed in the AFL during the 1960s. Called the "bump and run," its most skilled practitioner was Willie Brown of the Oakland Raiders. Brown came right up to the line of scrimmage to hit the receiver, and he would continue to bump him as they ran down the field together.

This tactic made it virtually impossible for the receiver to run a precise route, and it also messed up the quarterback's timing. Brown was so successful that other AFL cornerbacks began using the bump and run and it spread into the NFL after the leagues merged in 1970.

Passing and scoring declined during the decade. In response, the league targeted the bump and run with a series of rules changes. The present rule allowing a defender to make contact with a receiver only once, within five yards of the line of scrimmage, was adopted in 1978. That, along with the change that moved the hash marks closer to the center of the field in 1972, has contributed to an increased use of zone defenses in the last fifteen years.

As already noted, the more conservative read and react defenses tend to use zone coverages almost exclusively. The most conservative zone is the "two-deep," which has been favored by the New York Giants for years. The four defensive backs cover the deep areas, with the linebackers covering the shallow areas. A patient quarterback with an accurate arm can pick the two-deep zone to pieces, but any off-target throw is likely to be intercepted. The defense worked well for the Giants when they were able to use Lawrence Taylor as a blitzer to force a quick throw.

Teams will often use the two-deep zone to prevent a quick score when they're ahead. Late in a half, when the offense is likely to throw to a sideline to stop the clock, a common defense is the double zone, with both safetymen covering the deep sideline areas and both cornerbacks covering shallow along the sideline. This type of zone looks almost like up-and-under coverage on the wide receivers. The difference is that the defenders will give the receivers a little more room than they would in true double coverage.

The most controversial coverage of all is the "prevent defense," a *very* deep two-deep zone that gives receivers—and runners—all kinds of room. Teams have frequently been criticized by writers and sportscasters for going into the prevent too early, or for using it at all.

The normal two-deep zone will give up relatively short passes. The prevent will give up medium-range and even fairly long passes in order to prevent the touchdown throw beyond coverage. An offense can often eat up big chunks of yardage against the prevent defense to get into scoring range.

It can also give up sizable runs, as the 49ers demonstrated in the 1981 NFC championship game against the Cowboys. Trailing 27–21 with less than five minutes to play, the 49ers were on their own 10-yard line. Dallas chose to go to the prevent defense. Using sweeps, draws, and short passes, the 49ers quickly moved 84 yards, and Joe Montana then hit Dwight Clark with a 6-yard touchdown pass to put San Francisco ahead. The drive consumed so little time that the Cowboys still had a reasonable chance to win after the ensuing kickoff, but a fumble killed their hopes.

The zone defense can be much more sophisticated than the two-deep, the double zone, or the prevent, and it usually is. Announcers often talk about "rotation" in connection with a zone defense, because the secondary and linebackers do rotate to get into coverage.

For example, to get into a strong-side zone against an offense that is strong to the right, the left cornerback moves up to cover the short zone, the strong safety moves to the left to cover the deep zone, the free safety moves left to cover the deep middle zone, the right corner drops back to cover the deep zone on his side of the field, and the right outside linebacker moves farther outside and somewhat to his right to cover the shallow zone there.

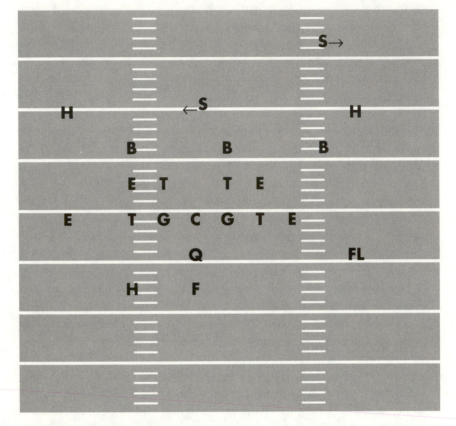

DOUBLE ZONE DEFENSE
The double zone is designed primarily to defend against sideline passes late
in the first half of the game. Cornerbacks cover the shallow areas; safetymen
the deep areas near the sidelines.

Although the zone sounds passive, and certainly looks passive on
paper, it isn't necessarily. A good defensive back will frequently cover a
receiver very closely when he's in his zone, and he can often afford to
gamble on an interception if he knows he has deep help.

Combination defenses can be played out of the basic zone. A team
that has an exceptionally good cover man at cornerback may use him to
cover the opposition's best receiver man-to-man while the rest of the
secondary is in zone coverage. And a linebacker is frequently assigned to
cover a specific running back to guard against a screen or a quick flare
pass.

As mentioned in the previous chapter, an offense often uses motion to
find out what kind of coverage is being used. Motion may also change the
nature of the coverage. If a strong-side zone was called, but the flanker

goes into motion across the formation to put both wide receivers on the weak-side, the defense will probably audible to a weak-side zone. Some teams use a defensive back, often the free safety, to call coverage audibles, while others make it the responsibility of the linebacker who calls the other audibles.

One important part of the defense is often overlooked. A defender on each side of the field is designated as the force man on running plays to that side. This designation is sometimes part of the defensive play call, and at other times it's automatically determined by the formation.

The force man's job is to come up fast against any kind of run to the outside. He doesn't necessarily have to make the tackle, but he has to take on blockers to keep them from getting other defenders, and he's supposed to "string out" the play by keeping the ball carrier from cutting downfield.

A cornerback is most often the force man, but the role is sometimes given to the strong safety or an outside linebacker. This can be a tricky job. If the play is designed to get to the sideline, the force man has to protect to the outside and make the runner cut back, into the defensive pursuit. On the other hand, he also has to prevent the runner from making a quick cutback, before the pursuit is there.

There are a couple of other important role players in many defensive situations. Against the pass, there's usually an "anchor" defender, most often a defensive lineman but sometimes a linebacker, who has to hold back somewhat to watch for a draw or a screen. This assignment often goes to a mobile defensive tackle who's not an outstanding pass rusher despite his mobility.

Quarterbacks who are good runners—Randall Cunningham of the Eagles, Steve Young of the 49ers, and Warren Moon of the Vikings (formerly of the Oilers), for example—present the defense with a special problem. To counteract the possibility of a long run, most defenses assign a "spy," who stays somewhat behind the line of scrimmage and moves with the quarterback. This player has to be ready to move up and make the tackle if the passer pulls the ball down, and he also has to be able to drop quickly back into a passing lane when he's certain the ball is going to be thrown.

Perhaps the biggest change in pro football over the last decade or so is the use of situational substitution. As offenses began bringing in special "packages" for special situations, defenses responded similarly. First there was the "nickel back," so called because he was a fifth defensive back used in passing situations, especially against an offense that had three wide receivers. Then came the "dime back," a sixth defender.

There are two different ways of playing up front when an extra defensive back comes in. The nickel back usually replaces a linebacker. Some 3–4 teams like to go to a four-man front to get extra pressure on the passer; they'll take out two linebackers to bring in a back and another linemen. Going to the dime defense, they may take out three linebackers. Conversely, some 4–3 teams will take out a defensive lineman for one of the extra backs in order to use blitzes from the outside.

The choice is based primarily on personnel. When the New Orleans Saints had Pat Swilling and Rickey Jackson as outside linebackers, a defensive lineman was expendable in passing situations. Even with only three linemen, the Saints had five people rushing the passer. But if the linebackers are not so mobile, better suited to stopping the run, the defense is better off bringing in another pass rusher up front.

There are two types of short yardage defenses. On the typical third-and-one, away from the goal line, teams typically use what is commonly called the "6–1." An extra defensive linemen or two may be brought in for this defense, but a 4–3 team with strong outside backers often leaves them in the game. The chief difference is that the interior linemen will play in the gaps between offensive linemen and the linebackers will be right up on the line of scrimmage and they'll play aggressively to stop the run.

On very short yardage situations and goal line situations inside the 5-yard line, the "gap 8" is the most common defense. Extra linemen have to be brought in, usually replacing a linebacker and the free safety, and eight players are massed to stop the run. As the name suggests, this defense also stations front-line defenders in the gaps. They're often called upon to "submarine"—drive low across the line and fall on their faces if necessary to keep the gaps closed. Because a running back may try to leap over the pile to get the first down or the touchdown, at least one defender will be assigned to make a similar leap to hit the ball carrier in midair and send him backwards.

THE POSITIONS

Let's take a look at the defense, position by position.

Nose Tackle

The nose tackle probably has the most thankless position in football. He's expected to be blocked early and often, taking a physical pounding from the offensive center, both guards, and perhaps a tackle or two. As a result, he doesn't usually make many plays, but by occupying blockers he makes it much easier for his teammates to get to the ball.

That role makes the nose tackle a key player in the 3–4 defense. One of the best around right now is Ray Childress of the Oilers. At 6-foot-6 and 276 pounds, he's taller than most at his position. More typical specimens are Tim Krumrie of the Bengals and Jeff Wright of the Bills, both 6-3 and about 275 pounds; Michael Carter of the 49ers, at 6-2 and 285 pounds; and Erik Howard of the Giants, who is 6-4 and 268 pounds.

At nose tackle, speed is subordinate to strength, although a quick first move is important. Perhaps most important of all is the player's willingness to sacrifice his body for the sake of the team.

Defensive Tackle

Defensive tackles in the 4–3 are not quite as anonymous as nose tackles. Some of the greats of the past, such as Bob Lilly, Merlin Olsen, and Alan Page, relied more on speed than sheer power. They were outstanding pass rushers as a result. Today's defensive tackles in general are much bulkier than those stars.

The role of the defensive tackle varies from team to team. In most cases, his job is quite similar to that of the nose tackle—take up space and occupy blockers. The physiques are similar, too, but a tackle in the 4–3 usually has to have more speed because he's so often used on stunts and loops in combination with the other tackle or a defensive end.

Partly because of the increased use of blitzes, tackles don't get as many sacks as they used to. However, they are called upon to get some kind of pressure up the middle and they're trained to get their hands up when they get near the quarterback to block his vision and possibly to deflect the ball.

Aggressive defenses like to put a tackle in the slot between a guard and the center to occupy two blockers, much like the nose tackle in the 3–4. Some of them station the other tackle between a guard and offensive tackle, while the defensive end on that side—usually the weak side—moves to the outside.

Again, the goal is generally to force the offense into a double team, or at least to confuse the blocking scheme. Defensive tackles used in this role are often built more like nose tackles, but they're usually much quicker. An outstanding example is Cortez Kennedy of the Seahawks, a 6-foot-3, 293-pounder who often shoots the gap between blockers before either of them can get a piece of him.

When the Dallas Cowboys won Super Bowls XXVII and XXVIII, they had two defensive tackles similar to Kennedy: Tony Casillas and Russell Maryland. Both played nose guard in a five-man line as collegians and were projected as nose tackles in the NFL. In fact, Casillas began his pro career as a nose tackle with the Falcons before his trade to Dallas in 1992.

The top defensive tackles in the NFL today range from an even 6 feet to 6-4 in height and from 265 to more than 300 pounds. The increase in weight over the last couple of decades has been dictated in large part by a corresponding increase in the size of the offensive linemen they're up against.

Defensive End

The "glamour" defensive lineman in modern pro football are usually defensive ends in the 4–3. They're often spotlighted in that alignment as outside linebackers are in the 3–4.

Perhaps the best in football right now are Reggie White of the Packers, Bruce Smith of the Bills, and Chris Doleman of the Falcons. They're similar in size. White and Doleman are 6-foot-5, while Smith is an inch shorter. Smith and Doleman weigh 275 and White is 10 pounds heavier.

All three of them combine great strength with exceptional speed and mobility. They can push blockers off the line of scrimmage with a bull rush, charge inside to get into the offense backfield quickly, or spin to the outside to get a good attack angle on the quarterback.

These three are intimidating defenders who can dominate a game like some of the great tackles of the past, such as Hall of Famers Lilly, Page, "Mean Joe" Greene, and Randy White. Because offenses have to focus on them, Smith and Reggie White often move around on the line of scrimmage, anywhere from an interior spot to a position well outside the defensive tackle. They make a lot of plays and, by tying up blockers and forcing changes in blocking schemes, they also enable teammates to make plays.

Every successful 4–3 team in the last decade has had an outstanding defensive end. Among them are Richard Dent (6-5 and 265 pounds) of the Bears and Charles Mann (6-6 and 272) of the Redskins.

In the 3–4, the defensive ends are not usually as noticeable, but there are exceptions. Reggie White starred in that defense as a rookie with the Philadelphia Eagles and Pierce Holt, 6-4 and 280 pounds, with out-standing in the 3–4 with the 49ers before joining the Falcons as a free agent in 1993.

Because the 3–4 does tend to emphasize the outside linebackers, ends in that defense are often used more like the tackles in the 4–3. Their role is to tie up blockers against the run. On pass plays, an end often takes an inside rush to clear the outside lane for a rushing linebacker.

Howie Long of the Raiders was one of the best 3–4 defensive ends for more than a decade. The 6-foot-5, 275-pounder was an aggressive, hard-charging defender who would probably have played tackle in the 4–3.

Whatever the alignment, defensive ends tend to be somewhat taller than tackles. Greater height gives them a better chance of deflecting a pass when they don't get to the quarterback. Current starters at the position range from 6-3 to 6-7 and from 265 to 300 pounds.

Some teams bring a player off the bench as a "designated pass rusher." The 6-foot-5, 245-pound Charles Haley, a former outside linebacker with the 49ers, fills that role as a defensive end in the Cowboys' 4–3 defense.

Linebackers

Linebackers are a special breed. Since "The Violent World of Sam Huff" aired on CBS in 1960, they've been stereotyped as hard-nosed, aggressive players. Joe Schmidt of the Lions, Ray Nitschke of the Packers, Dick Butkus of the Bears, and many other middle linebackers were cast in that role by the media.

The fact is, linebackers can't usually be too aggressive. While they have to react quickly to the ball, they also have to be careful not to get pulled out of position by fakes and trick plays. Linebackers are taught to read keys, but the great ones subliminally read the entire offense.

Coaches and commentators like to refer to "instinct" when they talk about the way an outstanding linebacker responds to a play. It's not really instinct—no one is born with the ability—but it is reflexive, based on game experience and hours of studying game films.

Since the retirement of Chicago's Mike Singletary, middle linebackers aren't nearly as prominent as they used to be, even in the 4–3 defense. Probably the best current pure middle linebacker is Sam Mills of the Saints. A *Sporting News* All-Pro in 1991 and 1992, Mills has an unusual physique for the role. Only 5-foot-9, he's a solid 225 pounds with great mobility. Like a small, fast running back, Mills can be hard to find behind his shield of gigantic linemen.

He and other middle linebackers are hurt by the fact that most All-Pro teams now include two inside linebackers, usually from teams that play the 3–4. An emerging star is Junior Seau, who joined the Chargers in 1990 as a middle linebacker in the 4–3 and was named to the Associated Press All-NFL team in 1992 and 1993. It's typical of modern defensive trends that Seau was moved to an outside spot the following season. Cornelius Bennett of the Bills, another former all-pro as an inside backer, has also been moved outside.

Perhaps the best inside linebacker around is Al Smith of Houston, who's relatively unknown compared to the many fine outside backers in the game. At 6-1 and 250 pounds, he's similar in build to past middle

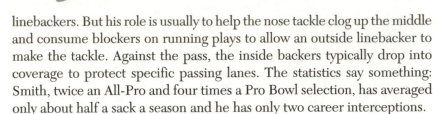

linebackers. But his role is usually to help the nose tackle clog up the middle and consume blockers on running plays to allow an outside linebacker to make the tackle. Against the pass, the inside backers typically drop into coverage to protect specific passing lanes. The statistics say something: Smith, twice an All-Pro and four times a Pro Bowl selection, has averaged only about half a sack a season and he has only two career interceptions.

A list of outside linebackers, starting with the recently retired Lawrence Taylor, sounds like a "Who's Who" of defense: Pat Swilling, Cornelius Bennett, Derrick Thomas, Wilbur Marshall, Monte Coleman, Rickey Jackson—all are well known to pro football fans, probably better known than Smith and Mills. Seth Joyner of the Eagles, Darryl Talley of the Bills, and Bryan Cox of the Dolphins are among the very good players who are often overlooked because of all those other stars at the position.

These backers are very similar in size. Taylor, the prototype, was 6-3 and 245 pounds; so are Thomas and Swilling. Bennett, Coleman, Jackson, and Joyner all stand 6-2 and weigh from 235 to 245. Cox and Talley are the tallest at 6-4. Talley weighs 235, Cox 241. Marshall is the smallest of the bunch at 6-1 and 231 pounds.

For sheer speed, none can beat Swilling, but all are faster than average for their size, even veterans Coleman and Marshall, who have slowed a bit with age.

Their roles vary somewhat. Swilling and Thomas, like Taylor, move around in the defense and are allowed to free-lance because they're so fast that they can compensate for mistakes. Swilling in particular often goes flying into the backfield on a blitz, then reverses direction and catches a runner from behind. After Swilling went from the Saints to the Lions in 1993, Jackson took over the free-lance role in New Orleans.

Other outside linebackers have to play within the confines of the defensive scheme. They have to react quickly to the run without over-pursuing. The weak-side backer is more likely to be used on blitzes, while the strong-side backer is more likely to drop into coverage, but there's no hard-and-fast rule.

Offensive coordinators like to run right at good outside linebackers, on the theory that they'll only catch the play from behind if you run away from them. But the best at the position are also strong enough to fight off blockers and still make the tackle.

CORNERBACKS

Playing cornerback in the NFL has never been an enviable job. The cornerback's nightmare is getting beat deep by a wide receiver in front of

50,000 fans and millions more watching on television. But someone who has nightmares won't succeed, because a cornerback can't dwell on past failures or worry about future failures.

Some of the best all-around athletes in football play the position. Speed is a requirement, but flat-out speed isn't enough; the cornerback has to be able to run backwards, for at least several yards, almost as fast as a wide receiver can run forward. Ideally, he's also pretty good-sized, a good leaper, and ambidextrous at knocking down passes. Oh yes—the ability to tackle larger running backs traveling at top speed is also in the job description.

Because of the prevalence of zone defenses, the job isn't as potentially embarrassing as it was in the days when man-to-man coverage ruled. If a receiver gets wide open nowadays, it isn't necessarily the fault of the nearest defender; quite likely, someone who is nowhere near the play blew his coverage, as sportscasters, sportswriters, and knowledgeable fans know. But the guilty party knows who he is, as do his coaches and teammates.

The best cornerbacks welcome man-to-man coverage because they love the challenge. And, because of their self-confidence, they're also often willing to gamble on an interception when a lesser defender would play it safe.

Although the bump and run all over the field is no longer allowed, a cornerback will often bump the receiver within the 5-yard limit, even in a zone defense. In man-to-man, he then has to be ready to run with the receiver. The bump requires strength; the run requires speed. Most of today's best cornerbacks are somewhat bigger than those of the past, but they don't give up any speed.

Rod Woodson of the Pittsburgh Steelers may be the very best right now. A world-class hurdler at Purdue, Woodson is an even 6 feet and weighs 200 pounds. He's a very hard hitter and an elusive runner when he gets his hands on the ball. An All-NFL selection five times in his first seven seasons, Woodson is a rarity in that he's also used as a kick returner. Coaches don't like to use a starter in that role because of the danger of injury, but Woodson is such a threat that he can't be left off the special teams.

Albert Lewis, 6-2 and 195, was a standout with the Kansas City Chiefs for eleven seasons before joining the Los Angeles Raiders in 1994. A perennial All-Pro selection, Lewis doesn't have Woodson's blazing speed, but he has uncanny anticipation. His height, long arms, and leaping ability often enable him to knock down a pass when it looks as if he's been beaten by a step or two. Like all outstanding corners, Lewis has what coaches call "a nose for the ball." In addition to 38 interceptions, he had 10 fumble recoveries through the 1993 season.

SAFETYMEN

The defensive safetymen have two completely different jobs. The strong safety is usually the biggest, strongest defensive back, and he's often the hardest hitter, pound for pound, on the team. He's not only responsible for the tight end in man-to-man coverage, he often functions virtually as another linebacker against the run. In fact, Hall of Famer Ken Houston was a linebacker in college before joining the Houston Oilers in 1967.

Steve Atwater of the Denver Broncos, an All-Pro in 1992 and 1993, is 6-foot-3 and 217 pounds. He's not only a punishing tackler, but a fine defensive back who had 21 interceptions in his first five seasons, an unusually high total for a strong safety.

By contrast, Henry Jones of the Bills is small for a strong safety, at 5-foot-11, but he's a solid 197 pounds and he has unusual speed for the position. He led the NFL with 8 interceptions and 263 return yards in 1992, when he scored two touchdowns on runbacks.

The free safety is the last line of defense. Even in a zone defense, he'll play basically in the center of the field, although he may be cheating somewhat in one direction or the other. He has to have speed; if the ball is thrown to a sideline, he's expected to get there about the same time, and he's got about twenty-five yards to run. He also has to have a cornerback's anticipation combined with the ability to avoid being faked out of position by a clever quarterback. If a pump fake gets the free safety moving one way, and the ball goes back to the other side of the field, the result might well be a touchdown.

Free safeties aren't as well known as they used to be, in part because of zone defenses; they can't roam quite as much to make interceptions as they used to. The 6-foot-1, 190-pound Mark Carrier of the Bears, who led the NFL with 10 interceptions as a rookie in 1990, is one of the best current players at the position.

Among the other top free safeties around are Tim McDonald, 6-2 and 215, of the 49ers; Eugene Robinson, 6-0 and 191, of the Seahawks, the NFL interception leader in 1993; and Todd Scott, 5-10 and 207, of the Vikings.

It's impossible to talk about modern defensive backs without mentioning Ronnie Lott, who's sure to go into the Pro Football Hall of Fame as soon as he's eligible. Known for his hitting, Lott was an All-Pro cornerback with the 49ers in 1981, when he intercepted seven passes and returned three of them for touchdowns.

Lott was moved to free safety in 1986 and he led the NFL with 10 interceptions to be named an All-Pro at that position. After going to the

Los Angeles Raiders in 1991, Lott became a strong safety and was again named to the All-Pro team. His 14-year NFL career apparently ended when the New York Jets released him after the 1994 season, in part because Lott had suffered two concussions and a neck injury.

Some coaches felt Lott should have been a strong safety all along because of his 6-foot-1, 203-pound size and his proven ability to take on ball carriers of any size. But he also had the speed, the anticipation, and the intelligence to excel at corner and free safety. No other player has ever mastered all three defensive backfield positions.

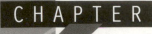

6

Special Teams

The most important player on a pro football team during the 1920s was usually the punter. Teams often punted on third down, even on second down when they were deep in their own territory. Field position was much more important than possession, because few teams could move the ball consistently, and possession was risky. Fumbles and interceptions were common, mainly because the rounder ball of the time was harder to hold on to and harder to throw.

A team's best punter was often a halfback or fullback, but there were exceptions. One of the great kickers of the era was Fats Henry, a 5-foot-10, 240-pound tackle, who had an 83-yard punt for Canton against the Akron Pros in 1923 and a 50-yard field goal by drop kick in 1922.

Because rosters were small and substitutions were severely limited by the rules, every team had several punters. If the best punter happened to be on the bench because of injury, fatigue, or a tactical substitution, someone else would take over the job. For example, when the Green Bay Packers won the first of three straight championships in 1929, they had one of the greatest punters of the era in Verne Lewellen. But four other Packers punted at one time or another that season.

The field goal attempt was an iffy proposition. Although the rounder ball was better suited to drop-kicking because of its truer bounce, that kicking style was unreliable. A good drop kick requires a perfect drop, perfect bounce, and perfect timing. The game-winning kick in the closing minutes was almost unheard of. By the fourth quarter, the field was thoroughly torn up by cleats, if it wasn't muddy. And, if it was muddy, the ball by then was so soggy that kicking it accurately for any distance was virtually impossible.

There was nothing automatic even about the extra point. The great Ernie Nevers scored all of the Chicago Cardinals' points in two consecutive 1929 victories, 19–0 over the Dayton Triangles and 40–7 over the Chicago Bears. He scored nine touchdowns in those two games, but kicked only five of the extra points. He missed two, had one blocked, and the fourth was never attempted because of a bad snap.

The closest thing to a "special team" during the 1920s and into the 1930s was the lineup when a kicker was someone like Fats Henry, who moved into the backfield and had to be replaced in the line by one of the backs.

The situation changed a little during the 1930s, but only a little. The goal posts were moved from the end line to the goal-line in 1933 and the diameter of the ball was reduced. The change in the ball made it easier to throw but more difficult to drop kick, and the place kick became more common.

Roster limits were increased to 24 in 1935, to 25 in 1936, and to 30 in 1938. There were still no true specialists, but "semi-specialists" began to emerge. The first of them was Jack Manders of the Chicago Bears. A reserve fullback behind Bronko Nagurski in 1933, Manders was an excellent place kicker who was often put in to attempt a field goal. He tied for the league lead with 6 field goals in 1933 and led the league with 10 in 1934, when he finished second in scoring. Ten field goals doesn't sound like much today, but Dutch Clark had led the league in 1932 with only three.

Paradoxically, as improved passing led to more touchdowns, the field goal became more important. Extra point percentages increased greatly because the goal posts were ten yards closer and place kickers were more accurate than drop kickers. Scores of 6–0, 7–6, and 13–12, which had been fairly common because of missed extra points during the 1920s, gave way to scores of 10–7, 13–10, and 17–14, and games were more often decided by a late field goal.

Even when a team scored a touchdown to win, the victory was often set up by an earlier field goal. In the first playoff between divisional champions, in 1933, Manders kicked three field goals to keep the Bears in the game. They were losing 21–16 with less than three minutes left when Nagurski passed to Bill Hewitt, who lateraled to Bill Karr for a 36-yard touchdown that won the title. Obviously, if Manders had missed one of his three field goal attempts, the Bears would have been in no position to win.

Several teams carried backup players because of their kicking ability. One of them was Armand Nicolai, a reserve lineman with Pittsburgh from 1934 through 1942. Nicolai twice tied for the NFL lead in field goals and he scored a total of 179 points, all on kicks, during his career.

But true specialization couldn't arrive until free substitution did, along with larger rosters. After the roster limit was increased to thirty-three players in 1948, a club could theoretically have eleven offensive players, eleven defensive players, and eleven special teams players. In practice, it couldn't be done. For one thing, backups were needed at each position. For another, the free substitution rule, adopted in 1943 for the duration of World War II, was done away with after the war ended and a team was allowed to send in only three players at a time.

In 1949, the NFL adopted free substitution on a one-season trial basis, and the rule became permanent in 1950. By 1952, the two-platoon system was firmly in place, and a handful of kicking and punting specialists had arrived on the scene.

A pioneer in specialization, as in so many things, was Paul Brown of the Cleveland Browns. When the Browns were organized to play in the new All-America Football Conference in 1946, Brown signed Lou Groza as a backup tackle. Groza was used primarily as a place-kicker in his rookie year. However, he was also an excellent offensive tackle who became a starter at that position in 1947. Groza didn't become a kicking specialist until 1959.

Similarly, the Browns had a great punter in Horace Gillom, who joined the team as a two-way end in 1947 and, like Groza, was primarily a specialist as a rookie. From 1948 on, he was used occasionally as a position player, but his chief value to the team was as a punter. In his last two seasons, 1955 and 1956, punting was Gillom's only job.

But, with the roster limit still at thirty-three, most coaches stayed away from specialists. The top place-kickers in the 1950s included quarterback Bob Waterfield of the Rams, halfback Doak Walker of the Lions, fullback Fred Cone of the Packers, and defensive end Sam Baker of the Redskins. Among the best punters were quarterback Norm Van Brocklin of the Rams, fullback Fred Morrison of the Bears, and defensive back Yale Lary of the Lions.

When the roster limit went up to thirty-six in 1959, more specialists appeared, but players like halfback Paul Hornung of the Packers and guard Steve Myrha of the Colts were still prized commodities because, by doubling as kickers, they, in effect, allowed a team to carry an extra player.

The limit was increased to thirty-seven in 1963 and to forty in 1964. By then, virtually every professional team had specialist kickers and punters.

The most notable sign of specialization was the arrival of soccer-style kickers, many of whom had never played American football before. Indeed, some of them had never seen American football before they began playing it.

The first of them was Pete Gogolak, a Cornell graduate who joined the Buffalo Bills in 1964. The second was his brother Charlie, from Dartmouth, who began kicking for the Boston Patriots in 1966.

At first scorned, even ridiculed, by some fans and sportswriters—not just because of their style of kicking but also because they tended to be under-sized by pro football standards—the soccer-stylers gradually won respect for distance as well as accuracy. The last old-style, straight-ahead kicker was Mark Moseley, who retired after the 1986 season.

The real pioneer of special teams was George Allen, who coined the phrase, along with "kamikaze squad" and "suicide squad." The fiery, emotional Allen became head coach of the Los Angeles Rams in 1966, after years as a defensive coach with the Chicago Bears.

Although the Rams had a rather stodgy offense, they became a winning team under Allen because of big plays by the defense and the special teams. He established the same pattern when he took over the Washington Redskins in 1971.

By using the adjective "special," Allen made his part-time players feel special, and he instilled pride in their accomplishments. His success inspired other coaches to put more emphasis on special teams. Their importance was formally acknowledged in 1984, when Pro Bowl ballots included a slot for a special teams player, aside from the kicker and punter.

Good play on special teams can often win a player a spot on the squad that he might not otherwise have won. A rookie fighting for a job as a team's fifth wide receiver might well be kept, ahead of a player with more sheer physical talent, if he shows the willingness to go all out on the punt and kickoff teams. And several backup offensive linemen have extended their professional careers for years because of their skill at snapping the ball on place kicks and punts.

John Madden has written that special teams players need to have "controlled fanaticism." But it's important to remember that "special teams" refers to six different units, and each is special in its own way. Madden was referring primarily to the punt and kickoff teams; players on those teams have to fly down the field recklessly—or fanatically—without losing control, because they have specific responsibilities.

The kickoff team is essentially made up of one kicker and ten tacklers. Sometimes the kicker is forced into being a tackler, and a number of the soccer-style kickers have become fairly adept at bringing runners down, often with cross-body blocks, but coaches hate to see it happen. For one thing, it means a long return has already taken place and, for another, there's always the risk of injury to the kicker.

Most teams number their players, from L-1 to L-5 on the left of the kicker and from R-1 to R-5 on the right of the kicker, with the "5" men nearest the sideline and the "1" men nearest the kicker.

The most important players on the kickoff team are the two closest to the kicker, L-1 and R-1, and the two farthest from him, L-5 and R-5. The L-1 and R-1 men are supposed to break up the wedge, while the L-5 and R-5 men have to stay in their lanes until they're absolutely certain the runner can't get to the sideline.

Since the wedge in front of the return man is made up of four players, it's not easy for two members of the kicking team to break it. These players have to be fast enough to get there quickly and big enough to take on two blockers apiece. They have to hit the gap between blockers. Sometimes, they function almost as blockers themselves, taking the wedge men out of the play. A few wedge breakers are adept at actually splitting blockers in order to make the tackle, but that's not their chief role.

The two men just to the outside of the wedge breakers, L-2 and R-2, are the surest open-field tacklers on the kickoff team. They're virtually expected to make the tackle, either by getting quickly around the wedge and breaking to the inside to get the ball carrier or by finding seams created by the wedge breakers.

The L-3, L-4, R-3, and R-4 men, like L-5 and R-5, have to stay in their lanes as they rush down the field, because an open lane is a virtual invitation to the return man to run for big yardage. They can close a little more quickly than the outside men, however, especially if the kick returner breaks through the wedge and up the middle.

Some teams have L-2 or R-2, or even both of them, slow down at about the 40-yard line of the return team and move toward the middle of the field to act as safety men. This tactic is used most often if the kicker needs protection because he probably can't make the tackle himself. When that's done, L-3 and R-3 have to close somewhat to the inside to protect two running lanes.

Everyone's job, obviously, is to prevent the long runback. The kicker can do that by simply booting the ball through the end zone, or at least deep into the end zone, to prevent any runback at all. Some kickers who lack strong legs have become skilled at kicking the ball toward the coffin corner, pinning the runner against a sideline so pursuit can close quickly from the other side of the field.

After a score, the kicking team has momentum on its side, at least temporarily. A long runback can turn the momentum around. On the other hand, pinning the other team inside its own 20-yard line maintains momentum. The importance of the kickoff is illustrated by the fact that, in recent seasons, the New York Giants and Denver Broncos have kept a strong-legged player on the roster just to handle kickoffs and the occasional long field goal, because their field goal kickers couldn't get the ball deep enough.

While the kickoff team is made up primarily of linebackers and defensive backs because of their speed and tackling ability, the punt team has to have offensive linemen, because the first job is to prevent the punt from being blocked.

In the regular punt formation, the five interior linemen are relatively tight. There are small gaps between them, but the gaps can't be wide enough to allow an opponent to charge through without contact. A wingback on each end of the line and just behind it is responsible for keeping any potential blocker from flying in from the corner. The punter stands thirteen yards deep. In front of him, a couple of yards behind the line of scrimmage and a yard or so to the side of his kicking foot, is a player sometimes called "the personal interferer." His role is to pick off anyone who penetrates with a chance to block the kick. He has to check the middle first, then make sure no one is coming in from either of the wings.

The two outside men on the line of scrimmage are the only players on the punting team who are allowed to go downfield before the ball is kicked. They're usually defensive backs, though a wide receiver is sometimes used in one of the spots. One of them is very likely to make the tackle, if there's a runback; ideally, they'll get downfield fast enough, and the kick will be high enough, to force a fair catch. Of course, these players have to be fast, but they also need strength, because the return team will try to block them at the line of scrimmage to slow their progress.

While the snapper may be the starting center, most teams like to have a backup lineman function as the long snapper for both the punt and field goal teams, because he has more time to work out with the special teams than a regular would.

A good long snapper delivers the ball quickly and accurately to the punter's hands. A great one—and there have been a few of them—can actually control the spiral on the snap so surely that the ball will arrive with the laces up so the punter doesn't have to waste a split-second turning it.

Then, of course, there's the punter himself. Some fans have asked why there are no soccer-style punters in pro football, especially after having seen some great long kicks during the 1994 World Cup tournament.

The answer is simple: Soccer players are trained not to handle the ball. A punter, above all, needs sure hands. He has to catch the ball cleanly before he can kick it, and he often has to handle a bad snap. If he can't handle the ball, it can be a gift of fifty or more yards to the opposition.

Punters are generally "real" football players, as opposed to place-kickers. A number of them were college quarterbacks. Ray Guy of the Raiders, possibly the best of all time, was the team's emergency quarterback and he also handled kickoffs for most of his career, though he didn't kick field goals.

While NFL record keeping emphasizes sheer distance on punts, coaches are more interested in the net yardage: The distance of the kick minus the distance it's returned or, in the case of a touchback, minus the 20 yards that the receiving team gains when the ball is brought out of the end zone.

Net yardage is related to hang time—the amount of time the ball is in the air. The magic number is 4.5 seconds. If a punt stays in the air that long, or longer, the receiver almost always has to call a fair catch. If the hang time is less than that, there's probably going to be a return. A punter who kicks the ball 40 yards with a 4.5 hang time consistently is more valuable than someone who punts it 45 yards with a 4.0 hang time.

Coaches used to prize coffin corner kickers, but the art of kicking the ball out-of-bounds inside the 10-yard line is now almost forgotten. With the hash marks closer to the center of the field, today's punter has a more difficult angle than those of the past. Also, an attempt to kick toward the sideline often results in a "shank"—a punt that slides off the side of the kicker's foot and goes only a short distance. After the offense has worked hard to get the ball to the opposition's 45-yard line, a shanked punt that goes out-of-bounds on the 28 is demoralizing. In effect, it subtracts twenty or more yards from what the offense has done.

Punters today are more often called upon for the "pooch" kick that goes high and a relatively short distance down the middle of the field, dropping somewhere inside the 10-yard line, where the punting team has a chance to down it before it crosses the goal line.

The NFL method of counting only distance penalizes many good kickers. Someone who punts the ball 45 yards into the end zone gets credit for all 45 yards; someone who has the kick downed at the 5-yard line gets credit for only 40 yards, but he's gained 15 yards more for his team.

However, players and coaches don't necessarily pay much attention to statistics. Rich Camarillo was selected for the Pro Bowl three years in a row, from 1991 through 1993, without leading his conference in punting. Rohn Stark was named the AFC's Pro Bowl punter after the 1992 season, although he averaged 2 yards less per punt than conference leader Greg Montgomery. Stark had a league-leading 22 punts inside the 20-yard line that season to Montgomery's 14.

When a team is pinned inside its own 5-yard line, the punter has to be closer to the line of scrimmage than usual, and a tight formation is used. The interior linemen have to be shoulder to shoulder, and the blocking backs are brought in close to the center. The chief danger is quick penetration up the middle. A rusher from the outside is less likely to be able to block the kick because he'll have a bad angle on the punter.

A bad snap, of course, can mean disaster in this situation. The snapper has two problems. First, he has to center the ball two or three yards shorter than usual, which can be difficult. Second, he's also responsible for preventing penetration, and he's probably confronted by three defenders, one on his nose and one on each shoulder. He has to concentrate on making a good snap first, before worrying about them.

The punter has to be very alert. If he does get a bad snap, or if he fails to handle the ball cleanly, he's undoubtedly better off taking a safety than letting the other team recover for a touchdown.

On a kickoff return, five men are stationed about 10 yards from the kicker. Their primary job is to slow down the middle men on the kicking team. A couple of them may cross over to block on the opposite side of the field from where they originally line up to get better blocking angles.

The four-man wedge lines up about the 20-yard line. As the kick goes past them, these four players will retreat somewhat, moving toward the ball.

There are two return men, stationed near the goal line and just about on the hash marks. If the kick is fielded by one of them in the end zone, the other return man has to size up the situation and tell him whether to run it out or not. He usually yells "Stay!" or "Go!"

As the ball carrier starts up field, the other return man joins the wedge. The runner should head right for the middle of the wedge, looking for a seam that he can break through. Once he finds an opening, his course is more or less pre-determined, since the special teams coach will have called a right, left, or middle return on the sideline.

After making their initial blocks, the five front men peel back. If the return is going to one side or the other, they'll try to set up a wall on that side of the field, to keep opponents away from the sideline, and the runner tries to get behind the wall so he can sprint up the alley along the sideline. On a middle return, the front men try to create a corridor in the middle of the field.

The men in the wedge are usually linemen, though many coaches like to have one fullback there to field the kick if it comes up short. The front men are likely to be interior linemen, tight ends, or fullbacks.

While there have been a few great open-field runners who excelled at punt and kickoff returns, somewhat different skills are required. Because he runs into a lot of traffic as he heads up through the wedge, a good kickoff returner has to be strong, so he may be a little bigger and not quite as fast as his team's punt returner.

A list of the NFL's best kick returners presents an interesting mixture of types. They include starting defensive backs Deion Sanders and Rod Woodson, both of whom also return punts; backup safety Alton Montgomery; kick return specialist Clarence Verdin, who is occasionally used as a third wide receiver; backup running backs Randy Baldwin, Eric Ball, and Johnny Bailey; and, finally, Eric Metcalf, Dave Meggett, and Mel Gray, who are also used as long-yardage and third-down running backs because of their speed.

Perhaps the most special of special teams are those used in onside-kick situations. This situation, of course, comes up only when a team has scored late in the game but is still trailing. (An onside kick is occasionally tried as a surprise maneuver earlier, but the regular kickoff team is then in the game, or it wouldn't be a surprise.)

Once a kickoff has gone ten yards, it's a free ball and can be recovered by either team. On an onside kick, the kicker will usually just dribble the ball along the ground. Both teams want players with good hands on the field, since the goal is to get possession of the ball. Wide receivers and defensive backs will predominate, with perhaps a running back or two.

The return team will generally keep its two kick returners in the game, but they'll be farther from the goal line than usual. They are there simply to prevent a long kickoff from being recovered by the kickers, which could result in a touchdown.

The other nine players are stationed the required 10 yards from the spot of the kick. It's legal for the receiving team to recover the ball *before* it's gone 10 yards, so a receiver may move toward the ball in an attempt to recover it quickly. If he touches it, though, he has to be sure he can gain possession, because the kick becomes a free ball when it's been touched by a receiver, even if it hasn't gone 10 yards yet.

The onside-kick team usually lines up like a regular kickoff team, with five players on each side of the kicker. Various tricks have been tried on onside-kicks at one time or another. The most common is to have the players from one side of the field sprint to the other side just before the kick in order to outnumber the receiving team. Occasionally, as the regular kicker approaches the ball, another player will come in from the side to kick it. Yet another surprise tactic, sometimes successful in the past but rarely attempted now, is to kick the ball fairly high but short, over the nine front men on the receiving team, in the hope that a speedster can get past them and recover the ball before they do.

Players on both teams have to remember that possession is paramount. If anyone gets his hands on the ball, he should wrap it up and fall down without attempting to advance it.

The team receiving a punt will usually try to set up a return. The standard formation has six interior linemen who will try to put some pressure on the punter, with three players on the outside. Two of them will be assigned to block the punting team's fastest outside man and the third will be on the other outside man.

Some teams use two deep return men, as on a kickoff, but most have one return man about 40 yards deep, in line with the punter, and another stationed 25 to 30 yards deep.

When the kick is in the air, one return man will call for it. Since he has to focus first on the ball, not on potential tacklers, the other is responsible for letting him know whether he should make a fair catch or attempt a runback.

A return man has to have a good field sense when he's deep in his own territory. The general rule is that he should not try to catch the ball inside his own 10-yard line. Quite often, however, a return man will field the ball on his 5-yard line because he has lost track of where he is.

The punt returner, like the punter, must have good hands. He has to make sure he catches the ball before he tries to do anything else. Once he catches it, his first move is all important. There are probably two opponents, the two outside men, very near him. The other deep man will try to block one of them. If the block is made, and if the runner can elude the other, he's likely to have a long return.

Meanwhile, the other members of the return team are peeling back. As on a left or right kickoff return, they try to set up a "picket line" on one side of the field or the other. The punt returner, after his first move, will usually try to get between the wall and the sideline.

Because the punt coverage players will tend to head toward the picket line, knowing that's where the return is supposed to go, the runner can occasionally gain a lot of yardage by going straight up the middle of the field and then breaking to the other side. It's his decision. But, if he tries it too often without significant results, he's likely to be replaced by someone who takes the return the way the special teams coach diagrammed it.

Speed, combined with that good first move, are more important on a punt return than on a kickoff return. As already noted, some players are good at both—notably Deion Sanders, Clarence Verdin, and Rod Woodson. Among the best punt returners are wide receivers Tim Brown and Arthur Marshall and defensive backs Terrell Buckley and Dale Carter.

In studying films of an opponent, a special teams coach may see a flaw that could set up a blocked punt. Maybe the punter is having trouble with the snap, or maybe he takes a little bit too much time in getting the kick away. It could be that one of the wing blockers is somewhat too eager to commit to the outside, so a rusher can take an inside lane against him. Or perhaps the snapper is slow to react to pressure up the middle after he delivers the ball.

If the coach thinks his team can get a block, there are two distinct philosophies about when to try it. Under Jimmy Johnson, the Dallas Cowboys often went for the block on the opposition's first punt. Johnson liked his team to get an early break and an early lead to put the pressure on the opponent. Some coaches prefer to wait for the crucial moment, when a blocked punt can either turn the game around or break it open.

The people most likely to block a punt are speedsters coming from the outside and strong, tall players coming up the middle. A perennial All-Pro as a special teams player is Steve Tasker, a 5-foot-9, 191-pounder. Though nominally a wide receiver, he's averaged only one reception a year in his eight seasons as a pro. Best known for his speed and tackling ability on Buffalo's kickoff and punt return teams, Tasker is also a threat as a punt blocker.

In Super Bowl XXVII, the Bills briefly took a 7–0 lead over Dallas because Tasker blocked a punt at the Cowboys' 16-yard line. Of course, they lost 52–17, so Tasker's effort went almost unnoticed, but at the time it seemed like a crucial play.

The best kick blocker in pro football history was Ted "Mad Stork" Hendricks, a 6-foot-7 outside linebacker with unusually long arms. Hendricks was used in the middle on both punts and place kicks. He had 25 blocks during his career, which would undoubtedly be a record except that official records of blocked kicks weren't kept while he was playing.

Blocking a punt, especially from the outside, is one of the most difficult feats in football. The natural impulse is to head toward the kicker, but running into him without touching the ball is a cardinal sin. Rushers are taught to take an angle toward a spot just in front of where the punter will be when he actually kicks the ball and then to dive through the air. It's surprising how often a defender misses the ball by not getting high enough or by having it go right between his hands. A successful block is often made with the face mask, helmet, or chest rather than with the hands or arms.

There are three key players on the field goal team: The snapper and the holder in addition to the kicker. The holder is often a backup quarterback, but some teams prefer to use their punter in that role. As already noted, a punter has to have good hands, and so does the holder.

Most teams have a long snapper who's used on both punts and field goals, but sometimes different people are used in those roles. The field goal snapper obviously doesn't have to be able to center the ball as far, but he has to get it to the holder quickly and accurately. At the same, he can't snap the ball too hard, or it will be difficult to handle. Ideally, he can control the spiral so the laces will be up when the holder makes his catch.

The holder, who is positioned 7 or 8 yards behind the line of scrimmage, has a split-second to field the ball with both hands, get it down, spot it with the index finger of his left hand, and get his right hand out of the way. (For a left-footed kicker, the spot is made with the right hand.) He may also have to turn the ball so the laces are facing forward. The timing is vitally important, because the kicker starts forward before the ball is actually spotted. If there's a delay, either he'll have to slow his approach or he'll get there too soon. In either case, he's very likely to miss the kick. A really good holder can often save the day with his ability to catch an off-target snap and still get the ball down in time.

And then, of course, there's the kicker. Like a golfer, he has to keep his head down and his eyes focused on the ball, not the target. Most kickers naturally look at the uprights while waiting, in order to line up the kick properly, but one of the best was Ray Wersching of the 49ers, who never looked at the goal posts. Wersching used the hash marks as his guides.

Generally speaking, soccer-style kickers are more effective on artificial turf than on grass. The now obsolete straight-ahead kicker had an advantage on grass, because he planted his foot with the toes pointed straight down the field and his cleats were more likely to anchor. A soccer kicker, however, plants his front foot at an angle and is more likely to lose his footing, especially on a wet or muddy field.

Obviously, the ideal kicker is both accurate and strong. But his psychological makeup is even more important than his kicking ability. The field goal kicker spends most of his time on the sideline. If he's young and unproved, he probably gets little respect from the "real" football players, who take a physical beating for twenty or thirty minutes of the game.

After all those other players have done all that work, the kicker is often, all of a sudden, thrust into the game to attempt a field goal that will mean victory if it's good, defeat if it's not. Some kickers who looked very good in practice have been unable to deal with that kind of pressure.

The best are very strong psychologically. They not only have to deal with the present pressure in the game-winning situation, they have to be able to forget past failures. A field goal kicker who gets down after a miss, like the cornerback who hangs his head when a receiver beats him, isn't going to last long. A number of kickers have had a good season or two only to fall into slumps from which they never recovered.

The first of the truly great soccer-style kickers was Jan Stenerud. He was unusual among the breed in that he was good-sized at 6-foot-2 and 190 pounds. A fine all-around athlete, he left his native Norway to attend Montana State on a skiing scholarship. In part because of his skiing, he had an exceptionally strong leg and he was also very accurate. Stenerud holds the professional career record with 373 field goals. He won a lot of games for the Chiefs, the Packers, and the Vikings.

Nick Lowery, long with the Chiefs but now a Jet, is likely to break that record. Even bigger than Stenerud at 6-foot-4 and 207 pounds, Lowery already has the best career percentage in history, at better than 80 percent, and he's one of only a handful of kickers to have booted two field goals of more than 50 yards in a game.

Two other current kickers who combine accuracy with strength are Pete Stoyanovich of the Dolphins and Morten Andersen of the Saints. Andersen holds the NFL career record with 22 field goals of 50 or more yards and he's not far behind Lowery in accuracy. Some other kickers who have had long careers because of shorter-range accuracy are Gary Andersen, Jim Breech, and Eddie Murray.

The defensive alignment on a place kick is similar to that used on a punt. The chief difference is that there are no deep men unless it's a very long field goal attempt. Because the holder is not as deep as the punter, it's difficult to block a kick with a rush from the outside, although it's been done.

Many soccer-style kickers have trouble getting the ball quickly into the air. A block is more likely to come with a push up the middle by a tall player who gets his hands up.

Although records weren't kept during his time, Bob St. Clair, an offensive tackle with the 49ers during the 1950s and 1960s, reportedly blocked ten kicks one season. St. Clair was put in the middle against kicks because he was 6-foot-9 and had tremendous strength at 265 pounds.

Ted Hendricks has already been mentioned because of his ability to block both punts and place kicks. There are no truly outstanding kick blockers in the NFL today, primarily because modern linemen tend to be shorter, though heavier, than those of the past.

There's no doubt that special teams have come a long way, baby, since the days of Lou Groza and Horace Gillom. Head coaches now routinely say that the game is one-third offense, one-third defense, and one-third special teams. A team that can win the battle in two of those three areas is likely to win the game.

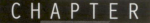

7

A Week in the Life

At a Packer-Bear game in Green Bay a few years ago, I sat in the press box next to Paul Wiggin. I remembered him from my years as a sports editor in Ohio during the early 1960s, when he was an undersized but very good defensive end for the Cleveland Browns. He later became head coach at his alma mater, Stanford. When I sat beside him in the Green Bay press box, he was an advance scout for the Minnesota Vikings, who were scheduled to play the Bears on Monday Night Football the following week.

It seemed to me that, with game films and videotape, a scout should be virtually obsolete. I said so to Wiggin. He grinned and explained, in some detail, what his job was.

Game films are severely edited. They include just play after play after play. They don't show the offensive team huddling, and they don't show the substitutions that take place between plays.

One of the advance scout's major concerns is to keep track of exactly what players are in the game in certain situations. With the amount of situational substitution that goes on nowadays, an advance scout may be more important than ever.

At one point in the game, the Bears faced a second and long situation. They brought in three wide receivers and had running back Neal Anderson lined up behind quarterback Jim Harbaugh, who was under center.

"They're going to run the draw play with Number 35," Wiggin said. (One thing I've noticed about scouts: They never use names, only numbers.)

Sure enough, Harbaugh handed the ball to Anderson, Number 35, on a draw and the Packers smothered him for a 2-yard loss. I asked Wiggin what had tipped him off.

"Every time the Bears use that package, with three wide receivers and the quarterback under center, they run the draw," Wiggin explained. "If they ever faked it and threw the ball, they'd probably have a touchdown."

The following Monday, I was in Atlanta watching the Bears and Vikings on television with my son-in-law. On second and long, the Bears lined up with the same package they'd used in Green Bay. "They're going to give it to Anderson on a draw play," I said.

They did. Minnesota middle linebacker Jack Del Rio charged into the backfield and tackled Anderson almost before he took the hand-off. My son-in-law was tremendously impressed by my deep insight into pro football.

A week of preparation for a game leads to that kind of play—a 5-yard loss on second down that forces the opposition into a passing situation where a sack for a further loss of yardage or an interception can lead directly to victory.

This chapter will take you through a week of preparation by an NFL team. But the preparation actually begins in training camp. So let's first take a quick look at what goes on during pre-season training and exhibition games.

Pro teams operate "mini-camps," three or four days in length, soon after the April draft of college players. These camps are intended primarily to give rookies a crash course in pro football, and to give the coaches a preliminary look at their new players. In addition to rookies, recently acquired veterans and players coming back from injuries are often invited to attend.

Full-scale training begins in early July. Rookies, other new players, and quarterbacks usually report three or four days before the other players. In the 1930s, the main purpose of the training camp was to get the players into shape. Most players now stay in pretty good shape during the off season, so that's a secondary purpose, although they still have to get into game condition, which is different.

Everything that's done during training camp and into the regular season is based on the team's playbook. The playbook is a loose-leaf notebook that contains diagrams of all the offensive and defensive formations, every running play, every type of blitz and pass coverage, and every pass pattern for every receiver position, including running back.

But it contains more than plays. The playbook usually begins with league rules pertaining to player conduct, followed by the team's own rules. There's also a glossary of terms. Even a veteran player may have to study the glossary thoroughly if he's with a new team, because the terminology might be quite different. For example, in numbering holes, some teams use odd numbers for the right side of the offense and even numbers for the left, but other teams reverse that. Similarly, on most teams the kickoff return men nearest the kicker are numbered L-1 and R-1, while the L-5 and R-5 players are those nearest the sidelines. A few teams, however, designate the players near the sidelines as L-1 and R-1, and the players nearest the kicker are L-5 and R-5.

The playbook can be intimidating to a rookie, especially if he's from a college that ran a relatively simple offense. He's already surrounded by enormous players who have established themselves as professionals. He not only has to prove to the coaches and to himself that he has the skills to play at this new level, he has to take a cram course studying a book that contains three or four hundred pages of diagrams.

Quarterbacks and offensive linemen have the hardest course of study. A quarterback is expected to know what every player is supposed to do on every play. An offensive lineman not only has to learn a couple of hundred running plays, his assignment on each play will change as the defensive alignment changes. That's one reason that very few rookies start in the offensive line.

The pre-season is obviously a very busy time for the coaches. They have four games in which to get the team ready for the regular season. And they're not only trying to get the players into shape and game-ready, they're also evaluating personnel to decide who should stay on the roster and who should be cut.

Generally speaking, younger players and backups will get quite a bit of action in the first couple of games. By the third exhibition game, the starters are likely to play at least the first half and possibly into the third quarter.

The approach to the fourth game depends largely on the kind of team a coach has. If he's coaching a team dominated by veterans that had a winning record the previous season, he may opt to let most of them sit it out, to avoid injuries and also to give his bench players more game experience. But if it's a younger team that needs to improve, he'll probably use his starters most of the way.

Every coach likes to win that last exhibition game to get his team headed into the regular season with a good attitude. But coaches have different philosophies about winning during the pre-season. Again, the philosophy may vary with the makeup of the team. If it's expected to be a contender, the coach probably wants a winning record. If it's a young team, winning is less important than getting a good, hard look at personnel.

Preparation for a game begins with the scouting report and films. Most coaches begin preparing by looking at film as soon as possible after a home game, the showers, and the post-game press conference. And some coaches bring their players in for a meeting on Monday, then give them Tuesday off. The day-by-day schedule may vary considerably, too. But this rough schedule is fairly typical of how any NFL team does it.

MONDAY

9 A.M.—The coaching staff looks at the film of Sunday's game, taking notes and grading players. Every player is graded on every play, based on the assignment he was supposed to carry out. Everything counts: The amount of time a linebacker holds up the tight end on the line of scrimmage, how well a back carries out his fake when he runs into the line without the ball—everything.

Meanwhile, injured players show up for treatment by the team trainer and evaluation by doctors. The head coach will check on their condition to get at least a preliminary idea of who will be available to play this week. Healthy players report on Tuesday.

1 P.M.—The coaches split into three groups to look at the edited films of the next opponent. Under NFL rules, teams have to exchange films of their previous two games. The films are broken down into reels for the offense, defense, and special teams.

Films are studied primarily for tendencies. The offensive coordinator wants to know what defensive alignment the opponent likes to use in various down-and-yardage situations and how the linebackers and defensive backs respond when a back or receiver goes in motion. The offensive line coach zeroes in more specifically on the kinds of moves defensive linemen and linebackers use to try to get into the offensive backfield to break up a running play or to sack the quarterback.

In another room, the defensive coordinator and the assistant defensive coaches are studying the opposition's offense. Again, the analysis covers the general and the specific. What formations does the team favor in various down-and-yardage situations, and what plays are run out of those formations? How do running backs respond to the threat of a blitz? What pass routes does a certain receiver seem to favor?

Meanwhile, the special teams coach is looking at film of the opposition's special teams, diagramming their formations and taking note of any tendencies that might lead to a blocked field goal or a long punt return.

6 P.M.—Typically, the coaches have food delivered as they assemble once more to begin putting together a game plan. They work with frequency charts that were developed during the film study. The advance scout is on hand with his own charts showing situational substitution and diagrams of unusual plays run yesterday by the opposition.

Some coaches think the game plan is over-rated. When Tommy Prothro was coaching the Los Angeles Rams, he said of game plans, "When you're up to your ass in alligators, it doesn't help to remember that you came to drain the swamp." He meant that if the game plan calls for grinding out yardage on the ground and wearing down the opposition's defense, it's not very useful if the team gets behind by three touchdowns early in the second quarter. But the game plan is, at least, a necessary evil. It's like an outline to a writer. It serves as an overall guide to what needs to be accomplished, even though it may bear little resemblance to the finished product.

Based on the game plan, the offensive coaches develop a "ready list." A team may have two hundred or more running plays in its playbook, but only about fifteen of them will be practiced for a given game, along with fifteen or twenty pass patterns out of an almost unlimited number of possible combinations.

The ready list is more than a list of plays. It includes a list of situations in which those plays will be run. If the opposition likes to come with an all-out blitz on third-and-long, for example, a quick pass to a running back or a fly pattern to a wide receiver might be called for. Maybe a very aggressive defensive lineman is targeted for a trap play. Or there might be a cornerback who tends to commit quickly on a short route, so it's possible to beat him deep on a hook-and-go.

The defensive coaches also prepare their own list of schemes to use in various situations. Like the offensive ready list, it's based partly on the frequency chart of what the opponent likes to do, partly on strengths and weakness of individual players.

Although the head coach has over-all responsibility for the game plan, it's developed through discussion, sometimes arguments, among the entire staff. This meeting may well last into early Tuesday morning, especially if the team is preparing for an unfamiliar opponent or for a particularly important game.

TUESDAY

9 A.M.—The players split into two groups, offense and defense, to watch the film of their game, listening to comments from the coaches. The projector is frequently stopped and the film wound back so a play can be watched again, often in slow motion. Sometimes, particularly if a player made a serious mistake, a play may be run several times—not to embarrass the player, but so he can see exactly what he did wrong and why. The two groups then watch the game films of their next opponent.

10 A.M.—The advance scout gives his report to the entire team, using a blackboard to diagram formations and plays. He usually has a comment on each opposing player, as well. For example, he might say something like, "Number 81 is tougher at catching the ball over the middle than he used to be. And the last time we played them, Number 43 was slowed down by an ankle, but he's healthy now and as fast as ever, so you have to worry about him breaking one."

11 A.M.—In sweat suits, players work out for an hour or so. The emphasis is on correcting mistakes that were spotted on the film. Some teams have their workout during the afternoon, but most give the players the rest of the day off.

12:30 P.M.—The coaches have another meeting to study frequency charts and probably some more film. If the opponent is a team they've played recently, they may watch film of that game to see what worked and what didn't. The ready list is expanded.

WEDNESDAY

One of the head coach's most important tasks today is to check on injuries—not just for himself, but for the league office. Each team has to file an injury report with the NFL, listing players as probable, questionable, or doubtful. There are two reasons for the report: First, to let the opposing head coach know who may or may not be playing on Sunday. Second, and perhaps more important, is the NFL's hard-nosed stance against gambling. The league obviously can't prevent gambling, but NFL policy is to avoid anything that might taint the outcome of a game. With the honest, forthright reporting of injuries, bookies and bettors can't take advantage of inside information to get an "edge." The injury report has to be updated on Thursday. Team reports appear in most newspapers, usually among the fine print listing the schedule for the week.

9 A.M.—Offensive and defensive units meet with their coaches to get a kind of preview of the game plan. Although the game plan and ready list aren't final yet, the plays and defensive schemes that they'll probably be using are diagrammed and restudied.

10:30 A.M.—After calisthenics, linemen work with their coaches while the rest of the players go through a passing drill. Then defensive players put on jerseys of a different color and pretend to be the opposition, while the offense runs plays designed to attack the defenses likely to be used in various down and yardage situations.

12:30 P.M.—Now the offense changes jerseys to run the opposition's favorite plays for an hour or more. Like the earlier offensive drill, this defensive drill is a rather light workout, basically noncontact.

2 P.M.—The players meet once more to receive their grades for the previous game. Awards are given out for high grades and for specific accomplishments, such as quarterback sacks, interceptions, downfield blocks that helped to spring a long run, and outstanding special teams play. The goal is to begin getting the team psychologically prepared for the following Sunday.

4:30 P.M.—As the last players shower, the coaches have one more meeting to go over everything they've done so far and everything they still need to do. There may be some last-minute soul searching here; the ready list will probably be cut down a bit because it's simply too long. And a couple of plays may be added.

Some coaches like to "script" plays. Bill Walsh, when he was with the 49ers, scripted as many as twenty-five plays to be run in sequence. Of course, the script could be interrupted for special situations that called for a special play, such as third and long or first and goal. But, aside from that, each play in the Walsh script was designed to find out something about the opposition defense. Although several Walsh disciples follow his policy of scripting a number of plays, other coaches simply script plays to be used in certain situations. For example, John Madden with the Oakland Raiders had plays that he wanted to be used the first time his team faced a second and long or a short-yardage situation.

When Vince Lombardi coached the Packers during the 1960s, he scripted just the first play his offense was going to run. In his book *Run to Daylight*, written with W. C. Heinz, Lombardi describes the play that Green Bay ran in a crucial game against the Detroit Lions. It was a fairly simple running play, but it sent three different blockers against Detroit's great middle linebacker, Joe Schmidt, because Lombardi wanted Schmidt to be watching for blockers coming from all directions for the rest of the game.

THURSDAY

This is undoubtedly the most important day of the week. It's the day the players learn, and begin working on, the things they have to do to win on Sunday.

9 A.M.—The offensive and defensive units meet separately with their coaches again. Copies of the game plan, ready list, and defensive schemes are distributed. The offensive coordinator goes over the opponent's defensive frequency chart, while the defensive coordinator does the same with the offensive frequency chart. Professional players are intelligent and knowledgeable about their sport; most of them want to know not only what they're supposed to do, but *why*. This meeting is meant to tell them why as well as what.

The defensive coordinator may tell his unit something like this, based on frequency charts: "On second and long, they line up with split backs 92 percent of the time, and the weak-side back goes in motion 65 percent of the time. They like to throw to him quickly to give him a chance to run with the ball, and he doesn't check off on the linebacker, so we're going to blitz from that side and cover him with the strong safety. That means the weak safety will usually be covering the tight end."

Meanwhile, the offensive coordinator may be saying something like this: "On second and long, they blitz both outside linebackers 85 percent of the time, because they really like to get you into a third and long so they can blitz again. This Number 53 on the outside is very quick. He had $3\frac{1}{2}$ sacks, five knockdowns, and seven pressures last week. We're going to pull the weak-side guard to handle him, and the weak-side back has to check off and help. That means the center is going to have to fill for the guard."

10:30 A.M.—The team breaks into even smaller units now: Receivers, offensive linemen, offensive backs, defensive linemen, linebackers, and defensive backs, each meeting with a single coach to study their individual assignments on each offensive play or each defensive scheme.

Since the playbook contains *everything*, at least in theory, there's nothing genuinely new. But, because of the nature of the opposition, there may be some plays on the offensive ready list that the team hasn't yet used this season. And even on a familiar play, the blocking scheme might change because of certain defensive tendencies. Similarly, the defensive coordinator might want to use a blitz combination or a type of zone coverage that he doesn't often use. At this point, the receivers coach, for example, is responsible for making certain that each receiver knows exactly what his assignment is on every play against every type of defense that the other team is likely to use.

11:30 A.M.—Now the players assemble on the practice field for a fairly brief workout. Again, they're in small groups, and they practice the assignments they've just studied.

1:30 P.M.—After a break for lunch, offensive and defensive units get together for another team practice, to work once more on the things they're going to do Sunday. The second-team offense works against the defense, running the opposition's favorite plays, while the offense runs the plays on its ready list against the backup defensive unit. These are more intense workouts than those held on Wednesday, with more contact, but they're still short of the all-out, full-contact scrimmages that NFL teams used to have, mainly because of the risk of injury in the 16-game season.

3:30 P.M.—Most of the players are now done for the day. But the quarterbacks meet with the offensive coordinator to go over the game plan one last time, and the special teams work out with their coach for about an hour.

FRIDAY

The players now get to taper off somewhat, with their most intense physical work behind them. The day usually begins with small group meetings at which players review their assignments. Such a meeting often features "pop" verbal quizzes. The offensive line coach, for example, may say to his starting right guard, "Second-and-ten, we're running our 21 lead draw against their nickel defense. What do you do?"

After the group meetings, which typically take a half-hour or forty-five minutes, the offense again runs its plays against the opposition's defenses, and the defense then rehearses its schemes against the opposition's offensive formations. These final run-throughs are no-contact workouts. The main goal of the day is mental sharpness.

If the team is going to be on the road, there's a flight to prepare for. If the team's at home, its players are aware that the other team is going to have a short day, so they want a short day, as well. Practice is usually over by noon.

SATURDAY

This is a day for light workouts and special teams practice. The home team works out in the morning and the visiting team has the afternoon. One goal of the visitors, especially on a grass field, is to check out the condition of the turf. If there's been recent rain, or if the field has been used for another sport or a rock concert, players want to know where the footing is good and where it's questionable.

SUNDAY

About four hours before kickoff, the team gathers for a meal. Usually breakfast, but if the game is being played at three or four P.M. because of national television, it's more like brunch. And, for one of those Sunday or Monday night games, it might be a late afternoon or early evening dinner.

Players show up in the locker room two hours before kickoff. Coaches are there, too, and they may move around with last-minute bits of advice or encouragement. Some coaches like to stay away, though. John Madden has written about the fact that, after his first year as a head coach, he decided to stay out of the locker room because he felt he was too hyper and got his players nervous.

Each player has his own way of preparing himself. Some joke around, some play cards, some sit and meditate, some read, some take a nap. Now and then there's a player—often one of the very best, like Fred Biletnikoff—who gets so keyed up that he has to throw up his pre-game meal.

Kickers start warming up on the field a half-hour before the game, and the rest of the team follows ten minutes later. The coin toss takes place—to be reenacted, shortly before kickoff, for the spectators and the television audience.

Teams retreat into their locker rooms once more, for just a few minutes, a few last words of advice, and possibly a quick pep talk, before the game begins.

Once they're back on the field for the kickoff, there's not much coaching to be done. Yes, there are coaches in the press box, calling plays and defensive formations, and television cameras focus on the head coach as he stands stoically or paces frantically. And, if it's a close game, there may be a time-out when an important decision is made on the sidelines.

But, if the coaching was effective during the week—if a team was physically, mentally, and emotionally prepared to play going in—there's a good chance of victory, even against a superior team. If the coaching wasn't as good as it should have been, there's a good chance of losing, even against an inferior team.

After the game, players have a brief respite in which they can shed their uniforms, shower, and get at least partially dressed. But the NFL requires that each dressing room be opened to accredited media personnel within fifteen minutes after the end of a game. Interviewers are free to talk to any players they choose; those who played key roles in the outcome, for better or for worse, are naturally popular targets. It's not unusual for a group of a dozen or more journalists to gather around a single player, who's barraged with questions while he zips up his pants and puts on his shirt.

Players who need treatment for injuries report to the trainer's room after showering. This room is off-limits to media, so it's often used as a refuge by athletes who don't want to be interviewed for one reason or another. Some players simply don't like answering questions; others are perfectly willing to talk after playing well in a victory but become tongue-tied after a loss or a poor personal performance.

The locker room scene isn't as frantic as it once was, because there are now more formal press conferences that begin about a half-hour after the game. The winning team usually goes first, although the visiting team may be up first if the timing of the flight home makes it necessary.

The head coach leads off, giving a brief analysis of the game from his point of view and answering some questions. Several players will also be on hand. The winning quarterback is almost always among them, along with others who played key roles: The kicker whose last-second field goal won the game, the defensive back whose interception set up the winning score, a running back or wide receiver who put up impressive numbers, a defensive lineman who made a key sack or two.

An assistant coach may also be invited to the press conference. If special teams played an important role in a victory, for example, the special teams coach will probably be there to explain how he orchestrated the performance.

An hour and a half to two hours after the game, players are finally ready to leave the stadium. First, there's a very brief team meeting. Occasionally, a head coach may really chew his team out if they played badly that day. But the coach is usually quite low-key. He wants his players to get past this game and begin getting ready, emotionally, for the next game.

The winning coach will generally congratulate his players on a job well done. He may say something like, "This was a good win today because we did all the things we have to do. We'll have to play just as well, or better, to win next Sunday, because we're going to be up against a better team away from home."

The loser may say something like, "We could have won today, but we made some crucial mistakes. If we avoid those mistakes next week, we can win, so let's all start thinking about how we can play better on Sunday. We'll start working on it Tuesday morning."

For the visiting team, there's a bus ride to the airport and the flight home. Players on the home team simply drive away, some with their wives, some with other players, some alone in their cars. Their coaches, though, remain at the stadium. They can start getting ready for the next game. They already have one game film of the opposition, from the previous week, and the film of their own game will also be ready for viewing within a short time.

Teams to Know

Akron Pros—One of the founding teams of the American Professional Football Association, the Pros won the league's first championship with an 8–0–3 record in 1920. Led by black player-coach Fritz Pollard, the Pros gave up only 7 points all season.

After playing only Ohio teams during what amounted to the regular season, the Pros went to Buffalo in December for a scoreless tie with the All-Americans, who had lost one game, and then played another scoreless tie in Chicago against the Decatur Staleys, who also had one loss.

The APFA was renamed the National Football League in 1922 and Akron was in the league through 1926. The 1926 team was called the Indians.

Arizona Cardinals—The St. Louis Cardinals moved to Phoenix in 1988. They've yet to have a winning season in that location.

Atlanta Falcons—The Falcons entered the NFL as an expansion team in 1966. They won the NFC Western Division title in 1980 but have yet to advance farther than that.

Baltimore Colts—The original Colts were in the All-America Football Conference from 1946 through 1949 and they were one of the teams that entered the NFL after the AAFC went out of business in 1950. However, the franchise folded before the 1951 season.

Baltimore wasn't without a team for very long. In 1953, the troubled Dallas Texans franchise settled there and took over the Colts' name. Led by quarterback Johnny Unitas, running back/receiver Lenny Moore, split end Ray Berry, and fullback Alan Ameche, the Colts won the 1958 NFL championship by beating the New York Giants 23–17 in the league's first overtime game. They repeated as champions in 1959.

With Earl Morrall replacing the injured Unitas for most of the season, the Colts won their third NFL title in 1968; Morrall was named the league's player of the year. However, the New York Jets upset Baltimore 16–7 to become the first AFL team to win the Super Bowl.

After the merger of the NFL and AFL in 1970, the Colts were one of three teams from the old NFL that moved into the American Football Conference. They won the AFC title that year and went on to beat the Dallas Cowboys 16–13 in Super Bowl V.

One of the most unusual transactions in NFL history took place in 1972, when Carroll Rosenbloom traded the Baltimore franchise to Robert Irsay for the Los Angeles Rams. The team floundered under Irsay's ownership and he moved the franchise to Indianapolis in 1984.

Boston Bulldogs—The Bulldogs were in the NFL for just one season, in 1929. They dropped out after compiling a 4–4–0 record.

Boston Redskins—George Preston Marshall was given an NFL franchise for Boston in 1932. The team was called the Braves that season, but the name was changed to the Redskins in 1933.

The Redskins won the 1936 Eastern Division championship. Attendance in Boston was so disappointing that Marshall moved the championship game against the Green Bay Packers to New York's Polo Grounds. The Packers won 21–6. The franchise moved to Washington in 1937.

Boston Yanks—Oddly, the Yanks entered the NFL during World War II, in 1944. The franchise disbanded after the 1948 season, but most of its players joined a new team, the New York Bulldogs, in 1949.

Boston Patriots—A charter member of the American Football League in 1960, the Patriots struggled to find a home field in Boston. At one time or another, they played at Harvard Stadium, at the Boston College and Boston University fields, and at Fenway Park, home of baseball's Red Sox.

Led by quarterback Babe Parilli and wide receiver/kicker Gino Cappelletti, who led the AFL in scoring with 113 points, the Patriots won the 1963 Eastern Division title, but they were blown away 51–10 by the San Diego Chargers in the league's championship game.

The team moved to the new Schaefer Stadium in Foxboro, MA, in 1971 and became known as the New England Patriots.

Brooklyn Dodgers—Yes, the football team. Brooklyn actually had two professional teams in 1926, the Lions in the NFL and the Horsemen in Red Grange's American Football League. That AFL lasted just one season and the NFL's Brooklyn franchise also folded after 1926.

The Dodgers entered the NFL in 1930 and remained in the league through 1944. The team was renamed the Tigers in 1944, but that didn't help. The Tigers lost all 10 of their games and the franchise went out of business after only three winning seasons in 15 years.

In 1946, another Brooklyn team called the Dodgers joined the new All-America Football Conference. They lasted through 1948 and won only eight games in three seasons.

Buffalo All-Americans—The All-Americans, a well-established team, joined the American Professional Football Association when it was founded in 1920. Aside from a 3–0 loss at Canton, they played only East Coast teams, mostly in nonleague games, that season. After compiling a 3–1–0 record in league play, the All-Americans tried for the championship by challenging Canton and Akron to games in early December.

Buffalo beat Canton 7–3 at the Polo Grounds on December 4 and played a scoreless tie against undefeated Akron in Buffalo the following day. The All-Americans finished third in the league's unofficial standings, with Akron winning the championship.

The team was renamed the Rangers in 1926 and the Bisons in 1927. The Buffalo franchise was inactive in 1928, but the Bisons returned to the NFL for one final season in 1929.

Buffalo Bills I—A new Buffalo Bisons franchise entered the new All-America Football Conference in 1946. Renamed the Bills the following year, Buffalo remained in the league until it merged with the NFL after the 1949 season.

On the surface, Buffalo looked like one of the AAFC's most successful operations. The Bills won the 1948 Eastern Division title, losing to Cleveland in the championship game, and home attendance was consistently good. Among the team's best players were quarterback George Ratterman, halfbacks Chet Mutryn and Rex Baumgardner, guard Abe Gibron, and defensive tackle John Kissell.

However, owner Jim Breuil had lost $700,000, mainly because of the high-priced contracts required to keep his stars from jumping to the NFL. When he was offered 25 percent of the Cleveland Browns in exchange for Baumgardner, Gibron, and Kissell in early 1950, he jumped at the chance.

Under the merger, only three AAFC teams were admitted to the NFL: the Browns, the San Francisco 49ers, and the Baltimore Colts. Despite a community fund drive to raise $200,000 in working capital, the pledge of 10,000 season tickets, and a promise from Commissioner Bert Bell that he'd do everything possible to get Buffalo into the NFL, the team was left out, in large part because owners didn't like the idea of having to play in snowy Buffalo late in the season.

Buffalo Bills II—After 11 years of waiting, Buffalo got another professional franchise in 1960, this time in the new American Football League. A strong defense and bruising runs by fullback Cookie Gilchrist helped take the Bills to AFL championships in 1964 and 1965. Those teams were conservatively quarterbacked by Jack Kemp most of the time, but they also had Daryle Lamonica, the "Mad Bomber," coming off the bench to throw deep when the offense was bogged down.

After the AFL-NFL merger in 1970, the Bills had indifferent success for a decade. They won division championships in 1980 and 1981 but lost in the first round of the playoffs both years.

Buffalo reemerged as a premier team under Marv Levy in the late 1980s. Featuring a pressure defense led by end Bruce Smith and linebacker Cornelius Bennett and a no-huddle offense led by quarterback Jim Kelly and running back Thurman Thomas, the Bills won six straight division championships and four consecutive AFC championships, from 1990 through 1993.

Despite an outstanding won-lost record during that period, the Bills have often been ridiculed for losing four straight Super Bowls, the last three by lopsided scores.

Canton Bulldogs—Organized as a semi-pro team in 1905, the Bulldogs disbanded after their coach was accused of conspiring to throw a game against the arch rival Massillon Tigers in 1907. Reorganized in 1914, the team signed Jim Thorpe for $250 a game. Under the management of Jack Cusack, the Bulldogs were the first team to establish the policy of signing all its players to exclusive contracts for a season.

The most famous player of the time, Thorpe was named figurehead league president when the American Professional Football Association was organized in 1920. Canton won league championships in 1922 and 1923. The franchise moved to Cleveland in 1924 and won a third straight title, then returned to Canton in 1925. The Bulldogs dropped out of the NFL after the 1926 season.

The Pro Football Hall of Fame is located in Canton because of the city's seminal role in the sport.

Chicago Bears—Originally the Decatur Staleys, the team moved to Chicago in 1921 and played as the Chicago Staleys for a season before being renamed the Bears. Under player-coach George Halas, the Bears used the T formation from the very beginning, while other teams ran out of the single-wing or the Notre Dame box.

Chicago won championships in 1921, 1932, 1933, 1940, 1941, 1944, 1946, 1963, and 1985. The 1933 title came in the first playoff game in NFL history, over the Portsmouth Spartans. Because of the publicity generated by that game, which was played indoors at Chicago Stadium, the league was reorganized into two divisions in 1934 to set up an annual post-season championship playoff.

Using a revamped version of the T formation, often with a split end and a man in motion, the Bears wiped out the Washington Redskins 73–0 in the 1940 championship game. Their success inspired other teams to switch to the T within the next several years.

Nicknamed the "Monsters of the Midway," the Bears have relied on a powerful running attack and strong defense for their success through the decades. The team's first great star was Bronko Nagurski, who played fullback on offense and tackle on defense from 1930 through 1937. They've had three of the best middle linebackers in pro football history, Bill George, Dick Butkus, and Mike Singletary, along with two of the game's premier runners, Gale Sayers and Walter Payton.

Chicago Cardinals—A charter member of the American Professional Football Association in 1920, the Cardinals won the league championship in 1925, mainly because of the outstanding play of quarterback Paddy Driscoll. Driscoll's 11 field goals easily led the league.

The official NFL history says the Cardinals in 1929 became the first team to hold an out-of-town training camp, to give fullback Ernie Nevers time to install the double wing attack he'd learned from Pop Warner at Stanford. Actually, the Duluth Eskimos had done exactly the same thing, for the same reason, in 1926.

The Cardinals had their best teams in 1947 and 1948. Led by the "Dream Backfield," with Paul Christman at quarterback, Pat Harder at fullback, and Charlie Trippi and Elmer Angsman at the halfback positions, the Cardinals won nine of their 12 regular season games and beat the Philadelphia Eagles 28–21 in the NFL championship playoff.

They were even better during the 1948 regular season, winning eleven of twelve, but this time they lost the title game to the Eagles 7–0 on a snow-covered field in Philadelphia.

The team slipped substantially during the 1950s. The Cardinals and the Chicago Bears had entered into the "Madison Street agreement," under which the Bears were to play north of Madison Street while the Cardinals played on the south side. In 1949, owner Charles Bidwill wanted to move into Dyke Stadium, on the north side of Madison. The Bears protested, Commissioner Bert Bell agreed, and the franchise moved to St. Louis in 1960.

Chicago Rockets—Chicago had a team in the All-America Football Conference for all four years of the league's existence, from 1946 through 1949. The team was called the Hornets in its final season.

Cincinnati Reds—In response to NFL President Joe Carr's effort to have more major cities represented in the league, the Reds were organized in 1933. It wasn't a successful venture. The team won only four games before being replaced on the schedule by the St. Louis Gunners late in the 1934 season.

Cincinnati Bengals—Summarily fired by the Cleveland Browns in 1962, after having been the team's only coach for 17 seasons, Paul Brown was inducted into the Pro Football Hall of Fame in 1967. The following year, he became general manager and coach of the Cincinnati Bengals, an expansion team in the American Football League.

The Bengals won a division title in 1970, only their third year of existence, and repeated in 1973. Brown retired from coaching after the 1975 season. Cincinnati also won a division championship in 1981 and the American Football Conference championship in 1988, but lost 20–16 to the San Francisco 49ers in the Super Bowl.

Cleveland Browns—When Mickey McBride bought a franchise in the All-America Football Conference in 1946, he made two lasting contributions to pro football. By hiring spare, nonroster players to drive for his taxicab company, he created the phrase "taxi squad." More important, he hired Paul Brown as his coach and named the team after him.

The Browns totally dominated the AAFC, winning all four of its championships. The AAFC folded after the 1949 season, but the Browns were admitted to the NFL, along with the San Francisco 49ers and the Baltimore Colts.

In their first six NFL seasons, the Browns won three titles in six championship playoff appearances. Those teams featured a "pass-and-trap" offense, with Otto Graham throwing to Mac Speedie and Dante Lavelli to set up runs by fullbacks Marion Motley and Fred "Curly" Morrison. Led by the great Jimmy Brown, they also won the NFL title in 1964.

Cleveland Tigers/Bulldogs/Indians—Cleveland has had a tangled history in pro football. The Tigers won just five games in the American Professional Football Association, in 1920 and 1921, then dropped out when the APFA became the National Football League before the 1922 season.

A new Cleveland team, the Indians, entered the NFL in 1923 and finished fifth out of 20 teams. Owner Sam Deutsch bought the defending champion Canton Bulldogs the following year, transferred the Canton players to Cleveland, renamed the team the Cleveland Bulldogs, and put the Canton franchise in mothballs.

Deutsch got the championship he'd been looking for. In 1925, he sold the Canton franchise back to Canton owners and lost several key players in the process. Cleveland dropped to twelfth place that season. Faced with competition from the Cleveland Panthers of Red Grange's American Football League in 1926, Deutsch folded his team.

Cleveland reentered the NFL with a new team, also called the Bulldogs, in 1927. That franchise lasted only one season. Another Cleveland Indian team was in the league in 1931 but won only two of ten games and disappeared.

Cleveland Rams—The Rams joined the NFL in 1937. Because of poor attendance during World War II, the franchise suspended operations in 1943, but resumed playing in 1944 and won the 1945 league championship behind rookie quarterback Bob Waterfield.

The city tripled the rent for the championship game and only 32,178 fans showed up, so owner Dan Reeves decided to move the team to Los Angeles in 1946.

Columbus Panhandles—Organized in 1905 as a company team, representing the Panhandle Division of the Pennsylvania Railroad, Columbus joined the American Professional Football Association when it was organized in 1920. The following year, Panhandle manager Joe Carr became president of the APFA, which became the NFL in 1922. Renamed the Tigers in 1923, Columbus remained in the NFL under new ownership through the 1926 season.

Dallas Cowboys—When the American Football League announced plans to begin playing in 1960, the NFL created a Dallas franchise to go head to head with the AFL's Dallas Texans. The Cowboys won the attendance battle despite losing records, forcing the Texans to move to Kansas City in 1963.

Tom Landry coached the Cowboys from the beginning through 1988. During the 1970s, they were nicknamed "America's team" because they attracted so many followers throughout the country. The Cowboys won NFC titles in 1970, 1976, and 1979. They beat the Miami Dolphins 24–3 in Super Bowl VI to win the 1971 NFL championship and they won the 1977 title by defeating the Denver Broncos 27–10 in Super Bowl XII.

During those years, the Cowboys featured such stars as quarterback Roger Staubach, running back Tony Dorsett, wide receiver Drew Pearson, defensive tackles Bob Lilly and Randy White, linebackers Lee Roy Jordan and Thomas "Hollywood" Henderson, and defensive backs Mel Renfro and Charlie Waters.

Landry was abruptly replaced by Jimmy Johnson in 1989 when the team was bought by Jimmy Jones, a former teammate of Johnson's at the University of Arkansas. Johnson produced NFL champions in 1992 and 1993 with an emphasis on defensive speed and a high-pressure offense that featured running back Emmitt Smith and the passing of Troy Aikman to Michael Irvin and tight end Jay Novacek.

Johnson suddenly announced his resignation early in 1994 because of a personality clash with Jones.

Dallas Texans I—In 1952, the NFL bought the assets of the financially troubled New York Yanks and sent the team's players to a new Dallas franchise. Attendance in Dallas was so poor that the Texans played all their games on the road for the second half of the season, then moved to Baltimore and became the Colts in 1953.

Dallas Texans II—Lamar Hunt tried unsuccessfully to buy the NFL's St. Louis Cardinals in 1959. He had hoped to move the team to Dallas. Instead, he organized the American Football League with his Dallas Texans franchise as one of the charter members.

The Texans won the 1962 AFL championship, beating the Houston Oilers 20–17 in the second overtime period. That remains the longest game in football history. However, the rival Dallas Cowboys of the NFL were a much more popular team, so the Texans moved to Kansas City and became known as the Chiefs in 1963.

Dayton Triangles—Organized as a town team in 1912, the Triangles joined the American Professional Football Association when it was organized in 1920. Dayton had winning records from 1920 through 1922, when the APFA became the NFL. However, the team then began to decline and dropped out of the league after the 1929 season.

Decatur Staleys—In 1919, the Staley Starch Company of Decatur, IL, hired George Halas as athletic director. He organized baseball, basketball, and football teams for the company. The football team entered the American Professional Football Association in 1920 and moved to Chicago the following season. After playing as the Chicago Staleys for a year, the team became known as the Bears, with Halas and Dutch Sternaman as co-owners.

Denver Broncos—One of the first four teams invited to join the new American Football League in 1960, the Broncos weren't particularly successful in the AFL because they usually had weak defenses. Their best years came after the AFL merged into the NFL in 1970.

The "Orange Crush" defense helped take Denver to the AFC championship in 1977, but they lost 27–10 to the Dallas Cowboys in the Super Bowl. The passing of strong-armed John Elway led them to conference championships in 1986, 1987, and 1989. The Broncos had good defenses built on speed rather than strength in those years, and they were overpowered by heavier offensive lines, losing 39–20 to the New York Giants in Super Bowl XXI, 42–10 to the Washington Redskins in Super Bowl XXII, and 55–10 to San Francisco in Super Bowl XXIV.

Detroit Heralds/Panthers/Wolverines—Like Cleveland, Detroit fielded several professional teams before landing a successful franchise. The Heralds existed as early as 1915 and joined the American Professional Football Association in 1920, but folded after the 1921 season.

The APFA became the NFL in 1922 and the Detroit Panthers spent two seasons, 1925 and 1926, in the league. They finished third in 1925 but dropped to a 4–6–2 record in 1926 and disbanded. The Wolverines had a 7–2–1 record in 1928 but left the league after that season.

Detroit Lions—Radio station owner George A. Richards bought the Portsmouth Spartans in 1934, moved the team to Detroit, and renamed it the Lions. Led by the great Dutch Clark at quarterback, they beat the New York Giants 26–7 to win the 1935 NFL championship.

The Lions had fine teams in the early 1950s. With Bobby Layne at quarterback, Leon Hart at end, and a great defensive backfield led by Jack Christiansen, they won titles in 1952 and 1953, defeating the Cleveland Browns in each championship game, 17–7 and 17–16.

Layne missed the 1957 title game, but Tobin Rote was more than adequate filling in. He passed for three touchdowns and ran for another in a 59–14 rout of the Browns. That avenged a lopsided 56–10 defeat by the Browns in 1954 that had prevented the Lions from winning a third consecutive championship.

Although the Lions have had some great players during the last thirty years, notably middle linebacker Joe Schmidt and running backs Billy Sims and Barry Sanders, they've mounted a championship threat only once, losing 41–10 to the Washington Redskins for the 1991 NFC title.

Duluth Eskimos—The Duluth Kelleys, originally a town team sponsored by the Kelley Hardware Store, joined the NFL in 1923. Ole Haugsrud bought the financially troubled team for a dollar in 1926 and signed his high school classmate, All-American fullback Ernie Nevers. The team became known as "Ernie Nevers' Duluth Eskimos."

Faced with a threat from Red Grange's American Football League, the NFL asked Haugsrud to take his team on the road for the season, and he agreed. According to Haugsrud, the team played 29 games in 110 days, although records and newspaper accounts apparently don't exist for some of the Eskimos' exhibition games.

Duluth was the first team to have an out-of-town training camp, at Two Harbors, Minnesota, so Nevers could install the double-wing offense he'd played in at Stanford. The Eskimos had a 6–5–2 league record in

1926. However, they slipped to 1–8–1 in 1927, after the AFL had folded, and Haugsrud agreed to withdraw the team in exchange for an option on the next Minnesota franchise in the NFL. As a result, he became a part owner of the Minnesota Vikings when that team was organized in 1960.

Evansville Crimson Giants—An independent team known as the Ex-Collegians in 1920, Evansville entered the American Professional Football Association in 1921 as the Crimson Giants. The APFA was renamed the National Football League in 1922 and Evansville dropped out after that season.

Frankford Yellowjackets—Representing a suburb of Philadelphia, the Yellowjackets were a strong independent team for years before joining the NFL in 1924. Because Pennsylvania law banned games on Sunday, Frankford often played two games on a weekend, at home on Saturday and away on Sunday.

In winning the 1926 NFL championship, the Yellowjackets played 17 regular season games, winning 14, losing 1, and tying 2. They had 11 wins against 3 losses and 2 ties in 1928 but finished second to Providence, which played only 11 games that year. After placing third with 10 victories and 5 ties in 19 games in 1929, Frankford dropped all the way to ninth place in 1930 and the franchise went out of business before finishing the 1931 season.

Green Bay Packers—Curly Lambeau was the only freshman to win a football letter at Notre Dame in 1918, but he had to go home to Green Bay because of tonsillitis before the school year ended. He organized a football team sponsored by the Indian Packing Company. In 1921, the Packers joined the American Professional Football Association, which became the NFL the following year.

Green Bay has had two very distinct dynastic periods. Featuring a passing attack under Lambeau, they won NFL titles in 1929, 1930, 1931, 1936, 1939, and 1944. Among their stars during that period were receivers Johnny Blood and Don Hutson, passers Arnie Herber and Cecil Isbell, tackle Cal Hubbard, guard Mike Michalske, and fullback-linebacker Clarke Hinkle, all of whom are in the Pro Football Hall of Fame, along with Lambeau.

After suffering through some very bad seasons, the Packers hired Vince Lombardi in 1959. Emphasizing a running attack, ball-control passing, and a strong defense, Lombardi took them to championships in 1961, 1962, 1965, 1966, and 1967, including victories in the first two Super Bowls.

Lombardi's Packers produced several more Hall of Famers, including quarterback Bart Starr, running backs Paul Hornung and Jimmy Taylor, offensive linemen Forrest Gregg and Jim Ringo, defensive end

Willie Davis, middle linebacker Ray Nitschke, and defensive backs Herb Adderley and Willie Wood.

Hammond Pros—One of the founding towns in the American Professional Football Association in 1920, Hammond played only three league games that season and lost all of them. The Pros won just five games during the next six years and dropped out of the NFL after the 1926 season.

Hartford Blues—When the American Football League, featuring Red Grange, announced plans to begin operating in 1926, the NFL responded by trying to add as many teams as possible to keep them out of the new league. The Hartford Blues was one of those stopgap teams. They spent just that one season in the NFL before dropping out.

Houston Oilers—Bud Adams was the first person Lamar Hunt contacted after Hunt decided to organize a new American Football League, to begin play in 1960. Adams agreed to put together a Houston franchise.

His Oilers won the first two AFL championships, in 1960 and 1961. Led by quarterback George Blanda, wide receiver Charlie Hennigan, and running back Billy Cannon, who had signed the sport's first $100,000 contract, the Oilers averaged 27.1 points a game in 1960 and an incredible 36.6 points in 1961.

Houston won its third straight division title in 1962, but lost to the Dallas Texans in the second overtime of the league championship game, still the longest game in football history.

The Oilers have had only spotty success since then. They did reach the AFC championship game in 1978 and 1979, losing to Pittsburgh both years. After quarterback Warren Moon left the Canadian Football League to join Houston in 1984, fans had high hopes, but the Oilers have been consistently disappointing in the playoffs since then despite good regular season records.

Kansas City Cowboys—The Kansas City Blues entered the NFL in 1924 and became known as the Cowboys in 1925. The team won only four games during those two seasons. The Cowboys were asked to play most of their games on the road in 1926, when the NFL faced its first rival, the American Football League. Kansas City finished third with an 8–3–0 record despite that handicap, but the franchise folded.

Kansas City Chiefs—Even though the Dallas Texans won the 1962 AFL championship, they couldn't compete for attendance with the NFL's Dallas Cowboys, so the franchise moved to Kansas City and became known as the Chiefs in 1963.

Behind the passing of Len Dawson, the receiving of Otis Taylor, and the running of Mike Garrett, the Chiefs won AFL championships in 1966 and 1969. They lost to the Green Bay Packers 35–10 in Super Bowl I, but beat the Minnesota Vikings 16–7 in Super Bowl IV, the last before the AFL-NFL merger took place in 1970.

The Chiefs haven't had much success since the merger. They've reached the playoffs only six times since then and have been eliminated in the first round four times, in the second round once and they lost the AFC Championship Game in 1993.

Kenosha Maroons—A strong semi-pro team for more than thirty years, extending into the 1940s, the Maroons were in the NFL for just one season, 1924, when they lost four games and tied one without a victory.

Los Angeles Buccaneers—Because the rival American Football League had a Los Angeles franchise in 1926, the NFL added the Buccaneers that season. Despite the name, the team was actually based in Chicago and played all of its games on the road.

Los Angeles Chargers—Barron Hilton of hotel fame was persuaded to start a Los Angeles franchise when the American Football League was organized in 1960, but the new team couldn't compete with the NFL's Los Angeles Rams. It moved to San Diego in 1961.

Los Angeles Dons—The Dons had a high-scoring offense during their four years in the All-America Football Conference, but they never ranked better than third in the league because of a poor defense. When the AAFC folded after the 1949 season, so did the Dons.

Los Angeles Raiders—In 1980, the Oakland Raiders announced plans to move to Los Angeles but refused to ask for approval from the NFL, which would have required a favorable vote by 21 of the 28 teams. After the league won a temporary injunction to block the move, the Los Angeles County Coliseum Commission brought a countersuit, joined by the Raiders.

A federal jury found the NFL in violation of the Sherman Anti-Trust Act and the move took place in 1982. The Los Angeles Raiders won the 1983 championship with a 38–9 victory over the Washington Redskins in Super Bowl XVIII.

Like the Oakland Raiders, the Los Angeles club has been noted for an aggressive defense and a deep passing attack that opens up opposing defenses for runs and shorter passes. In recent years, managing general partner Al Davis, one of the least liked executives in pro football, has threatened to move the franchise to several other cities.

Los Angeles Rams—Because of poor attendance and impending opposition from the Cleveland Browns of the All-America Football Conference, the NFL's Cleveland Rams moved to Los Angeles in 1946. They were the first genuine major professional West Coast franchise in any sport. The Rams also made history, in a quiet way, by signing two black players from UCLA, end Woody Strode and halfback Kenny Washington, the first blacks to play in the NFL since 1933.

In the late 1940s, the Rams developed an exciting passing offense, with quarterbacks Bob Waterfield and Norm Van Brocklin throwing to Tom Fears, Crazy Legs Hirsch, and Bob Boyd. The three-end offense pioneered by Los Angeles became the standard "pro set" during the 1950s and well into the 1960s. Los Angeles won the 1951 NFL championship with a 24–17 victory over the Cleveland Browns.

Using a totally different approach, a strong defense and ball-control offense, the Rams won seven straight division titles, from 1973 through 1979. However, they were NFC champions just once, in 1979, when they lost 31–19 to the Pittsburgh Steelers in the Super Bowl. In 1995 the franchise moved to St. Louis.

Los Angeles Wildcats—Named for George "Wildcat" Wilson, an All-American halfback at the University of Washington in 1925, the Wildcats played in Red Grange's American Football League in 1926. Like their NFL rivals, the Buccaneers, the Wildcats played all of their games on the road. The AFL, and the Wildcats, lasted just one season.

Louisville Brecks—Originally a semi-pro team representing the Breckinridge Athletic Club of Louisville, the Brecks joined the American Professional Football Association in 1921. The APFA became the NFL in 1922 and the Brecks dropped out after the 1923 season.

Louisville Colonels—Like the Los Angeles Buccaneers, the Colonels were added to the NFL to make it seem bigger and more geographically dispersed in its battle with the American Football League of 1926. Based in Chicago, this "Louisville" team played all of its games on the road and left the league when the AFL folded after the season.

Miami Dolphins—The AFL's first expansion team, in 1966, Miami became a contender by hiring Coach Don Shula away from the Baltimore Colts in 1970, when the league merged into the NFL. Behind the running of Larry Csonka, Jim Kiick, and Mercury Morris, the ball-control passing of Bob Griese, and the "no-name defense," the Dolphins won three straight AFC championships, from 1971 through 1973.

After losing 24–3 to the Dallas Cowboys in Super Bowl VI, following the 1971 season, Miami won all 17 games in 1972, including a 14–7 win over the Washington Redskins in Super Bowl VII. The Dolphins also won Super Bowl VIII, 24–7 over the Minnesota Vikings.

In Shula's 25 years with the team, Miami has been first or second in the AFC's Eastern Division 21 times. The Dolphins won AFC titles in 1982 and 1984, but lost in the Super Bowl both years. Since 1983, Miami has relied on the passing of quarterback Dan Marino for most of its offense, but the defense has often been shaky.

Miami Seahawks—The All-America Football Conference gave Miami its first major professional franchise when it began operating in 1946, but attendance was dismal. The team moved to Baltimore and became known as the Colts in 1947.

Milwaukee Badgers—Milwaukee joined the NFL in 1922 and dropped out after the 1926 season. The team's major contribution to football history was its involvement in the controversial championship race of 1925. The Badgers had actually finished the season and disbanded when they were asked to play a final game against the Chicago Cardinals. The team that was hastily put together for a 59–0 loss included four high school players. As a result, the franchise was fined $500 and Cardinal quarterback Arthur Folz, who had served as Milwaukee's manager and coach for that game, was banned from the NFL for life.

Minneapolis Marines/Redjackets—The Minneapolis Marines started the 1921 season in the NFL, but left the league after winning only one of four games. They returned in 1922, then dropped out again after the 1924 season, with just three total victories.

Another Minneapolis team, the Redjackets, won only two NFL games during the 1929 and 1930 seasons.

Minnesota Vikings—The Vikings were originally supposed to join the AFL in its first season, 1960, but Max Winter was offered an NFL franchise for 1961 and he decided to take it. The AFL then added Oakland to replace Minnesota.

Under Bud Grant, the Vikings were one of the NFL's best teams from 1969 through 1980, winning nine division titles. They were NFL champions in 1969 and NFC champions in 1973, 1974, and 1976 but they lost in all four Super Bowl appearances.

With Fran Tarkenton at quarterback, those Minnesota teams pioneered ball-control through a short passing attack, but their greatest strength was the "Purple People Eaters" defense, led by linemen Alan Page, Carl Eller, and Jim Marshall.

In Tarkenton's final season, 1978, the Vikings won another division title but lost in the first round of the playoffs. They won two more division championships during the 1980s without much playoff success. Dennis Green took over the team as the second black coach in modern history in 1992 and has guided them to two NFL Central Division titles in three seasons, but the Vikings still haven't been able to get past their first playoff game.

Muncie Flyers—The Flyers were in the American Professional Football Association at the beginning of its first season in 1920, but they left the league after losing 45–0 in their only game. In 1921, Muncie tried again, this time staying in the league long enough to lose two games.

New Orleans Saints—When Congress passed the Professional Sports Act of 1967, allowing a merger between the NFL and the AFL, the bill's chief sponsors were Senator Russell Long and Congressman Hale Boggs, both of Louisiana. Three weeks later, the NFL announced that New Orleans had been awarded an expansion franchise.

The Saints made the playoffs for the first time in 1987 and they repeated in 1991 and 1992, but they lost in the first round each time.

New York Brickley's Giants—Charles Brickley, a great drop kicker from Harvard, organized New York's first football team in 1921. He was so well known that the squad was called "Brickley's Giants." However, the Giants dropped out of the American Professional Football Association after losing their only two games.

New York Bulldogs—Made up largely of players from the defunct Boston Yanks franchise, the Bulldogs spent just one season, 1949, in the NFL.

New York Giants—In 1925, bookmaker Tim Mara was persuaded to buy a New York franchise in the National Football League. (Bookmaking was then a legal occupation.) The Giants struggled through their first season but were saved financially when Red Grange showed up with the Chicago Bears on a post-season barnstorming tour to attract more than 70,000 fans.

A strong defense led by player-coach Steve Owen at tackle, complemented by the passing of Harry Newman to Red Badgro and Ray Flaherty and the powerful running and kicking of Ken Strong, took the Giants into the first three NFL championship playoffs, from 1933 through 1935. They beat the Chicago Bears 30–13 in the famous 1934 "Sneakers Game." Trailing 10–0 at half-time, the Giants switched from cleats to sneakers to get better traction on the icy Polo Grounds field and they won going away.

New York also reached the championship game in 1938, 1939, 1941, 1944, and 1946, but they won only once, beating the Green Bay Packers 23–17 in 1938. During the late 1950s and early 1960s, the Giants were perennially in contention. Defense, now led by middle linebacker Sam Huff, was again one of the keys, and the team also had fine passers in Charlie Conerly and Y. A. Tittle, throwing to Kyle Rote, Frank Gifford, and Del Shofner.

The Giants crushed the Chicago Bears 47–7 to win the 1956 championship. They lost the 1958 championship 23–17 to the Baltimore Colts in the first overtime game in NFL history. New York lost to Baltimore again in 1959, to the Packers in 1961 and 1962 and to the Bears in 1963.

After years in the doldrums, the Giants reemerged in the 1980s. With Lawrence Taylor anchoring a strong corps of linebackers and quarterbacks Phil Simms and Jeff Hostetler running a conservative ball-control attack based on runs and short passes, they beat the Denver Broncos 39–20 in Super Bowl XXI after the 1986 season and defeated the Buffalo Bills 20–19 in Super Bowl XXV after the 1990 season.

New York Yankees I—Red Grange's manager, C. C. Pyle, was turned down for a New York franchise in the NFL in 1926, so he formed the first American Football League, with Grange starring for the New York Yankees. The league lasted just one season, but the Yankees were admitted to the NFL in 1927. They folded after the 1928 season.

New York Yankees II—The Yankees won the All-America Football Conference Eastern Division title in 1946 and 1947, the first two years of the league's existence, but lost to the Cleveland Browns in both championship games. They dropped to third place in 1948 and to last place in 1949, after merging with the financially troubled Brooklyn Dodgers. The AAFC went out of business after that season.

New York Yanks—The Yanks were in the NFL for just two seasons, 1950 and 1951. The team was transferred to Dallas in 1952 and became the Baltimore Colts the following season.

New York Titans/Jets—The Titans, owned by broadcaster Harry Wismer, entered the AFL in its first season, 1960. Although they had a respectable 19 victories in three seasons, Wismer was operating on very little capital and the team went bankrupt in 1963. The franchise was then purchased by Sonny Werblin, who completely reorganized the operation as the New York Jets.

Werblin brought the AFL its first major burst of publicity in 1965, when he signed quarterback Joe Namath to an unprecedented $400,000 contract. The Jets soon had an explosive offense, with Namath passing to George Sauer and Don Maynard while fullback Jim Nance consistently ripped off yardage on the ground. They won the 1968 AFL title.

The Baltimore Colts were favored by as much as three touchdowns over the Jets in Super Bowl III, but Namath brashly guaranteed victory. Then he produced it. Crossing up Baltimore's defense by going to short passes and quick runs, the Jets became the first AFL team to win the Super Bowl with a 16–7 victory that was more impressive than the score indicated. The team went into decline after that moment of glory, in part because Namath suffered from knee problems. The Jets have reached the playoffs only five times since then and have never gone beyond the second round.

Newark Tornadoes—The Orange, New Jersey, Tornadoes moved to Newark in 1930 and the franchise folded after winning just one game that season.

Oakland Raiders—Oakland was a last-minute addition to the AFL in 1960, after the Minnesota Vikings announced that they were going to the NFL. In 1963, owner Wayne Valley hired Al Davis as general manager and head coach. Davis turned the Raiders into the league's most feared team, built on an intimidating defense and the threat of the long pass to loosen up opposing defenses.

After serving briefly as AFL commissioner in 1966, Davis returned to Oakland as managing general partner. With "Mad Bomber" Daryle Lamonica at quarterback, backed up by 39-year-old George Blanda, who was also the team's place kicker, the Raiders won the 1967 AFL title but lost to the Green Bay Packers 33–14 in Super Bowl II.

The AFL and NFL formally merged in 1970. A powerful offense, featuring left-handed quarterback Ken "Snake" Stabler, tight end Dave Casper, wide receivers Cliff Branch and Fred Biletnikoff, and strong running by Mark Van Eeghen, took Oakland to the championship in 1976, when the Raiders beat the Minnesota Vikings 32–14 in the Super Bowl. In 1980, it was the defense that led the way, starring linebacker Ted Hendricks, cornerback Lester Hayes, and end John Matuszak. The Raiders finished only second in their division that year but became the first wild card team to win the Super Bowl, beating the Philadelphia Eagles 27–10.

A planned move to Los Angeles in 1980 had been blocked by a court injunction, but the Raiders won the legal battle in 1982 and have played in the Los Angeles Coliseum since then.

Known principally as a defensive strategist, Coach Greasy Neale devised the original Eagle defense at Philadelphia in 1949, primarily to stop the Los Angeles Rams' high-scoring passing attack. It worked; the Eagles beat the Rams 14-0 for the NFL championship that season. *Courtesy Philadelphia Eagles*

Oorang Indians—Sponsored by the Oorang Kennels of Marion, OH, the Indians played all of their NFL games on the road in 1922 and 1923. Led by Jim Thorpe, the team was made up entirely of native Americans, including players with names such as Eagle Feather, Red Fang, and

Joe Little Twig. Although the Indians had two future Hall of Famers in Thorpe and Joe Guyon, they won a total of only four games in their two seasons.

Orange Tornadoes—The Duluth Eskimo franchise, inactive in 1928, was transferred to Orange, New Jersey, in 1929. The Tornadoes spent just one season in Orange and moved to Newark in 1930.

Philadelphia Quakers—The Quakers won the championship of the first AFL in 1926, the only year that league operated. They did it with strong defense, giving up only 52 points in ten games. The AFL's weakness was thoroughly exposed when the New York Giants, who'd finished seventh in the NFL, whipped the Quakers 31–0 in a post-season exhibition game.

Philadelphia Eagles—Bert Bell, who was to become the first NFL commissioner in 1946, founded the Eagles in 1933. The team struggled for years and Bell sold his interest in 1941 to become part owner of the Steelers. In 1943 the Eagles temporarily merged with the Pittsburgh Steelers because of the World War II manpower shortage.

After the war, Philadelphia became an NFL power. Led by the running of Steve Van Buren and passes from Tommy Thompson to Pete Pihos, the Eagles won three straight Eastern Division titles, from 1947 through 1949. They beat the Chicago Cardinals 7–0 on Van Buren's 5-yard touchdown run for the 1948 NFL championship and shut out the Los Angeles Rams 14–0 in the 1949 title game.

The heroes of their 1960 championship team were Chuck Bednarik, who averaged well over thirty minutes a game, playing both center and linebacker, and quarterback Norm Van Brocklin, whose favorite target was Tommy MacDonald. The Eagles beat the Green Bay Packers 17–13 for the title.

A group of spirited overachievers won Philadelphia the 1980 NFC championship, but the Eagles were overpowered 27–10 by the Oakland Raiders in Super Bowl XV. During the last several years, quarterback Randall Cunningham and a fine defense have helped keep the Eagles in contention, but they haven't had much success in the playoffs.

Pittsburgh Pirates/Steelers—When Art Rooney started the Pittsburgh NFL franchise in 1933, he named it after the baseball team, as was common at the time. The Pirates were renamed the Steelers in 1940.

During World War II, the undermanned team was forced to merge twice, with the Philadelphia Eagles in 1943 and with the Chicago Cardinals in 1944. Rooney tried coach after coach without much success until he hired Chuck Noll in 1969. Noll built the "Steel Curtain" defense around tackle "Mean Joe" Greene, linebackers Jack Lambert and Jack Ham, and defensive back Mel Blount.

That defense was complemented by a ball-control offense featuring the running of fullback Franco Harris and the leadership and accurate passing of quarterback Terry Bradshaw to Lynn Swann and John Stallworth.

Named the "team of the decade" for the 1970s, the Steelers won four Super Bowls in six years. They beat the Minnesota Vikings 16–6 in Super Bowl IX, after the 1974 season, and defeated the Dallas Cowboys 21–17 the following year. Pittsburgh beat the Cowboys again, 35–31, in Super Bowl XIII after the 1978 season and won Super Bowl XIV 31–19 over the Los Angeles Rams.

Portsmouth Spartans—Long a strong independent team, the Spartans joined the NFL in 1930. They finished the 1932 season in a first-place tie with the Chicago Bears, setting up the league's first post-season playoff game. Because of bitter cold and heavy snow, the contest was played indoors at Chicago Stadium.

The field was only 60 yards long from goal line to goal line, but neither team could score during the first three quarters. Portsmouth, hampered by the absence of star quarterback Dutch Clark, lost the ball on an interception in the fourth quarter and the Bears faced a fourth-and-goal situation at the 2-yard line. Fullback Bronko Nagurski faked a run into the line, then pulled up and threw a touchdown pass to Red Grange. Portsmouth Coach Potsy Clark insisted that Nagurski hadn't been five yards behind the line, as required by the rules at that time, but officials ruled it a touchdown and the Bears later scored a safety to win 9–0.

In 1934, the franchise moved to Detroit and the team became known as the Lions.

Pottsville Maroons—Pottsville was in the NFL only from 1925 through 1928, but old-timers haunted the league well into the 1980s, insisting that the Maroons should have been awarded the 1925 championship. What would be a major controversy today went almost unnoticed at the time because of the enormous amount of attention devoted to Red Grange's post-season tour with the Chicago Bears.

A strong running attack, led by fullback Tony Latone, and fine kicking by Charlie Berry, who led the NFL with 74 points, gave Pottsville a 10–2–0 record, including a season-ending 21–7 win over the Chicago Cardinals, who "finished" at 9–2–1.

The Maroons then played an exhibition game on December 12 against a team of Notre Dame all-stars at Shibe Park in Philadelphia. The Frankford Yellowjackets, who played the same day in nearby Frankford Stadium, protested this invasion of their territory. NFL President Joe Carr suspended Pottsville and told the Cardinals to play a couple more games. They won 59–0 over a hastily assembled Milwaukee Badgers team that included four high school players and then beat the Hammond Pros 13–0.

The Cardinals were awarded the league championship over Pottsville's protests. After finishing third in 1926, the Maroons had two consecutive losing seasons and dropped out of the league.

Providence Steam Roller—The Steam Roller existed as a semi-pro team before and for many years after its seven seasons in the NFL, from 1925 through 1931. Providence played on the league's most unusual field, a velodrome that made its money on bicycle racing.

Coached by Jimmy Conzelman and starring George "Wildcat" Wilson at halfback and Gus Sonnenberg at tackle, the Steam Roller won the 1928 NFL championship on defense, giving up just 42 points in eleven games.

Racine Legion/Tornadoes—Originally an American Legion semi-pro team, as the name suggests, Racine entered the NFL in 1922, played just about .500 ball for three years, and left the league after the 1924 season. When the NFL beefed up to 22 teams in 1926 to counter the threat of the first AFL, Racine spent another season in the league with a team called the Tornadoes.

Rochester Jeffersons—The Jeffersons joined the American Professional Football Association when it was formed in 1920, but played only one league game that season. They remained in the league through 1925 without ever having a winning record.

Rock Island Independents—A charter member of the American Professional Football Association in 1920, Rock Island jumped to the American Football League when it was organized in 1926. The AFL folded after that season. Rock Island continued to field an independent team for a number of years, but never again played in a major professional league.

San Diego Chargers—Unable to compete for fans with the NFL's Rams, the Los Angeles Chargers moved to San Diego in 1961, after the first season of the AFL's existence. With Tobin Rote and John Hadl throwing to Lance Alworth, the league's finest receiver, the Chargers amassed 399 points during the 1963 season and won the AFL championship by whipping the Boston Patriots 51–10. San Diego lost the next two league championship games.

During the late 1970s and early 1980s, the Chargers had some good teams, using the "Air Coryell" passing offense espoused by Coach Don Coryell. Starring Dan Fouts at quarterback, Kellen Winslow at tight end, and Wes Chandler and Charlie Joiner at wide receiver, San Diego lost to Cincinnati in the 1981 AFC title game.

San Francisco 49ers—The 49ers were one of the best teams in the All-America Football Conference during the four years of that league's existence, from 1946 through 1949, but they were never quite as good as the Cleveland Browns, who won all four championships.

The AAFC folded in 1950 and San Francisco entered the NFL. The 49ers had a number of good teams in ensuing years, but didn't approach championship quality until 1970, when they won the first of three straight NFC Western Division titles. Led by the passing of John Brodie to wide receiver Gene Washington and tight end Ted Kwalick, the 49ers reached the NFC championship game in 1970 and 1971, but lost to the Dallas Cowboys both times. They also won the Western Division title in 1972, only to be eliminated in the first round of the playoffs.

Bill Walsh became the team's head coach in 1979 and installed an offense featuring the short passing attack to set up runs and longer passes. In Walsh's system, Joe Montana emerged as one of the best quarterbacks in history. Receivers Dwight Clark and Jerry Rice and all-purpose running back Roger Craig also starred on offense, while hard-hitting defensive back Ronnie Lott led a pressure defense.

San Francisco beat the Cincinnati Bengals 26–21 in Super Bowl XVI, after the 1981 season. Under Walsh, the 49ers also won Super Bowl XIX 38–16 over the Miami Dolphins and Super Bowl XXIII 20–16 over Cincinnati. Long-time assistant George Seifert then replaced Walsh and coached San Francisco to a 55–10 victory against the Denver Broncos in Super Bowl XXIV.

After losing to the Dallas Cowboys in the NFC championship game in 1992 and 1993, the 49ers beat Dallas for the 1994 title and became the first team to win five Super Bowls with a 49–26 victory over the San Diego Chargers. Montana's replacement, Steve Young, became the second player in history to be named player of the year for the regular season and Super Bowl MVP. He threw six touchdown passes to break Montana's Super Bowl record.

Seattle Seahawks—Seattle entered the NFL as an expansion franchise in 1976. The Seahawks reached the playoffs three times during the 1980s and lost 30–14 to the Oakland Raiders in the 1983 AFC championship game.

Staten Island Stapletons—Based in the little town of Stapleton on Staten Island, this team was built around the great running back and kicker Ken Strong. The Stapletons entered the NFL in 1929 and dropped out after the 1932 season. Strong then became a star with the New York Giants.

St. Louis All-Stars/Browns—The first St. Louis entry in the NFL, in 1923, the All-Stars were also sometimes known as the Browns. The team lasted only one season.

St. Louis Gunners—A powerful independent team that often played exhibition games against NFL opponents, the Gunners joined the league during the 1934 season, replacing the hapless Cincinnati Reds. St. Louis played only three league games and won just one of them, then dropped out of the NFL to resume independent play.

St. Louis Cardinals—The Chicago Cardinals moved to St. Louis in 1960, partly to open up the Chicago television market for the Bears. After reaching the playoffs only three times in 28 seasons, the franchise moved to Phoenix in 1988. In 1995 the Rams moved to town to once again give St. Louis fans a pro football team to cheer on.

Tampa Bay Buccaneers—The Buccaneers joined the NFL in 1976. After losing 26 consecutive games, Tampa Bay reached the playoffs faster than any expansion team in history by winning the NFC Central Division title in 1979. However, the Bucs lost 9–0 to the Los Angeles Rams in the NFL championship game and have gone into the playoffs only twice since then.

Toledo Maroons—When the American Professional Football Association became the NFL in 1922, Toledo joined the renamed league and finished a surprising fourth. The franchise folded after a 3–3–2 record in 1923.

Washington Senators—Ostensibly representing Washington, D.C., the Senators entered the American Professional Football Association in 1922 and played all six of their games on the road before dropping out.

Washington Redskins—Because of poor attendance in Boston, the Redskins moved to Washington in 1937. Mainly because of the passing of Sammy Baugh, Washington appeared in six NFL championship games during the next nine seasons. The Redskins won twice, beating the Chicago Bears both times, 28–21 in 1937 and 14–6 in 1942. They also suffered the worst defeat in playoff history, a 73–0 loss to the Bears in 1940.

After years in the doldrums, the team began a return to respectability under Vince Lombardi in 1969 and under George Allen in the early 1970s. The 'Skins made it to the Super Bowl in 1972, but lost to Miami. But it took Joe Gibbs and his one-back offense to produce championship teams. Under Gibbs, the Redskins appeared in four Super Bowls and won three of them. They beat the Miami Dolphins 27–17 in Super Bowl XVII, after the 1982 season, then defeated the Denver Broncos 42–10 in Super Bowl XXII and the Buffalo Bills 37–24 in Super Bowl XXVI. Gibbs resigned after the 1992 season and Washington's fortunes abruptly declined.

9 FS

People to Know

Herb Adderley—A running back at the University of Michigan, Adderley was moved to defense when he joined the Green Bay Packers in 1961. The speedy, 6-foot, 200-pounder returned an interception 60 yards for a touchdown in Green Bay's 33–14 victory over the Oakland Raiders in Super Bowl II.

Adderley went to the Dallas Cowboys in 1970 and retired after the 1972 season with 48 career interceptions and 7 touchdowns. He was a starter for three Super Bowl champions, two in Green Bay and one in Dallas. Adderley was inducted into the Pro Football Hall of Fame in 1980.

Troy Aikman—As a quarterback at the University of Oklahoma and UCLA, Aikman completed 401 of 637 passes for 5,436 yards and 40 touchdowns. He became the Dallas Cowboys' starting quarterback as a rookie in 1989 and led the team to two straight NFL championships in 1992 and 1993.

The 6-foot-4, 222-pound Aikman had 22 completions in 30 attempts for 273 yards and 4 touchdowns in Super Bowl XXVII, and he completed 19 of 27 for 207 yards in Super Bowl XXVIII.

Marcus Allen—The 1981 Heisman Trophy winner as a running back at USC, Allen set NCAA records that season with 2,432 rushing yards and eight 200-yard games. He joined the Los Angeles Raiders of the NFL in 1982 and was named rookie of the year after leading the league with 14 touchdowns.

Allen led the league's rushers with 1,759 yards in 1985. He went to the Kansas City Chiefs as a free agent in 1993 and led the AFC with 15 touchdowns that season.

Lance Alworth—As a running back at the University of Arkansas, Alworth was the NCAA's top punt returner in 1960 and 1961. He became a wide receiver with the AFL's San Diego Chargers in 1962 and was named to the All-AFL team seven years in a row, from 1963 through 1969.

Known as "Bambi" because of his speed and grace, Alworth ended his career with the NFL's Dallas Cowboys in 1970 and 1971. He caught 542 passes for 10,266 yards, an 18.9 average, and 85 touchdowns in his eleven professional seasons. In 1978, Alworth became the first AFL player inducted into the Pro Football Hall of Fame.

Dick Anderson—Anderson was an All-American defensive back at the University of Colorado in 1967 and he was named the AFL's defensive rookie of the year with the Miami Dolphins in 1968. A safety man as a professional, Anderson was one of the leaders of Miami's "no-name defense."

The Dolphins won American Football Conference championships from 1972 through 1974 and Anderson was an All-Pro all three years. A knee injury kept him out of action for most of 1975 and all of 1976 and he retired after the 1977 season with 34 career interceptions.

Ottis (O.J.) Anderson—Anderson rushed for 193 yards in his first professional game with the St. Louis Cardinals in 1979 and set a rookie record with 1,605 yards for the season. He had four 1,000-yard seasons in the next five years, but saw only limited action in 1985 because of a foot injury.

Traded to the New York Giants in 1986, Anderson didn't become a starter again until 1989, when he gained 1,023 yards. He was named most valuable player in New York's 20–19 win over the Buffalo Bills in Super Bowl XXV, when he had 102 yards on 21 rushes.

Doug Atkins—The 6-foot-8, 275-pound Atkins went to the University of Tennessee on a basketball scholarship and also played defensive tackle on the football team. He became a defensive end with the NFL's Cleveland Browns in 1953.

In 1955, the Browns traded him to the Chicago Bears, where he spent eight seasons and was named to the All-Pro team in 1960 and 1963. He finished his career with the New Orleans Saints in 1969. An amazingly agile pass rusher who often jumped over blockers to get at the quarterback, Atkins is a member of the Pro Football Hall of Fame.

Red Badgro—Badgro played end for the New York Yankees of the NFL in 1927, after starring at the University of Southern California, then left football temporarily to play as a part-time outfielder with the St. Louis Browns.

He returned to football with the New York Giants in 1930 and finished his NFL career with the Brooklyn Dodgers in 1936. Called by Red Grange "One of the best half-dozen ends I ever saw," Badgro was an All-Pro in 1931, 1933, and 1934. He scored the first touchdown ever in an NFL championship game, on a 29-yard pass against the Chicago Bears in 1933. Badgro was inducted into the Pro Football Hall of Fame in 1981, at the age of seventy-eight and forty-five years after his retirement.

Lem Barney—A defensive back and punter at Jackson State University, the 6-foot-2, 190-pound Barney joined the Detroit Lions in 1967. He led the NFL with 10 interceptions, running back 3 of them for touchdowns, and was named the league's defensive rookie of the year.

An All-Pro in 1968, 1969, and 1972, Barney played in ten Pro Bowls during his eleven-season career with the Lions. He retired after the 1977 season with 56 interceptions. Barney scored 11 touchdowns, 8 on interception returns, 2 on punt returns, and 1 on a kickoff return. He was elected to the Pro Football Hall of Fame in 1992.

Cliff Battles—A four-sport star and Phi Beta Kappa at West Virginia Wesleyan College, Battles joined the Boston Braves of the NFL in 1931. A 6-foot-1, 200-pounder with speed, he was the first runner in NFL history to gain more than 200 yards in a game, with 215 yards on only 16 carries against the New York Giants in 1932, when he led the NFL in rushing with 737 yards on 146 attempts.

The Braves became the Redskins in 1932 and moved to Washington, D.C., in 1937, when Battles led the league in rushing again with 874 yards on 216 carries. An All-Pro in 1931, 1936, and 1937, Battles quit over a salary dispute and became an assistant college coach in 1938. He's a member of the College and Pro Football Halls of Fame.

Sammy Baugh—An All-American tailback at Texas Christian University in 1936, Baugh joined the Washington Redskins the following season. He led the team to the NFL championship as a rookie, throwing touchdown passes of 33, 55, and 78 yards to beat the Chicago Bears 28–21.

During his 16 seasons, the Redskins appeared in five championship playoffs and won twice. Baugh's greatest year was 1943, when he became the only player ever to lead the NFL in passing, punting, and interceptions. He moved from tailback to T formation quarterback and became an offensive specialist in 1944.

"Slinging Sammy" Baugh led the NFL in passing, punting, and interceptions in 1943. He spent 16 seasons with the Washington Redskins and held most of the league's passing records when he retired in 1952. *Courtesy Pro Football Hall of Fame*

When he retired after the 1952 season, Baugh held most of the league's records for passing. His completion percentage of 70.3 percent in 1945 and his average of 51.4 yards a punt in 1940 are still records. He later coached Hardin-Simmons University and the New York Titans of the AFL.

Baugh is a member of the College and Pro Football Halls of Fame.

Chuck Bednarik—After serving in the Air Force during World War II, Bednarik was an All-American center/linebacker at the University of Pennsylvania in 1947 and 1948 and then joined the Philadelphia Eagles. An All-Pro as an offensive center in 1950, he was moved to linebacker the following season and was named to the All-Pro team at that position six years in a row, from 1951 through 1956.

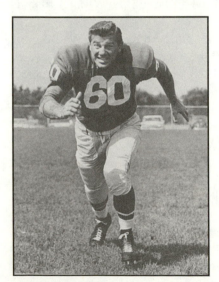

Chuck Bednarik of the Philadelphia Eagles was the NFL's last two-way player, as an offensive center and defensive linebacker. He played 58 minutes in Philadelphia's 17–13 win over the Green Bay Packers in the 1960 championship game. *Courtesy Philadelphia Eagles*

Bednarik became the last of the NFL's full-time two-way players in 1960, when the Eagles were decimated by injuries. In the championship playoff game against the Green Bay Packers, Bednarik made a touchdown-saving tackle on Packer fullback Jim Taylor with time running out to preserve a 17–13 victory.

Bednarik retired after the 1962 season with 20 career interceptions. He is a member of the College and Pro Football Halls of Fame.

Bobby Bell—An All-American defensive tackle at the University of Minnesota in 1962, Bell played defensive end with the AFL's Kansas City Chiefs for two seasons and became an outside linebacker in 1965. He was named to the All-AFL and All-AFC team at that position eight consecutive years.

The 6-foot-4, 225-pound Bell had a mammoth upper body, a 32-inch waist, and great speed. He retired after the 1974 season with eight career touchdowns, six on interception returns, one on a fumble recovery, and one on a kickoff return. Bell was inducted into the Pro Football Hall of Fame in 1983.

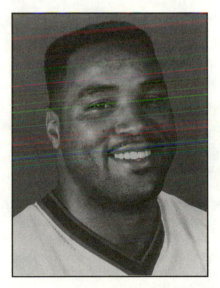

The 1986 Lombardi Award winner at the University of Alabama, Cornelius Bennett has been a starting linebacker with the Buffalo Bills since his rookie year and he's missed only one Pro Bowl in his eight seasons with Buffalo. *Courtesy Buffalo Bills*

Cornelius Bennett—Bennett won the 1986 Lombardi Award as the outstanding college lineman of the year as a linebacker at the University of Alabama. Chosen in the first round of the NFL draft by the Indianapolis Colts, he went to the Buffalo Bills in a three-team trade and immediately became a starter.

The 6-foot-2, 238-pound Bennett has played in the Pro Bowl every year except 1989 and he helped lead the Bills to four straight NFC championships, from 1990 through 1993, but they lost all four Super

Bowls. Through the 1993 season, he had 40½ quarterback sacks, 4 interceptions, and 12 fumble recoveries.

Hall of Fame receiver Raymond Berry caught 12 passes for 194 yards and a touchdown when the Baltimore Colts beat the New York Giants 23–17 in the 1958 NFL championship game. It was the first overtime game in football history. *Courtesy Pro Football Hall of Fame*

Raymond Berry—A most unlikely star, the 6-foot-2, 187-pound Berry caught only 33 passes in his three-year career at Southern Methodist University. A part-time player for two seasons with the Baltimore Colts, he became a starter in 1957.

Using intelligence and hard work to make up for a lack of physical skills, Berry led the NFL with 56 regular season receptions and 9 touchdown catches when the Colts won the 1958 NFL championship. He added 12 catches for 194 yards and a touchdown in the famous 23–17 overtime title victory over the New York Giants.

He also led the league with 74 receptions, 959 yards, and 14 touchdown catches in 1959 and with 74 receptions and 1,298 yards in 1960. Berry retired after the 1967 season with 631 career catches for 9,275 yards, both records at the time, and 68 touchdowns.

A member of the Pro Football Hall of Fame, Berry coached the New England Patriots to a 51–41 record from 1984 to 1989.

Fred Biletnikoff—An All-American end at Florida State in 1964, Biletnikoff didn't become a starter with the Oakland Raiders until 1967. He quickly established himself as one of the best receivers in pro football, catching 40 or more passes for ten straight seasons, including a league-leading 61 in 1971.

Biletnikoff was named the most valuable player in Super Bowl XI, when he caught 4 passes for 79 yards, setting up three of Oakland's touchdowns in a 32–14 victory over the Minnesota Vikings. He retired after the 1978 season with 589 career receptions for 8,974 yards and 76 touchdowns. He was inducted into the Pro Football Hall of Fame in 1988.

George Blanda—The longest career in football history began when Blanda joined the Chicago Bears in 1949 out of the University of Kentucky. He spent ten seasons with Chicago, mostly as a place kicker and backup quarterback, before retiring in 1959.

He came out of retirement in 1960 to become the starting quarterback for the Houston Oilers in the new AFL and led the league in completions in 1961, 1963, 1964, and 1965. Used primarily as a kicker in 1966, Blanda was the league leader in scoring that year.

Houston traded him to the Oakland Raiders in 1967. In 1970, at the age of forty-three, he was named the Associated Press male athlete of the year for an astounding five-week period during which he threw five touchdown passes and kicked three last-second field goals to give Oakland four victories and a tie. Blanda retired after the 1974 season with an NFL career record of 2,002 points. He was inducted into the Pro Football Hall of Fame in 1981.

Johnny Blood—John McNally adopted the name "Johnny Blood" to preserve his college eligibility after playing for two years at St. John's College in Minnesota. He spent fifteen years in the NFL under that name, beginning with the Milwaukee Badgers in 1925.

Blood had his greatest seasons with the Green Bay Packers, where he became the league's first outstanding deep receiver. He helped the Packers win championships in 1929, 1930, 1931, and 1936. His 10 touchdown receptions in 1931 is still the NFL record for a running back. Blood joined the Pittsburgh Steelers as player-coach in 1937 and retired during the 1939 season. Blood became a charter member of the Pro Football Hall of Fame in 1963.

Mel Blount—The key defensive back in the Pittsburgh Steelers' "Steel Curtain" defense, Blount (pronounced "Blunt") joined the team out of Southern University in 1970. The 6-foot-3, 205-pounder was an aggressive cover man and exceptionally hard hitter.

An all-conference choice from 1975 through 1977, Blount helped lead the Steelers to NFL championships in 1974, 1975, 1978, and 1979. He retired after the 1983 season with 57 career interceptions and three touchdown returns and was elected to the Pro Football Hall of Fame in 1989.

Terry Bradshaw—Bradshaw was the first player chosen in the 1970 NFL draft, by the Pittsburgh Steelers, out of Louisiana Tech. He took over as the team's starting quarterback in 1971. The Steelers won four Super Bowls under Bradshaw's leadership, after the 1974, 1975, 1978, and 1979 seasons.

The team's success was based largely on a ball-control running attack and a strong defense, but the 6-foot-3, 215-pound Bradshaw gave them a deep passing threat, and he was at his best in big games. In Super Bowl X, after the 1975 season, he threw a 64-yard pass to Lynn Swann for the winning touchdown in a 21–17 victory over the Dallas Cowboys.

Bradshaw was named the NFL player of the year in 1978 and he was the most valuable player in Super Bowls XIII and XIV, passing for more than 300 yards in each game. He retired after the 1983 season with 2,105 completions in 3,901 attempts for 27,909 yards and 212 touchdowns, and he was inducted into the Pro Football Hall of Fame in 1989.

Jim Brown—A rare combination of speed and power, Brown was an All-American in both football and lacrosse at Syracuse University as a senior, and he also lettered in basketball for three years. He was the NFL's rookie of the year with the Cleveland Browns in 1957.

The 6-foot-2, 238-pound Brown rushed for more than 1,000 yards in seven of the next eight years and he led the league in rushing every season except 1962, when he finished second. An eight-time All-Pro running back, he was named player of the year in 1958, 1963, and 1965.

Brown retired in the summer of 1966, when he was just thirty. A member of the Pro Football Hall of Fame, he gained 12,312 yards on 2,359 carries and scored 106 touchdowns rushing and 20 on pass receptions.

Paul Brown—Brown was a successful high school coach for twelve seasons before going to Ohio State in 1941. He had an 18–8–1 record through 1943 and then coached the Great Lakes Naval Training Station team. Brown took over the Cleveland Browns, who were named for him, in 1946 and guided them to four AAFC championships.

When the AAFC folded in 1950, the Browns entered the NFL, winning six divisional titles and three league championships in their first six seasons.

Brown pioneered the meticulous planning that is now taken for granted in pro football. He had the first full-time coaching staff, he analyzed game films much more extensively than any other coach of his time, and he was the first to hold regular classroom instruction for his players. The Browns had a 167–53–8 record in his seventeen seasons, through 1962.

After being inducted into the Pro Football Hall of Fame in 1967, Brown became coach of the new Cincinnati Bengals in the AFL. He had a 55–56–1 record and won two division titles with Cincinnati, then retired after the 1976 season.

Rosey Brown—A Little All-American tackle at Morgan State in 1952, Brown became an offensive starter as a rookie with the New York Giants and was quickly recognized as one of the best tackles ever. Though 6-foot-3 and 255 pounds, Brown was remarkably quick and agile as well as powerful. He spent thirteen seasons with the Giants and was an All-Pro eight straight years, from 1956 through 1963.

Brown retired after the 1965 season and was inducted into the Pro Football Hall of Fame in 1975.

Willie Brown—Brown signed as a free agent with the AFL's Denver Broncos out of Grambling in 1963 and was traded to the Oakland Raiders in 1967. A pioneer of the "bump and run" method of coverage, Brown was named to the AFL or AFC all-star team ten years in a row, from 1964 through 1973.

He spent twelve seasons with the Raiders, during which they averaged more than ten victories a season. Brown set a Super Bowl record with a 75-yard interception return in Oakland's 32–14 win over the Minnesota Vikings in Super Bowl XI, after the 1976 season. He retired in 1979 with 54 career interceptions and became a member of the Pro Football Hall of Fame in 1984.

Buck Buchanan—A star in basketball and track as well as football at Grambling, Buchanan was the first player chosen in the 1963 AFL draft, by the Kansas City Chiefs. The 6-foot-8 defensive end weighed about 270 pounds when he became a professional, but often reached 300 pounds and more during his career. Despite his size, he had great agility and speed and was an outstanding pass rusher.

An All-AFL selection from 1966 through 1970, Buchanan retired after the 1975 season. He was inducted into the Pro Football Hall of Fame in 1990.

Dick Butkus—Butkus was an All-American center-linebacker at the University of Illinois in 1963 and 1964 and became the Chicago Bears' starting middle linebacker in 1965, his rookie season. The 6-foot-3, 245-pounder was a seven-time All-Pro, though a knee injury forced his retirement after only nine years with the Bears.

He intercepted 22 passes and recovered 25 fumbles during his pro career. Butkus was named to the Pro Football Hall of Fame in 1979.

Earl Campbell—After winning the 1977 Heisman Trophy as a running back at the University of Texas, Campbell was the first round draft choice of the Houston Oilers. He led the league in rushing four years in a row, 1978 through 1981, and won the 1979 Bert Bell Trophy as the NFL's most valuable player.

The 5-foot-11, 230-pound Campbell had surprising speed to complement his power and could often break off long runs. After 1981, injuries limited his playing time, and he retired in 1985. He gained 9,407 yards on 2,187 career carries and scored 74 touchdowns. Campbell was inducted into the Pro Football Hall of Fame in 1991.

Tony Canadeo—Nicknamed the "Gray Ghost of Gonzaga" for the small Washington college he attended, Canadeo joined the Green Bay Packers in 1941 but didn't become a full-time starter as a single-wing tailback until 1943. He spent 1945 in the service, then returned to the team as a halfback in the T formation.

In 1949, Canadeo led the NFL with 1,052 yards, averaging 5.1 yards per attempt. He was only the third player in history to rush for more than 1,000 yards a season. He retired after the 1952 season with 4,197 yards on 1,025 attempts, and he also had 2,843 yards on receptions and returns. He entered the Pro Football Hall of Fame in 1974.

Guy Chamberlin—A halfback and end at the University of Nebraska, Chamberlin played for the independent Canton Bulldogs in 1919 and then joined the Decatur Staleys in the newly formed American Professional Football Association.

He became Canton's player-coach in 1922, when the APFA was renamed the NFL. Chamberlin guided Canton to two straight championships and the team won a third straight in 1924, after moving to Cleveland. He won his fourth title in five seasons as player-coach of the Frankford Yellowjackets in 1926.

After one season as a player for the Chicago Cardinals, he coached the team in 1928 and then retired from football. Chamberlin became a charter member of the Pro Football Hall of Fame in 1963.

Jack Christiansen—Christiansen joined the Detroit Lions as a kick returner and defensive back in 1951, after graduating from Colorado State, and soon became as much of a threat to score as most offensive players. An All-Pro for seven straight years, from 1952 through 1958, he led the NFL in interceptions twice and in punt return average once.

Christiansen retired after the 1958 season with 46 career interceptions and 13 touchdowns, 3 on interception returns, 8 on punt returns, and 2 as a running back. He was inducted into the Pro Football Hall of Fame in 1970.

Dutch Clark—One of the least known of the great pro players, Clark was also one of the most versatile. He graduated from Colorado College in 1930 but didn't enter the NFL until the following year, with the Portsmouth Spartans. After being an All-Pro quarterback each of his first two seasons, Clark left pro football in 1933.

He returned after the Spartans became the Detroit Lions in 1934 and was an All-Pro for four seasons in a row. Clark became player-coach of the team in 1937. Injuries forced him to retire after the 1938 season. A fine runner, passer, kicker, kick returner, and defensive back, Clark led the NFL in scoring three times in his eight seasons. He became a charter member of the Pro Football Hall of Fame in 1963.

George Connor—Connor joined the Chicago Bears after being an All-American tackle at Notre Dame in 1946 and 1947. The 6-foot-3, 240-pounder was named an All-Pro from 1949 through 1951. He then became an outside linebacker on defense while remaining at offensive tackle and was an All-Pro at both positions in 1952 and 1953.

Connor played only at linebacker for the next two seasons, then retired. He was elected to the Pro Football Hall of Fame in 1975.

Jimmy Conzelman—A quarterback at Washington University in St. Louis, Conzelman played for the Great Lakes Naval Training Station team in 1918. George Halas, a teammate at Great Lakes, signed Conzelman to play for the Decatur Staleys (now the Chicago Bears) in 1920.

Conzelman spent most of his NFL career as a player-coach, with the Rock Island Independents in 1922, the Milwaukee Badgers in 1923 and 1924, the Detroit Panthers in 1925 and 1926, and the Providence Steam Roller from 1927 through 1929. He guided Providence to the league championship in 1928.

After coaching at his alma mater for several years, Conzelman took over the Chicago Cardinals in 1946 and won a second championship in 1947. He retired after the Cardinals lost 7–0 to the Philadelphia Eagles in the 1948 title game and was elected to the Pro Football Hall of Fame in 1964.

Roger Craig—Craig was a key player for the San Francisco 49ers in three Super Bowl champions. He joined the team out of the University of Nebraska in 1983 and two years later he became the first player in history to gain more than 1,000 yards both rushing and receiving in a single season. He also set a record for running backs with 92 receptions.

The 6-foot-2, 219-pound Craig scored 3 touchdowns in San Francisco's 30–16 win over the Miami Dolphins in Super Bowl XIX after the 1984 season and he averaged 133 yards a game during the playoffs in 1988 and 1989. The 49ers won the NFL title both years. He later played for the Los Angeles Raiders and Minnesota Vikings.

Larry Csonka—A hard runner and punishing blocker, the 6-foot-3, 235-pound Csonka was an All-American fullback at Syracuse University in 1967 and then joined the Miami Dolphins. He gained more than 1,000 yards three years in a row, from 1971 through 1973.

In Miami's 24–7 win over the Minnesota Vikings in Super Bowl VIII, after the 1973 season, Csonka rushed for 145 yards on 33 carries and scored two touchdowns to win the Most Valuable Player award. After playing in the World Football League in 1975, Csonka finished his career with the New York Giants from 1976 through 1978 and with the Dolphins in 1979.

Csonka is a member of the College and Pro Football Halls of Fame.

Randall Cunningham—The top all-time career rusher among pro quarterbacks with more than 4,000 yards, the 6-foot-4, 205-pound Cunningham joined the Philadelphia Eagles in 1985 out of the University of Nevada–Las Vegas and became the team's starter in 1986.

He threw 21 or more touchdown passes four years in a row, from 1987 through 1990 and had 19 in 1992, when he completed more than 60 percent of his attempts. Cunningham missed most of the 1991 and 1993 seasons because of injury.

Willie Davis—A star at Grambling, Davis was drafted by the Cleveland Browns in 1958 but didn't become a starter until he was traded to the Green Bay Packers two years later. The 6-foot-3, 245-pound defensive end played for teams that won five NFL championships and the first two Super Bowls.

Davis started 162 consecutive games with the Packers. A five-time All-Pro, he retired after the 1969 season and was inducted into the Pro Football Hall of Fame in 1981.

Lenny Dawson—Purdue's starting quarterback for three years, Dawson never became a starter in five seasons with the Pittsburgh Steelers and Cleveland Browns. He joined the Dallas Texans of the AFL in 1962 and was named the league's player of the year, completing 61 percent of his passes and throwing for 29 touchdowns.

The team moved to Kansas City and became known as the Chiefs in 1963. Dawson won four AFL passing titles and was the most valuable player in the Chiefs' 23–7 victory over the Minnesota Vikings in Super Bowl IV after the 1969 season. He retired in 1976 with 2,136 completions and 252 touchdown passes in 3,741 attempts. Dawson entered the Pro Football Hall of Fame in 1987.

Eric Dickerson—Dickerson was an All-American running back at Southern Methodist in 1982 and was rookie of the year and NFC player of the year with the Los Angeles Rams in 1983, when he led the NFL with 1,808 yards rushing. Blessed with remarkable speed for his size, the 6-foot-3, 230-pounder set a record with 2,105 yards the following season.

He was the NFL rushing leader again in 1986 and in 1988, when he was with the Indianapolis Colts. The controversial Dickerson, who was often in trouble with coaches and management, missed much of the 1990 and 1991 seasons and retired in 1993 because of physical problems.

A five-time All-Pro, Dickerson rushed for more than 1,000 yards in seven straight seasons, a league record.

Mike Ditka—The first tight end inducted into the Pro Football Hall of Fame, "Iron Mike" played at the University of Pittsburgh and joined the Chicago Bears in 1961. He was named rookie of the year. Outstanding as both a blocker and a receiver, the 6-foot-3, 225-pound Ditka set a record for tight ends with 76 catches in 1964 and was an All-Pro four times.

He ended his playing career with the Philadelphia Eagles in 1967 and 1968 and with the Dallas Cowboys from 1969 through 1972, then became head coach of the Bears in 1982. His 1985 team lost only one game and whipped the New England Patriots 46–10 in the Super Bowl. Ditka left coaching after the 1992 season to become a television commentator.

Art Donovan—After serving in the Marines, Donovan was a three-year starting tackle at Boston College and entered pro football with the old Baltimore Colts in 1950. The team became the New York Yanks in 1951 and the Dallas Texans in 1952 before returning to Baltimore.

Donovan was an All-Pro defensive tackle from 1954 through 1957 and he starred on Baltimore's first championship team in 1958. Nicknamed "Fatso" because his weight often ballooned to more than 300 pounds in the off season, he retired during training camp in 1962 and was inducted into the Pro Football Hall of Fame in 1968.

Tony Dorsett—Speed, vision, and incredible cutting ability made Dorsett a great runner. Twice an All-American at Pittsburgh, he won the 1976 Heisman Trophy and then joined the Dallas Cowboys, where he was named the NFL's rookie of the year. He gained more than 1,000 yards his first six years as a pro.

Dorsett was traded to the Denver Broncos in 1988 and retired because of a knee injury in training camp the following year. His 12,379 career yards is second all-time to Walter Payton. In 1994, Dorsett was elected to the Pro Football Hall of Fame.

Paddy Driscoll—An outstanding kicker and dangerous runner, Driscoll played at Northwestern and with the Great Lakes Naval Training Station team in 1918, then joined the independent Hammond Pros. When the American Professional Football Association was organized in 1920, he became the quarterback for the Chicago Cardinals.

Driscoll set a league record with 27 points in a single game in 1923, tied one with a 50-yard field goal the following season, and set another by kicking four field goals in a 1925 game. In 1926, Driscoll was traded to the Chicago Bears. He retired after the 1929 season and was elected to the Pro Football Hall of Fame in 1965.

Bullet Bill Dudley—An amazingly versatile player, Dudley was an All-American halfback at the University of Virginia in 1941 and then led the NFL in rushing with the Pittsburgh Steelers. He served in the Army during World War II and was the league's rushing leader again in 1946.

The 5-foot-10, 175-pound Dudley was traded to the Detroit Lions in 1947, when he scored 13 touchdowns, 4 on runs, 7 on pass receptions, and

1 each on punt and kickoff returns. He also threw 2 touchdown passes that season. Dudley played for the Washington Redskins in 1950 and 1951 and retired after rejoining Washington briefly in 1953.

In 9 NFL seasons, Dudley gained 3,057 yards rushing, 1,303 on pass receptions, 1,515 on punt returns, 1,743 on kickoff returns, and 459 on interception returns. He also punted for a 38.2 average, kicked 121 extra points and 23 field goals, and scored 44 touchdowns. He is a charter member of the Pro Football Hall of Fame.

Turk Edwards—Edwards was an All-American tackle as a junior at Washington State in 1930. Two years later, he joined the Boston Braves, who became the Boston Redskins in 1933 and moved to Washington in 1937. Very big for his time at 6-foot-2 and 260 pounds, Edwards was a four-time All-Pro.

He was forced to retire with a knee injury early in the 1940 season and he later coached the Redskins for three years. Edwards was inducted into the Pro Football Hall of Fame in 1969.

John Elway—In his career at Stanford, Elway passed for 9,349 yards and 77 touchdowns. He was the first player chosen in the 1983 NFL draft, by the Baltimore Colts, but he refused to sign and was traded to the Denver Broncos. Elway became a starter in 1984 and led Denver to AFC championships in 1986, 1987, and 1989. However, the Broncos lost in all three Super Bowls.

The Associated Press named him the NFL player of the year in 1987, when he passed for 3,198 yards and 19 touchdowns. A fine athlete, Elway has a strong arm that makes him particularly dangerous when he scrambles out of the pocket. He's also a fiercely competitive leader who has taken the Broncos to many last-minute victories.

Weeb Ewbank—A high school and college coach for many years, Ewbank was forty-seven when he became head coach of the Baltimore Colts in 1954. He built a team that won consecutive NFL championships in 1958 and 1959 but was fired after the 1962 season. Ewbank then took another major rebuilding job with the New York Jets of the AFL.

His patience with young players, particularly quarterback Joe Namath, was rewarded with an AFL championship in 1968 and the Jets shocked the football world by beating the Colts 16–7 in Super Bowl III. Ewbank retired after the 1973 season. The only coach to win championships in both leagues, he was inducted into the Pro Football Hall of Fame in 1978.

Tom Fears—When he joined the Los Angeles Rams out of UCLA in 1948, Fears was a defensive back for one game but was then moved to offensive end. He led the NFL in receptions his first three seasons in the league and was also the leader in touchdown passes with 9 in 1949 and in reception yardage with 1,116 in 1950. His 18 catches against the Green Bay Packers that year is still the NFL single-game record.

A great clutch receiver, the 6-foot-2, 215-pound Fears caught a 74-yard touchdown pass that beat the Cleveland Browns 24–17 in the 1951 championship game. He also had three touchdowns in the Rams' 24–14 win over the Chicago Bears for the 1950 Western Division title. Fears retired after the 1956 season with exactly 400 catches and 38 touchdowns. He was the first head coach of the New Orleans Saints in 1967, and became a member of the Pro Football Hall of Fame in 1970.

Beattie Feathers—The first NFL player to gain more than 1,000 yards, Feathers did it in 1934 as a rookie with the Chicago Bears, when he had 1,004 yards in 101 attempts. His 9.9 average is still the league record.

A 1933 All-American at the University of Tennessee, the speedy, 5-foot-10, 185-pound Feathers played in the NFL through 1940, but injuries hampered him from 1935 on and he gained a total of less than 1,000 yards during those six seasons.

Ray Flaherty—After graduating from Gonzaga University, Flaherty played for the Los Angeles Wildcats of the first AFL in 1926, then with the NFL's New York Yanks and New York Giants. An end, he led the league with 21 receptions in 1932.

Flaherty retired after the 1935 season and became coach of the Boston Redskins in 1936. The team moved to Washington in 1937 and won the NFL championship that year. Flaherty also guided them to the 1942 title and then entered the Navy. He later coached the New York Yankees and Chicago Hornets in the All-America Football Conference. His 82–41–5 record won him induction into the Pro Football Hall of Fame in 1976.

Len Ford—Ford played college football at Morgan State and the University of Michigan. He was an offensive end with the Los Angeles Dons of the All-America Football Conference in 1948 and 1949, then joined the Cleveland Browns, who moved him to defense.

An All-Pro from 1951 through 1955, the 6-foot-5, 260-pound Ford spent the 1958 season with the Green Bay Packers before retiring. He was inducted into the Pro Football Hall of Fame in 1976.

Daniel Fortmann—Fortmann graduated from Colgate in 1936, at twenty, and became the youngest player ever to sign an NFL contract. He immediately took over as a starting guard with the Chicago Bears. An All-Pro from 1938 through 1943, the 6-foot, 210-pound Fortmann played for NFL champions in 1940, 1941, and 1943.

He retired after the 1943 season to practice surgery. Fortmann was elected to the Pro Football Hall of Fame in 1985.

Dan Fouts—Because he played for poor teams at Oregon, Fouts wasn't chosen until the third round of the 1973 draft, but he became the San Diego Chargers' starting quarterback as a rookie. During the eight seasons from 1979 through 1986, Fouts averaged 24 touchdown passes a year.

He set NFL records with 4,082 yards passing in 1979, 4,715 yards in 1980, and 4,802 yards in 1981. Named the NFL player of the year in 1982, Fouts retired after the 1987 season and was inducted into the Pro Football Hall of Fame in 1993.

Benny Friedman—An All-American at the University of Michigan in 1925 and 1926, Friedman was the finest passer of his era. After playing in the NFL with the Cleveland Bulldogs and the Detroit Wolverines, he went to the New York Giants in 1929 and threw a record 20 touchdown passes to lead them to a 13–1–1 season, though they finished second to the Green Bay Packers.

Friedman remained with the Giants through 1933 and retired after playing one game with the Brooklyn Dodgers in 1934. For years, he campaigned for election to the Pro Football Hall of Fame, but never made it. However, he is a member of the College Football Hall of Fame.

Frank Gatski—"Gunner" Gatski played football at Marshall University and then Auburn after serving in World War II. He joined the Cleveland Browns of the All-America Football Conference in 1946. The 6-foot-3, 235-pounder played center and linebacker as a rookie and became Cleveland's starting center in 1947.

The AAFC folded after the 1949 season and the Browns entered the NFL. Gatski was an All-Pro from 1951 through 1953 and in 1955. He retired after spending the 1956 season with the Detroit Lions and was elected to the Pro Football Hall of Fame in 1985.

Bill George—The first of the true middle linebackers, George was also one of the best. He played tackle at Wake Forest and became the Chicago Bears' middle guard in 1952. George began dropping out of the line on passing situations and, because he was still so effective at playing the run, the Bears began using him at linebacker on every down.

Both strong and fast, the 6-foot-2, 230-pounder was an All-Pro for eight consecutive seasons, 1955 through 1962. He went to the Los Angeles Rams for the 1966 season and then retired. George was inducted into the Pro Football Hall of Fame in 1974.

Joe Gibbs—After fifteen seasons as an assistant college and professional coach, Gibbs took over the Washington Redskins in 1981. A pioneer of the one-back offense, which he helped develop as an assistant with the San Diego Chargers, Gibbs guided the Redskins to five division titles and Super Bowl victories after the 1982, 1987, and 1991 seasons.

He retired abruptly after the 1992 season with a 124–60–0 record.

Frank Gifford—A single-wing tailback at Southern California, Gifford was a defensive back as a rookie with the New York Giants in 1952. He became a starter at running back in 1952 and was named the NFL's player of the year in 1956, when he accounted for 1,422 yards rushing and receiving.

The 6-foot-1, 195-pound Gifford was an All-Pro from 1955 through 1957 and in 1959. After a year in retirement, he returned to the Giants as a flanker in 1962 and retired for good after the 1964 season. He has been a broadcaster on ABC's "Monday Night Football" for most of its existence. Gifford is a member of the College and Pro Football Halls of Fame.

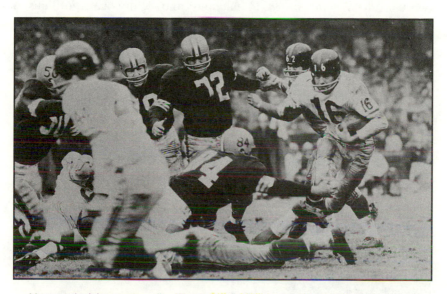

Now a television personality, Frank Gifford (16) began his professional career as a defensive back for the New York Giants in 1952. He then became a running back and, after a year of retirement, returned to the team as a wide receiver. *Courtesy New York Giants*

Sid Gillman—Gillman graduated from Ohio University in 1934, played pro football for a season, then coached college football until 1955, when he took over the Los Angeles Rams. In 1960, he became the first coach of the AFL's Los Angeles Chargers, who moved to San Diego the following year.

A pioneer in the use of the pass to set up the running game, Gillman guided the Chargers to five Western Conference titles and the 1963 AFL championship. He became general manager of the Houston Oilers in 1971 and coached the team in 1973 and 1974. Gillman, who had a 123–104–7 record, was elected to the Pro Football Hall of Fame in 1983.

Otto Graham—An All-American in both basketball and football, Graham spent two years in the Navy after graduating from Northwestern in 1944 and then joined the Cleveland Browns of the new All-America Football Conference. With Graham at quarterback, the Browns had a 52–4–2 record and won all four AAFC championships.

After the league folded in 1950, the Browns entered the NFL. They won three more titles in the next six years. Graham threw four touchdown passes in their 30–28 championship victory over the Los Angeles Rams in 1950. He passed for three touchdowns and ran for three more in a 56–10 win over the Detroit Lions in 1954, and had two touchdown passes and two touchdown runs in a 38–14 championship victory over the Rams in 1955. The NFL's player of the year in 1953 and 1955, Graham was inducted into the Pro Football Hall of Fame in 1965.

Red Grange helped make pro football a popular sport when he went on a post-season barnstorming tour with the Chicago Bears in 1925, immediately after playing his last game for the University of Illinois. *Courtesy Pro Football Hall of Fame*

Red Grange—Grange was to football what Babe Ruth was to baseball during the 1920s. An All-American halfback at Illinois from 1923 through 1925, he scored on runs of 95, 67, 56, and 45 yards the first four times he touched the ball against Michigan in 1924. He later scored on a 12-yard run and threw a 23-yard touchdown pass. Despite a muddy field, Grange gained 363 yards on 36 carries against Pennsylvania as a senior.

Nicknamed "Number 77," the "Galloping Ghost," and the "Illinois Flash," Grange stirred controversy by leaving school to tour with the Chicago Bears immediately after his final college game. The tour attracted more than 70,000 fans in New York and 75,000 in Los Angeles, by far the largest crowds to turn out for pro football at that time.

Grange played for the New York Yankees in the AFL, which was organized around him, in 1926 and was with the team in the NFL in 1927.

He missed the entire 1928 season with a serious knee injury and then played for the Bears from 1929 through 1934. Although not the runner he had been, Grange was named an All-Pro in 1931 and 1932. He is a member of the College and Pro Football Halls of Fame.

Bud Grant—A three-sport star at Minnesota, Grant played professional basketball with the Minneapolis Lakers for two years and was then a starting end for the Philadelphia Eagles in the 1952 and 1953 seasons. After four years with the Winnipeg Blue Bombers of the Canadian Football League, he became the team's head coach and won four championships in ten seasons.

With the Minnesota Vikings from 1966 through 1983, Grant coached 11 Central Division champions and took his team to four Super Bowls without winning. He returned to coach the team in 1985 and then retired permanently with a 168–108–5 record. He was inducted into the Pro Football Hall of Fame in 1994.

Joe Greene—"Mean Joe" never liked his nickname, which was given to him because his North Texas State team was called the "Mean Green." The 6-foot-4, 260-pound Greene joined the Pittsburgh Steelers as a defensive tackle in 1969 and was a key player on the "Steel Curtain" defense that helped take Pittsburgh to four Super Bowl championships during the 1970s.

An All-Pro from 1970 through 1977 and the defensive player of the year in 1972 and 1974, Greene lined up at an angle, with his lead shoulder pointed at the gap between offensive linemen. He was so quick that he could often burst through the line before being blocked.

Greene retired after the 1981 season and was elected to the Pro Football Hall of Fame in 1987.

Forrest Gregg—Gregg joined the Green Bay Packers as an offensive tackle in 1966 after playing both offense and defense at Southern Methodist. The 6-foot-4, 250-pounder was unusually fast for his size and was often used to pull on running plays. He played primarily at guard in 1961 and 1965 because of injuries to other players.

An All-Pro eight years in a row, from 1960 through 1967, Gregg played for the Dallas Cowboys in 1971 before retiring. He later coached the Cleveland Browns, Cincinnati Bengals, and the Packers. Gregg was inducted into the Pro Football Hall of Fame in 1977.

Bob Griese—A three-year starter at Purdue, Griese became the Miami Dolphins' starting quarterback as a rookie in 1967. Like Bart Starr with the Packers, he was the perfect leader for an offense that emphasized ball-control through runs and short passes. An accurate short passer and excellent ball-handler, he was skilled at sizing up defenses and calling audibles.

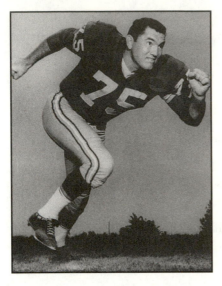

An All-Pro eight years in a row—from 1960 to 1967—Forrest Gregg was an offensive tackle most of the time but he also played guard when necessary. A member of five Green Bay Packer championship teams, Gregg was also a successful coach after retiring as a player. *Hank Lefebvre Photo/ Collection of Lee L. Lefebvre*

An All-Pro in 1971 and 1977, Griese led the Dolphins to victories in all 17 of their games in 1972. He attempted only 18 passes in Super Bowls VII and VIII, but completed 14 of them for 161 yards in two Miami victories. Griese retired after the 1980 season and was elected to the Pro Football Hall of Fame in 1990.

Lou Groza—Groza was the first true kicking specialist. After two years at Ohio State, he saw military service during World War II and joined the Cleveland Browns of the All-America Football Conference in 1946. The Browns entered the NFL when the AAFC folded in 1950.

A starting offensive tackle from 1947 through 1959, Groza missed the 1960 season with an injury, but returned as a kicking specialist from 1961 through 1967. He retired with 1,608 career points, a record at the time, and was inducted into the Pro Football Hall of Fame in 1974.

Joe Guyon—Though not nearly as well known as his teammate, Jim Thorpe, Guyon was one of the finest all-around players of the 1920s. A tackle and halfback at Carlisle Indian School from 1911 through 1913, he spent a final college season at Georgia Tech in 1917. From 1919 through 1925, he played guard, tackle, halfback, and quarterback for the Canton Bulldogs, Cleveland Indians, Oorang Indians, and Kansas City Cowboys.

After sitting out the 1926 season, he played for the New York Giants in 1927 and then retired. The 6-foot-1, 195-pounder was a speedy runner, a powerful tackler and blocker, and a fine punter and drop kicker. He was inducted into the Pro Football Hall of Fame in 1966.

"Papa Bear" George Halas founded the Decatur Staleys in 1920, moved the team to Chicago in 1921, and re-named it the Bears in 1922. He coached the team for a total of 40 seasons and won 7 NFL champion-ships. *Courtesy Pro Football Hall of Fame*

George Halas—Halas played end at Illinois and with the Great Lakes Naval Training Station before organizing a football team for the Staley Starch Company of Decatur, IL, in 1920. The Decatur Staleys moved to Chicago in 1921 and became known as the Bears the following season, when Halas became co-owner.

The Bears' player-coach through 1929, Halas replaced himself with Ralph Jones for three years, then took over as coach again in 1933. He served as head coach through 1941, from 1946 through 1955, and from 1958 through 1967. The Bears were NFL champions in 1921, 1932, 1933, 1937, 1940, 1943, 1946, and 1963. Halas, who had a 325–151–31 record, was affiliated with the team until his death.

Halas made many contributions to pro football. He suggested that the American Professional Football Association be renamed the NFL in 1922, and he teamed with George Preston Marshall to formulate several rules changes that transformed the sport in 1933. His commitment to the T formation, culminating in a 73–0 defeat of the Washington Redskins in the 1940 championship game, led other pro teams to adopt the offense during the ensuing decade. "Papa Bear" became a charter member of the Pro Football Hall of Fame in 1963.

Jack Ham—An All-American at Penn State in 1970, Ham became a starting outside linebacker with the Pittsburgh Steelers in 1971. He was an All-Pro from 1973 through 1979 and the NFL defensive player of the year in 1975.

Somewhat under-sized at 6-foot-1 and 225 pounds, Ham had outstanding speed and the ability to diagnose plays quickly. He retired after the 1982 season with 32 career interceptions and 19 fumble recoveries. A starter on four Super Bowl champions, Ham was inducted into the Pro Football Hall of Fame in 1988.

John Hannah—The 6-foot-3, 265-pound Hannah was an All-American guard at Alabama in 1972 and a starter for the New England Patriots from 1973 until he retired after the 1985 season. An All-NFL selection in 1980, 1981, 1984, and 1985, Hannah was also named to the all-conference team in 1974, 1976, 1978, and 1979, and he was selected as one of the guards on the quarter-century AFL-NFL team for the 1960–1984 period.

Hannah was elected to the Pro Football Hall of Fame in 1991.

Franco Harris—Primarily a blocking fullback at Penn State, Harris was the NFL's rookie of the year with the Pittsburgh Steelers in 1972, when he rushed for 1,055 yards. He had seven other seasons of more than 1,000 yards during his thirteen-year pro career.

The 6-foot-2, 225-pound Harris was a fine blocker and receiver as well as an outstanding runner. He played for four Super Bowl champions and was named MVP in Pittsburgh's 16–6 win over the Minnesota Vikings in Super Bowl IX, after the 1974 season, when he gained 158 yards on 34 attempts. His most famous single play was the "immaculate reception" in a 1972 playoff game against the Oakland Raiders. Pittsburgh was trailing 7–6 with five seconds left when Harris caught a pass that bounced off a defender's shoulderpads and ran it in for a 60-yard touchdown that won the game.

Harris was inducted into the Pro Football Hall of Fame in 1990.

Ed Healey—Healey played end at Dartmouth, graduating in 1916, and didn't enter pro football until 1920, when he was twenty-five years old. He played tackle with the Rock Island Independents until the Chicago Bears bought his contract during the 1922 season. It was the first player sale in NFL history.

The 6-foot-3, 220-pounder was unusually fast. He once prevented a safety by catching a Bear halfback who was running the wrong way with an interception and tackling him short of the end zone. Healey retired after the 1927 season and was elected to the Pro Football Hall of Fame in 1964.

Pudge Heffelfinger—The first known professional player, Heffelfinger was a legend in his lifetime. At Yale, he was named as a guard to the first three All-American teams, from 1889 through 1891. Because of his speed, he was the first guard to pull out of the line and lead interference.

After graduating in 1892, Heffelfinger began playing for the Chicago Athletic Association team, which toured the east that fall. He was paid $500 to play for the Duquesne Athletic Club of Pittsburgh against the Allegheny Athletic Club on November 12. Heffelfinger scored the game's only touchdown, running 35 yards with a fumble.

Heffelfinger played fifty-one minutes in a charity all-star game in 1922, when he was fifty-four. His final appearance in uniform came in another charity game shortly before his sixty-fifth birthday in 1933, when he played nine minutes. He's a member of the College Football Hall of Fame

Mel Hein—In fifteen seasons of professional football, Hein was forced out of a game by injury only once. He captained Washington State in 1930, when he was named All-American center, and he joined the New York Giants the following year. The 6-foot-2, 225-pounder starred as a linebacker as well as an offensive center throughout his career.

An All-Pro eight consecutive seasons, from 1933 through 1940, he was named the league's most valuable player in 1938. He planned to retire after the 1941 season to coach Union College in Schenectady, but continued playing with the Giants through 1945 because of the World War II manpower shortage. During those four years, he spent the week in Schenectady and played for the Giants on Sundays without any practice.

Hein is a member of the College and Pro Football Halls of Fame.

Ted Hendricks—Hendricks was an All-American defensive end at Miami in 1967 and 1968 and became an outside linebacker with the Baltimore Colts in 1969. The 6-foot-7, 220-pound Hendricks was known as the "Mad Stork" because of his physique and all-out style of play.

A six-time All-Pro, Hendricks excelled as a kick blocker and pass rusher. He played for the Green Bay Packers in 1974 and the Oakland Raiders from 1975 through 1983 before retiring. Hendricks was inducted into the Pro Football Hall of Fame in 1990.

Fats Henry—Despite his roly-poly appearance, the 5-foot-10, 230-pound Henry was a very quick, agile athlete who starred in baseball, basketball, and track as well as football at Washington and Jefferson. He was an All-American tackle as a senior in 1919.

Henry entered pro football with the Canton Bulldogs from 1920 through 1923 and from 1925 through 1926. He retired after serving as player-coach with the Pottsville Maroons in 1927 and 1928, but spent a final season with the Staten Island Stapletons in 1930. A crushing blocker and outstanding defensive lineman, Henry was probably the best kicker of his time. He set records with a 50-yard drop-kicked field goal in 1922, an 83-yard punt the following year, and 49 consecutive extra points by drop kick.

Henry became a charter member of the Pro Football Hall of Fame in 1963.

Arnie Herber—A native of Green Bay, Herber joined the Packers in 1930 after playing only briefly in college. An outstanding long passer, he teamed with Johnny Blood and later with Blood and Don Hutson to give the Packers the NFL's most dangerous passing attack.

Herber was the NFL's passing leader in 1932, 1934, and 1936. He threw a 43-yard touchdown pass to Hutson and a 52-yard pass to Blood to set up another touchdown in Green Bay's 21–6 win over the Washington Redskins in the 1936 championship game. Herber retired after the 1940 season but played for the New York Giants in 1944 and 1945. He was inducted into the Pro Football Hall of Fame in 1966.

Bill Hewitt—Hewitt played end and fullback at Michigan and became a starting end for the Chicago Bears in 1932. Nicknamed the "Offside Kid" because of his fast start, he was an All-Pro with the Bears in 1933 and 1934 and with the Philadelphia Eagles in 1936 and 1937. He was the first player to represent two different teams on the All-Pro squad.

The 5-foot-11, 195-pound Hewitt played without a helmet until 1939, when the NFL began requiring helmets. He retired after that season but played with the merged Philadelphia-Pittsburgh squad in 1943. Hewitt was elected to the Pro Football Hall of Fame in 1971.

Clarke Hinkle—A three-year starter as a fullback at Bucknell, Hinkle signed with the Green Bay Packers in 1932. The solid, 5-foot-10, 205-pounder was an outstanding linebacker as well as a tough, durable runner.

An All-Pro from 1936 through 1938 and in 1941, his final season, Hinkle was also the Packers' chief punter through most of his career and he sometimes kicked extra points and field goals. He was inducted into the Pro Football Hall of Fame in 1964, and he's also a member of the College Football Hall of Fame.

Crazylegs Hirsch—Hirsch was an outstanding running back at Wisconsin and Michigan. After military service in World War II, he entered pro football with the Chicago Rockets of the All America Football Conference in 1946.

With the Los Angeles Rams in 1949, Hirsch became the first full-time flanker in the three-end offense. He was brilliant in 1951, when he had 66 catches for 1,495 yards and 17 touchdowns. He averaged 22.7 yards a catch and his average touchdown reception that season was an incredible 47.8 yards.

Hirsch retired after the 1957 season. He was inducted into the Pro Football Hall of Fame in 1968.

Paul Hornung—The 1956 Heisman Trophy winner as a quarterback at Notre Dame, Hornung seemed to be a flop as a professional until Vince Lombardi took over the Green Bay Packers and made him the starting left halfback and place kicker. An outstanding clutch player, the 6-foot-2, 220-pound Hornung set a record with 176 points in 1960, an average of 14.7 per game.

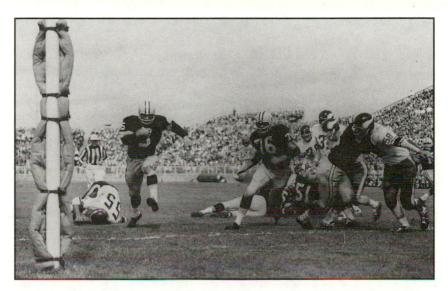

Paul Hornung runs to daylight and scores for the Green Bay Packers against the Minnesota Vikings in a 1960 game. Hornung had a record 176 points in just twelve games that season. *Hank Lefebvre Photo/Collection of Lee L. Lefebvre*

He was named the NFL's player of the year in 1961, when he again led in scoring. Hornung set a playoff record with 19 points in the Packers' 37–0 championship victory over the New York Giants. However, injuries hampered him for the rest of his career and he was suspended for the entire 1963 season for betting on games. He retired in 1967 and was inducted into the Pro Football Hall of Fame in 1986.

Ken Houston—Houston played linebacker at Prairie View A & M but was moved to strong safety when he joined the Houston Oilers in 1967. The 6-foot-3, 198-pounder had both speed and strength and was a fine tackler and ballhawk. He was traded to the Washington Redskins in 1973 and retired after the 1980 season.

Houston was named to all-conference teams in 1971 and from 1974 through 1977. He had 49 career interceptions and a record 9 touchdowns on interception returns. He was elected to the Pro Football Hall of Fame in 1986.

Cal Hubbard—One of the first agile giants of football, the 6-foot-5, 250-pound Hubbard had a unique career as a pro football player and major league umpire. He played tackle and end at Centenary College in Louisiana and Geneva College in Pennsylvania before signing with the New York Giants in 1927.

In 1929, Hubbard went to the Green Bay Packers, who promptly won three straight championships. Because teams refused to run at him, he began dropping off the line of scrimmage and operating virtually as a linebacker. Hubbard was an All-Pro from 1931 through 1933. He finished his playing career with the Giants and Pittsburgh Steelers in 1936.

An American League umpire from 1936 through 1957, Hubbard became the league's supervisor of umpires in 1958. He's the only man enshrined in both the Baseball Hall of Fame and the Pro Football Hall of Fame.

Sam Huff—After playing offensive and defensive tackle at West Virginia, Huff signed with the New York Giants in 1956 and became a middle linebacker. An All-Pro in 1958 and 1959, he became one of the best-known players in football because of the 1960 CBS television special, "The Violent World of Sam Huff."

The 6-foot-1, 230-pound Huff was traded to the Washington Redskins in 1964. He retired in 1968 but played a final season with Washington in 1969. Huff was inducted into the Pro Football Hall of Fame in 1982.

Pro football's first great receiver, Don Hutson played for three NFL champions in his eleven years with the Green Bay Packers. When he retired after the 1945 season, he held virtually every NFL receiving record. *Courtesy Pro Football Hall of Fame*

Don Hutson—The 6-foot Hutson weighed only 160 pounds and didn't become a starting end at Alabama until 1934, his senior season, when he was an All-American. Gifted with speed, dazzling moves, great hands, and exceptional running ability after he caught the ball, he compiled some amazing numbers after joining the Green Bay Packers in 1935.

Hutson caught an 83-yard touchdown pass on his first NFL play and was an All-Pro nine times in eleven seasons. He retired after the 1945 season with a host of records, including 489 career receptions, 8,010 reception yards, 99 touchdown catches, and 825 points. He also set NFL records with 14 receptions in a game, 74 receptions in a season, 4 touchdown receptions in a game, 17 touchdown receptions in a season, 237 yards in a game and 1,211 yards in a season. His 138 points in 1942 was a record until 1960.

Hutson became a charter member of the Pro Football Hall of Fame in 1963.

Jimmy Johnson—A two-way player and world-class hurdler at UCLA, the 6-foot-2, 188-pound Johnson was a part-time defensive back as a rookie with the San Francisco 49ers in 1961 and played wide receiver in his second year. He took over as a starting cornerback in 1963 and remained there until he retired after the 1976 season.

A conference all-star five times, Johnson had 47 career interceptions and returned two of them for touchdowns. He was inducted into the Pro Football Hall of Fame in 1994.

John Henry Johnson—Johnson was the rookie of the year in the Canadian Football League in 1953, after playing at Arizona State, and he signed with the San Francisco 49ers the following year. At 6-foot-2 and 225 pounds, he was a powerful runner and blocker, sometimes accused of dirty play by opponents because of his all-out attacking style.

Overshadowed by halfbacks Hugh McElhenny and Joe Perry with the 49ers, Johnson went to the Detroit Lions in 1957 and the Pittsburgh Steelers in 1960. He had his best seasons with Pittsburgh, rushing for more than 1,000 yards in 1962 and 1964. Johnson retired after the 1966 season and was inducted into the Pro Football Hall of Fame in 1987.

Charley Joiner—After playing defensive back at Grambling, Joiner became a wide receiver with the Houston Oilers in 1969. At 5-foot-11 and 180 pounds, he was used primarily as a deep receiver in his early years but became a possession receiver later in his career.

Joiner was traded to the Cincinnati Bengals in 1972 and to the San Diego Chargers in 1976. He retired after the 1986 season with 750 career receptions, then the NFL record.

Deacon Jones—The 6-foot-5, 260-pound Jones joined the Los Angeles Rams in 1961 after playing at South Carolina State and

Mississippi Vocational. He quickly became the best pass rusher in pro football, recording 26 sacks in 1967.

A key player in the Rams' "Fearsome Foursome" defensive line, Jones was an All-Pro from 1965 through 1970 and was named the NFL's defensive player of the year in 1967 and 1968. He ended his career with the San Diego Chargers in 1972 and 1973 and the Washington Redskins in 1974. He was inducted into the Pro Football Hall of Fame in 1980.

Stan Jones—An All-American tackle at Maryland in 1953, Jones became a starter at offensive tackle with the Chicago Bears in 1954 and was moved to guard the following season. After being named an All-Pro four times, the 6-foot-1, 250-pounder became a defensive tackle in 1963 and helped the Bears win the NFL championship that season.

He finished his career with the Washington Redskins in 1966. A pioneer in using weight training, Jones has served as strength coach for several NFL teams. He was inducted into the Pro Football Hall of Fame in 1991.

Sonny Jurgensen—Jurgensen joined the Philadelphia Eagles in 1957 out of Duke University. In 1961, his first season as a starter, he set an NFL record by passing for 3,723 yards and tied a record with 32 touchdown passes. The Eagles traded him to the Washington Redskins in 1964.

Jurgensen broke his own record with 3,747 passing yards in 1967, when he was the NFL passing champion. He won the title again in 1969. An All-Pro in 1961 and 1969, Jurgensen retired after the 1974 season. He was elected to the Pro Football Hall of Fame in 1983.

Jim Kelly—After playing at Miami, Kelly spent two seasons with the Houston Gamblers of the U.S. Football League and then joined the Buffalo Bills in 1986. Calling most of his own plays in Buffalo's no-huddle offense, Kelly led the NFL by completing 63.3 percent of his passes in 1990 and by throwing 33 touchdown passes in 1991.

Kelly helped lead the Bills to four straight AFC championships, from 1990 through 1993, but they lost all four Super Bowls.

Leroy Kelly—Kelly joined the Cleveland Browns out of Morgan State in 1964. Used as a kick returner and backup to Jim Brown during his first two seasons, he took over as a starter after Brown retired in 1966.

In 1967, Kelly became one of only eight players to win the rushing "triple crown" by leading the league with 1,205 yards, a 5.1 average, and 11 rushing touchdowns. He also led the NFL with 1,269 yards and 16 touchdowns in 1968, when he was named the league's player of the year.

The 6-foot, 205-pounder retired after the 1973 season with a total of 89 touchdowns and he was elected to Pro Football Hall of Fame in 1994.

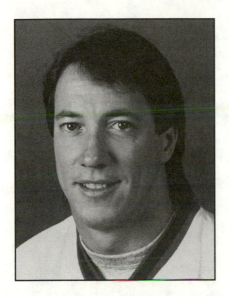

Jim Kelly calls most of the Buffalo Bills' plays in the no-huddle offense and is also a fine passer. He helped to lead the Bills to four straight AFC championships, but they have yet to win a Super Bowl. *Courtesy Buffalo Bills*

Walter Kiesling—Kiesling graduated from St. Thomas College in Minnesota in 1926 and spent two seasons with the Duluth Eskimos. A 6-foot-2, 245-pound guard, he went to the Pottsville Maroons in 1928, the Chicago Cardinals in 1929, the Chicago Bears in 1934, the Green Bay Packers in 1935, and the Pittsburgh Steelers in 1937.

An All-Pro in 1932, Kiesling retired as a player after the 1938 season. A long-time assistant coach with several professional teams, Kiesling also had several brief stints as a head coach with the Steelers. He was inducted into the Pro Football Hall of Fame in 1966.

Bruiser Kinard—Mississippi's football captain in 1937, Kinard also played basketball and ran the 440-yard dash in college. A tackle at only 190 pounds, he eventually reached 215 pounds as a professional without losing much of his speed.

Kinard entered the NFL with the Brooklyn Dodgers in 1938. After spending 1945 in the Navy, he joined the New York Yankees of the All-America Football Conference in 1946 and retired after the 1947 season. An All-Pro in 1940, 1941, 1943, and 1944, he missed only one game in his nine professional seasons. Kinard was inducted into the Pro Football Hall of Fame in 1971.

Curly Lambeau—After winning a letter as a freshman fullback at Notre Dame in 1918, Lambeau went home to Green Bay because of tonsillitis and never returned to college. In 1919, he formed the Green Bay Packers, named for the Indian Packing Corporation, which gave Lambeau $500 for uniforms and equipment.

In 1921, the Packers entered the American Professional Football Association, which became the NFL the following year. Lambeau was player-coach through 1928 and continued coaching through 1950. An early proponent of the forward pass, he guided the team to championships in 1929, 1930, 1931, 1936, 1939, and 1944.

Lambeau also coached the Chicago Cardinals in 1951 and 1952, the Washington Redskins in 1953 and 1954 before retiring with a 229–134–22 record. He became a charter member of the Pro Football Hall of Fame in 1963.

The founder of the Green Bay Packers in 1919, Curly Lambeau was player-coach of the team until 1929 and he continued coaching the Packers through 1950, producing six NFL champions. Lambeau was the first professional coach to emphasize the forward pass. *Stiller Photo/Collection of Lee L. Lefebvre*

Jack Lambert—A three-year starting middle linebacker at Kent State, Lambert was the only rookie to start for the Pittsburgh Steelers in 1974, when they won their first NFL championship. The 6-foot-4, 220-pounder was named the league's defensive player of the year in 1976.

Lambert also played for Super Bowl champions in 1975, 1978, and 1979. A three-time all-conference selection, he appeared in nine consecutive Pro Bowls. He retired after the 1984 season and was elected to the Pro Football Hall of Fame in 1990.

Tom Landry—After serving in World War II, Landry played football at the University of Texas and joined the New York Yankees of the All-America Football Conference as a defensive back and punter in 1949. He went to the New York Giants after the AAFC folded the following season.

He took over as head coach of the Dallas Cowboys when that team entered the NFL in 1960 and guided them through the 1988 season, compiling a 250–162–6 record. The Cowboys won 14 division championships, five conference titles, and two Super Bowls under Landry. The NFC coach of the year in 1975, he was dismissed after three straight losing seasons.

Dick Lane—Lane asked the Los Angeles Rams for a tryout in 1952 after attending Scottsbluff Junior College in Nebraska and spending two years in the Army. The Rams tried the speedy 6-foot-2, 210-pounder at wide receiver, then put him at cornerback. As a rookie, he intercepted 14 passes, still the NFL record, and ran two of them back for touchdowns.

Nicknamed "Night Train" after a hit song of the era, Lane was traded to the Chicago Cardinals in 1954 and to the Detroit Lions in 1960. He retired after the 1965 season with 68 career interceptions and 5 touchdowns. A five-time All-Pro, he was voted the best cornerback of the NFL's first fifty years in a 1969 poll and he was inducted into the Pro Football Hall of Fame in 1974.

Jim Langer—The Pittsburgh Steelers cut Langer during the 1970 pre-season, after he had played at South Dakota State, and he signed with the Miami Dolphins. Langer was at center for every offensive play when the Dolphins won all seventeen of their games, including the Super Bowl, in 1972.

Langer was named to the all-AFC team six years in a row, from 1973 through 1978. He spent the 1980 and 1981 seasons with the Minnesota Vikings before retiring and he was inducted into the Pro Football Hall of Fame in 1987.

Willie Lanier—Lanier joined the AFL's Kansas City Chiefs in 1967 after being a Little All-American at Morgan State. He was Kansas City's starting middle linebacker for eleven seasons and was named to all-AFL and all-AFC teams seven times.

The 6-foot-1, 245-pound Lanier, who had a 50-inch chest and 34-inch waist, was very fast as well as strong. He retired after the 1977 season with 27 interceptions and 15 fumble recoveries. Lanier was inducted into the Pro Football Hall of Fame in 1986.

Steve Largent—The nation's college leader with 14 touchdown receptions in both 1974 and 1975, Largent went to the Seattle Seahawks out of Tulsa University in 1976. Only 5-foot-11 and 185 pounds, he was a very durable and consistent receiver who gained more than 1,000 yards on receptions from 1978 through 1986, except for the strike-shortened 1982 season.

When he retired after the 1989 season, Largent held NFL records with 819 receptions, 13,089 yards, and 100 touchdown catches.

Yale Lary—A two-way halfback and punter at Texas A & M, Lary become a starting safety with the Detroit Lions as a rookie in 1952 and he took over the team's punting the following season. A four-time All-Pro, he led the NFL in punting three times.

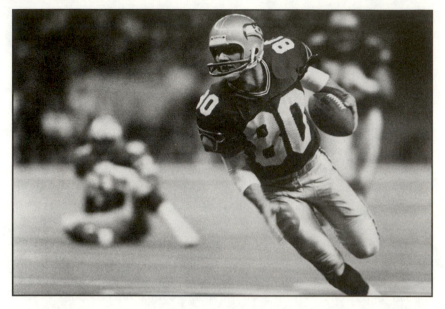

Inducted into the Pro Football Hall of Fame in 1995, Steve Largent of the Seattle Seahawks held NFL career records for passes caught, yardage, and touchdown receptions when he retired after the 1989 season. *Courtesy Seattle Seahawks*

Lary retired after the 1964 season with 50 career interceptions and an average of 44.3 yards per punt. He was elected to the Pro Football Hall of Fame in 1979.

Dante Lavelli—Lavelli was drafted into the Army in 1942, during his freshman year at Ohio State. He rejoined his college coach, Paul Brown, with the Cleveland Browns in the All-America Football Conference in 1946 and led the league with 40 receptions and 843 yards.

Nicknamed "Glue Fingers," Lavelli was a great clutch receiver. He caught the winning touchdown pass in Cleveland's 14–9 victory over the New York Yanks for the 1946 AAFC championship. The Browns joined the NFL after the AAFC folded in 1950 and beat the Los Angeles Rams 30–28 for the title that year, with Lavelli catching 11 passes, 2 for touchdowns.

Named to four all-league teams, Lavelli retired after the 1956 season. He entered the Pro Football Hall of Fame in 1975.

Bobby Layne—An All-American quarterback at Texas in 1947, Layne was with the Chicago Bears in 1948 and the New York Bulldogs in 1949. He started for the Detroit Lions from 1950 through 1958, leading the team to NFL championships in 1952 and 1953.

A fiery competitor who "couldn't do anything but beat you," in the words of a rival coach, Layne was known for winning games in the closing minutes. He took the Lions 80 yards in six plays to beat the Cleveland Browns 16–10 with seconds remaining in the 1953 championship game.

Layne went to the Pittsburgh Steelers in 1958 and retired after the 1962 season. He was inducted into the Pro Football Hall of Fame in 1967.

A great leader although not a great pure passer, quarterback Bobby Layne guided the Detroit Lions to NFL championships in 1952 and 1953. *Courtesy Detroit Lions*

Tuffy Leemans—A fullback at George Washington University, Leemans was moved to halfback when he joined the New York Giants in 1936. He led the league in rushing and was the only rookie named to the All-Pro team. Leemans was an All-Pro again in 1939.

A head injury forced his retirement after the 1943 season. Leemans rushed for 17 touchdowns, threw 25 touchdown passes, and had 3 touchdown receptions. He was elected to the Pro Football Hall of Fame in 1978.

Bob Lilly—Lilly, an All-American tackle at Texas Christian University, was the first player chosen in the college draft by the Dallas Cowboys in 1961. The 6-foot-5, 260-pounder became the key player in Dallas's "Doomsday Defense."

An eight-time All-Pro, Lilly missed only one game in his fifteen seasons with Dallas. He set a Super Bowl record by tackling Miami quarterback Bob Griese for a 29-yard loss when Dallas beat Miami 24–3 for the 1971 NFL championship. Lilly retired after the 1974 season and was inducted into the Pro Football Hall of Fame in 1980.

Larry Little—After playing at Bethune-Cookman College, Little signed with the San Diego Chargers as a free agent in 1967 and was traded to the Miami Dolphins in 1969. His combination of strength and speed made him one of the best guards in football.

An All-AFC selection from 1971 through 1974, Little played for two Super Bowl champions, including the undefeated 1972 Dolphins. He retired after the 1980 season. Little was elected to the Pro Football Hall of Fame in 1993.

James Lofton—A track star and All-American wide receiver at Stanford in 1977, the 6-foot-3, 190-pound Lofton was the NFL's rookie of the year with the Green Bay Packers in 1978. He was traded to the Oakland Raiders in 1987, went to the Buffalo Bills in 1989, and returned to the Raiders in 1993.

Lofton is the NFL career leader with 14,004 yards on receptions. He ranks fourth all-time with 764 receptions and tenth with 75 touchdown catches through the 1993 season.

Vince Lombardi—Lombardi was one of the "Seven Blocks of Granite" as a guard at Fordham in 1935 and 1936. He spent ten years as a high school coach and seven years as a college assistant before joining the New York Giants' staff in 1954. With the Giants, Lombardi helped develop a powerful offense that took the team to four division titles and the 1956 NFL championship.

As coach of the Green Bay Packers from 1959 through 1967, Vince Lombardi produced five NFL champions and the winners of the first two Super Bowls. Lombardi built a powerful running attack by adding single-wing blocking principles to the T formation. *Hank Lefebvre Photo/ Collection of Lee L. Lefebvre*

In 1959, he became coach and general manager of the Green Bay Packers. Lombardi quickly built the best team in football, winning championships in 1961, 1962, 1965, 1966, and 1967. The Packers also won the first two Super Bowls. After spending the 1968 season as Green Bay's general manager, he returned to coaching with the Washington Redskins, but died of cancer after only one season there.

Lombardi had a 105–35–6 record in regular season games and was 9–1 in the playoffs. He was inducted into the Pro Football Hall of Fame in 1971.

Ronnie Lott—An All-American at Southern California, Lott joined the San Francisco 49ers as a starting cornerback in 1981. He led the NFL with 10 interceptions in 1986 and was then moved to free safety. He became a strong safety with the Oakland Raiders in 1991, when he had a league-leading 8 interceptions.

The 6-foot-1, 203-pound Lott was named an All-Pro at all three positions. A very hard hitter with a nose for the ball, he went to the New York Jets as a free agent in 1993.

Sid Luckman—Luckman was a single-wing tailback at Columbia University before joining the Chicago Bears in 1939. He became their starting quarterback the following year, when the Bears developed the modern T formation. A fine ball-handler, excellent passer, and very intelligent signal-caller, Luckman helped take the Bears to championships in 1940, 1943, and 1946.

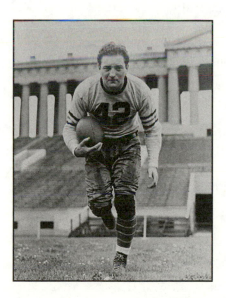

The first modern T-formation quarterback, Sid Luckman guided the Chicago Bears to NFL championships in 1940, 1943, and 1946. He still shares the league record with 7 touchdown passes in a single game. *Courtesy Chicago Bears*

The Bears' 73–0 win over the Washington Redskins in the 1940 title game led most other NFL teams to adopt the T formation within a short time. Luckman was the league's player of the year in 1943, when he set an

NFL record with 7 touchdown passes in a game. He also passed for five touchdowns in Chicago's 41–21 championship win over the Redskins, and he scored the winning touchdown on a 19-yard run when they beat the New York Giants 21–14 for the 1946 title.

Luckman retired after the 1950 season. He was elected to the Pro Football Hall of Fame in 1965.

Link Lyman—After playing at the University of Nebraska, Lyman entered pro football with the Canton Bulldogs in 1922. The 6-foot-2, 240-pounder was listed as a tackle, but he frequently moved on defense, often lining up in a gap, he could use his speed to charge into the offensive backfield.

The Bulldogs won two NFL titles in Canton and a third in 1924, when they were temporarily based in Cleveland. Lyman went to the Frankford Yellowjackets in 1925 and to the Chicago Bears in 1926. He was out of football in 1929 and 1932 and he retired after the 1934 season. Lyman was inducted into the Pro Football Hall of Fame in 1964.

John Mackey—The first great tight end, Mackey wasn't inducted into the Pro Football Hall of Fame until 1992, twenty years after his retirement, because of his long-time leadership of the NFL Players' Association. The 6-foot-2, 220-pounder joined the Baltimore Colts in 1963 after playing at Syracuse. An outstanding blocker, he had great speed that allowed him to average more than 20 yards per reception in 1963 and 1965.

When the Colts beat the Dallas Cowboys 16–13 in Super Bowl V, after the 1970 season, Mackey had a 75-yard touchdown catch on a tipped ball. He became president of the Players' Association that year and led the 1971 strike. Mackey retired after spending the 1972 season with the San Diego Chargers.

John Madden—A tackle at California Poly-San Luis Obispo, Madden suffered a career-ending knee injury as a rookie with the Philadelphia Eagles in 1959. He coached at the college level until joining the Oakland Raiders' staff in 1967 and he became Oakland's head coach in 1969.

In ten seasons, Madden took the Raiders to seven division titles and the 1976 NFL championship. He retired after the 1978 season with a 112–39–7 record and became a popular television commentator with CBS and FOX.

Gino Marchetti—After serving in World War II, Marchetti played at the University of San Francisco and joined the Dallas Texans of the NFL in 1952. The team folded after that season and he went to the new Baltimore Colts franchise. The 6-foot-4, 240-pound defensive end soon became the league's premier pass rusher.

An All-Pro from 1957 through 1962, Marchetti was named the NFL's player of the year in 1958, when the Colts beat the New York Giants 23–17 to win the championship in the first overtime game in history. He retired after the 1964 season, but played briefly in 1966 before retiring permanently. Marchetti was inducted into the Pro Football Hall of Fame in 1972.

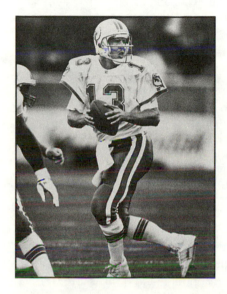

Gifted with a strong arm and a very quick release, quarterback Dan Marino of the Miami Dolphins has passed for more than 4,000 yards in a season for a record five times. *Courtesy Miami Dolphins*

Dan Marino—Because Marino had a disappointing senior season at the University of Pittsburgh, he was only the sixth quarterback chosen in the 1983 draft, but he turned out to be the best. A starter with the Miami Dolphins as a rookie, he won the Bert Bell Trophy as the NFL's player of the year in 1984, when he passed for 5,084 yards and 48 touchdowns, both records.

Because of his quick release, the 6-foot-3, 220-pound Marino is very hard to sack. He threw 759 consecutive passes without being thrown for a loss from 1988 into the 1989 season. Marino has set career records by passing for 4,000 or more yards in five different seasons.

Ollie Matson—An outstanding two-way back at the University of San Francisco, the 6-foot-2, 220-pound Matson was also a world-class sprinter who won a bronze medal in the 400-meter relay at the 1952 Olympics. He then joined the Chicago Cardinals and was an All-Pro defensive back as a rookie.

After a year in the Army, he became a running back in 1954. Matson was traded to the Los Angeles Rams in 1959. He spent the 1963 season with the Detroit Lions and was with the Philadelphia Eagles from 1964 through 1966. In his 14 professional seasons, Matson accounted for a total of 12,799 yards and 72 touchdowns on rushes, pass receptions, and kick returns. He was elected to the Pro Football Hall of Fame in 1972 and is also a member of the College Football Hall of Fame.

Don Maynard—Maynard joined the New York Giants as a wide receiver in 1958 out of Texas Western, but he was cut after catching just five passes. He then spent a year in the Canadian Football League and joined the New York Titans of the new AFL in 1960. The team was renamed the Jets in 1963.

The 6-foot-1, 185-pound speedster was one of the AFL's outstanding deep receivers, especially after Joe Namath became the Jets' starting quarterback. Maynard averaged more than 20 yards a catch four times, with a high of 22.8 in 1968. He retired after spending the 1973 season with the St. Louis Cardinals and was inducted into the Pro Football Hall of Fame in 1987.

George A. McAfee—An All-American halfback at Duke in 1939, the 6-foot, 177-pound McAfee joined the Chicago Bears in 1940. An outstanding breakaway runner, he returned a kickoff 93 yards for a touchdown in his first professional game and he tied the NFL record with 12 touchdowns in 1941.

McAfee spent nearly four years in the Navy, rejoining the Bears late in the 1945 season. He retired after the 1950 season with a total of 4,767 yards and 35 touchdowns on rushing, receptions, and returns. McAfee was elected to the Pro Football Hall of Fame in 1966 and he's also a member of the College Hall of Fame.

Mike McCormack—After graduating from Kansas, McCormack joined the New York Yanks of the NFL as an offensive tackle and linebacker in 1951. He then spent two years in the Army and went to the Cleveland Browns in 1954, when he was a starter at defensive middle guard.

McCormack was moved to tackle in 1955 and he served as Cleveland's offensive captain until he retired after the 1962 season. He later coached the Philadelphia Eagles, Baltimore Colts, and Seattle Seahawks. McCormack was inducted into the Pro Football Hall of Fame in 1984.

Hugh McElhenny—McElhenny joined the San Francisco 49ers in 1952 out of the University of Washington and was named the NFL's rookie of the year, averaging 7 yards per carry. The 6-foot-1, 198-pounder was gifted with speed and great cutting ability. An All-Pro in his first two seasons, he was limited to only 64 carries because of a knee injury in 1954, but he still scored 6 touchdowns.

He went to the Minnesota Vikings in the 1961 expansion draft and finished his career with the New York Giants in 1963 and the Detroit Lions in 1964. In 13 professional seasons, McElhenny gained 11,369 yards and scored 60 touchdowns on rushes, receptions, and kick returns. He was inducted into the Pro Football Hall of Fame in 1970.

Mike Michalske—A guard and fullback at Penn State, Michalske joined the New York Yankees of the American Football League in 1926. The Yankees entered the NFL in 1927 but folded in 1929 and Michalske went to the Green Bay Packers. He was a starting guard on three championship teams in his first three seasons.

The 6-foot, 210-pound Michalske was a four-time All-Pro. He retired in 1936 but returned to the Packers for the 1937 season. Michalske was elected to the Pro Football Hall of Fame in 1964.

Wayne Millner—Millner was an outstanding clutch receiver whose touchdown catch with seconds to play gave Notre Dame an 18–13 victory over Ohio State in 1935. He joined the Boston Redskins in 1936. The team moved to Washington the following season.

When Washington beat the Chicago Bears 28–21 for the 1937 NFL championship, Millner scored on touchdown passes of 55 and 78 yards. After serving in the Navy for three years, he finished his career with Washington in 1945 and was inducted into the Pro Football Hall of Fame in 1968.

Bobby Mitchell—A running back at Illinois, the 6-foot, 195-pound Mitchell joined the Cleveland Browns in 1958 and had 232 yards rushing in one game in 1959. In 1962, the Browns traded him to the Washington Redskins, where he became a wide receiver and led the NFL with 72 receptions and 1,384 yards.

An All-Pro in 1962 and 1964, he retired after the 1968 season with 91 career touchdowns and was elected to the Pro Football Hall of Fame in 1983.

Ron Mix—Mix started at tackle for three years at Southern California and joined the Los Angeles Chargers of the newly formed AFL in 1960. The team moved to San Diego the following season. The 6-foot-4, 255-pounder was an excellent downfield blocker because of his unusual speed.

An All-AFL selection from 1960 through 1968, he retired after the 1969 season but returned to play for the Oakland Raiders in 1971. Mix was a unanimous choice for the all-time All-AFL team and he was inducted into the Pro Football Hall of Fame in 1979.

Art Monk—The 6-foot-3, 210-pound Monk joined the Washington Redskins as a wide receiver in 1980 after being a running back at Syracuse. Because of his size, leaping ability, and sure hands, he was the team's chief possession receiver for most of his career.

Monk set a record with 106 receptions in 1984 and he had 7 receptions for 113 yards in Washington's 27–24 Super Bowl win over the

Buffalo Bills after the 1991 season. He left the Redskins with a career record of 888 catches after the 1993 season and signed with the Jets.

The only player to be named Most Valuable Player in the Super Bowl three times, Joe Montana quarterbacked the San Francisco 49ers to four Super Bowl champion-ships and was named the Associated Press male athlete of the year in 1989 and 1990. *Courtesy San Francisco 49ers*

Joe Montana—As a quarterback at Notre Dame, Montana won a reputation for leading his team to last-minute victories. He joined the San Francisco 49ers in 1979 and became a starter the following year, when he led the NFL with a 64.5 completion percentage. Montana played on four Super Bowl champions and is the only player to be named Super Bowl MVP three times. The Associated Press male athlete of the year in 1989 and 1990, he missed most of the 1991 and 1992 seasons with an injury and was traded to the Kansas City Chiefs in 1993. Montana retired after the 1994 season.

Lenny Moore—The 6-foot-1, 198-pound Moore joined the Baltimore Colts out of Penn State in 1956 and was named the NFL's rookie of the year. In twelve seasons with Baltimore, he was used as both a running back and a wide receiver. He caught 6 passes for 101 yards in the team's 23–17 overtime win over the New York Giants for the 1958 NFL championship.

In 1964, he scored a record 20 touchdowns rushing and receiving. A five-time All-Pro, Moore retired after the 1967 season with a total of 12,393 yards and 106 touchdowns. He was inducted into the Pro Football Hall of Fame in 1975.

Marion Motley—After a brief college career, Motley played for Paul Brown with the Great Lakes Naval Training Station team in 1945 and went with Brown to the Cleveland Browns of the All-America Football Conference the following year. The 6-foot-1, 238-pound fullback was a powerful blocker and runner who had a record 3,024 yards rushing in the league's four years.

The AAFC folded in 1950 and the Browns entered the NFL. Motley led the league in rushing that season but was hampered by injuries the next three years. He sat out the 1954 season and retired after a brief comeback attempt in 1955. Motley, who averaged 5.7 yards a carry during his career, was elected to the Pro Football Hall of Fame in 1968.

Anthony Munoz—The 6-foot-5, 285-pound Munoz joined the Cincinnati Bengals out of Southern California in 1980. An All-Pro seven times in his first twelve seasons, he missed most of 1992 with an injury and retired. Many experts consider Munoz the greatest offensive tackle in NFL history.

George Musso—A four-year starter at James Millikin College in Illinois, Musso joined the Chicago Bears in 1933 and was an All-Pro tackle in 1935. He then moved to guard and was named an All-Pro at that position in 1937. Nicknamed "Big Bear," the 6-foot-2, 270-pound Musso was a crushing blocker and outstanding defensive lineman. He played for four NFL championship teams before retiring after the 1944 season. Musso was inducted into the Pro Football Hall of Fame in 1982.

Bronko Nagurski—Nagurski was a fullback and defensive tackle at Minnesota. An All-American in 1929, he joined the Chicago Bears the following year. A hard, punishing runner, the 6-foot-2, 225-pounder was used at both tackle and linebacker on defense and he sometimes played offensive tackle after 1935.

An All-Pro from 1932 through 1934, Nagurski retired from football to become a professional wrestler in 1938. He returned to the Bears for the 1943 season before retiring permanently. Nagurski was elected a charter member of the Pro Football Hall of Fame in 1963.

Joe Namath—Named to some All-American teams as Alabama's quarterback in 1964, Namath signed with the AFL's New York Jets for a reported $400,000 the following year, bringing the young league instant publicity and respectability. He immediately became the team's starter and was named rookie of the year.

The brash Namath was sometimes criticized for his flamboyant lifestyle, but "Broadway Joe" passed for a record 4,007 yards in 1967 and took the Jets to the AFL championship in 1968, when he was named the league's player of the year. Namath then guaranteed victory over the favored Baltimore Colts in Super Bowl III and helped deliver it, completing 17 of 28 passes in the Jets' 16–7 win.

Namath retired after spending one season with the Los Angeles Rams in 1977. He was inducted into the Pro Football Hall of Fame in 1985.

Ernie Nevers—Nevers was an All-American fullback at Stanford in 1923 and again in 1925 after missing most of his junior season with an injury. As the tailback in the double wing, he was a triple threat who handled the ball on every play. The 6-foot-1, 205-pounder entered the NFL with the Duluth Eskimos in 1926.

After sitting out the 1928 season, he spent three years with the Chicago Cardinals. Nevers set a record by scoring all of his team's points in a 40–6 win over the Chicago Bears in 1929. He retired after the 1931 season and was elected a charter member of the Pro Football Hall of Fame in 1963. He also belongs to the College Hall of Fame.

Ray Nitschke—A fullback and linebacker at Illinois, Nitschke became the Green Bay Packers' starting middle linebacker as a rookie in 1958. The 6-foot-3, 235-pounder played for five championship teams and was named most valuable player in Green Bay's 16–7 victory over the New York Giants for the 1962 title.

He retired after the 1972 season and was inducted into the Pro Football Hall of Fame in 1978.

Chuck Noll—Noll graduated from the University of Dayton in 1953 and was a linebacker and offensive guard with the Cleveland Browns for seven seasons. He spent nine years as an assistant coach before taking over the Pittsburgh Steelers in 1969.

Noll built an aggressive defense and ball-control offense that brought Pittsburgh four Super Bowl championships during the 1970s. He retired after the 1991 season with a 209–156–1 record. Noll was elected to the Pro Football Hall of Fame in 1993.

Leo Nomellini—The 6-foot-3, 284-pound Nomellini was an All-American tackle at Minnesota in 1948 and 1949. He joined the San Francisco 49ers in 1950 and was an All-Pro offensive tackle twice. Then he moved to defensive tackle and won All-Pro honors four more times. He retired after the 1963 season and was inducted into the Pro Football Hall of Fame in 1969.

Merlin Olsen—Olsen won the 1961 Outland Trophy as the nation's top college lineman at Utah State and then joined the Los Angeles Rams. The 6-foot-5, 270-pounder became the top player on the "Fearsome Foursome" defense, a five-time All-Pro defensive tackle who played in four straight Pro Bowls, a record.

Olsen retired after the 1976 season to become a television commentator. He was inducted into the Pro Football Hall of Fame in 1982 and is also a member of the College Hall of Fame.

Jim Otto—In the ten-year history of the AFL, Otto was its only all-league center. He joined the Oakland Raiders as a free agent from the University of Miami in 1960 and was the All-AFL center from then through 1969. After the AFL merged into the NFL in 1970, Otto was the All-AFC center for another three seasons.

The 6-foot-2, 255-pounder retired after the 1974 season. He was inducted into the Pro Football Hall of Fame in 1980.

Steve Owen—Owen played tackle at Phillips University in Oklahoma and was with the Kansas City Cowboys of the NFL in 1924 and 1925, then joined the New York Giants. He took over as the team's coach in 1931.

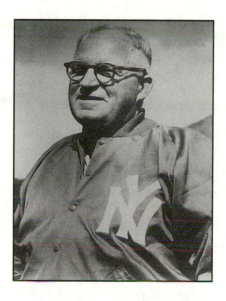

Steve Owen emphasized defense in his twenty-three years as coach of the New York Giants, from 1931 through 1953. He guided the team to NFL championships in 1934 and 1938. *Courtesy New York Giants*

In twenty-three seasons, Owen took the Giants to eight NFL championship games, but they won only twice, in 1935 and 1938. A believer in fundamentals and solid defense, he designed the "umbrella defense" that eventually became the modern 4–3. After the Giants held the Cleveland Browns to only 21 points in three games in 1950, most other NFL teams began using the defense.

Owen resigned after the 1953 season with a 153–108–17 record. He was inducted into the Pro Football Hall of Fame in 1966.

Alan Page—An All-American defensive end at Notre Dame in 1966, Page became a defensive tackle with the Minnesota Vikings and anchored their "Purple People Eater" defense. At 6-foot-4 and 240 pounds, he was amazingly quick at rushing the passer right up the middle.

Page was named the NFL's player of the year in 1971, when he had 10 quarterback sacks and 3 safeties. He was released by the Vikings in 1978 and joined the Chicago Bears. Page retired after the 1981 season without ever missing a game. An All-Pro from 1968 through 1976, he was elected to the Pro Football Hall of Fame in 1988.

Ace Parker—A 1936 All-American at Duke, where he was a triple-threat tailback in the single wing, Parker joined the NFL's Brooklyn Dodgers in 1937. He also played professional baseball for several years.

Parker was the NFL's player of the year in 1940, when he scored 5 touchdowns, threw 10 touchdown passes, punted for a 38-yard average, and kicked 19 conversions. After nearly four years in the Army during World War II, he ended his professional career with the Boston Yankees in 1945 and the New York Yankees of the All-America Football Conference in 1946.

He was inducted into the Pro Football Hall of Fame in 1972 and he's also a member of the College Hall of Fame.

Jim Parker—Parker won the Outland Trophy as the nation's best college lineman in 1956, when he was an All-American guard at Ohio State. He became a tackle with the Baltimore Colts and was an All-Pro at that position four years in a row. The Colts then moved him to guard and he won All-Pro honors four more times.

Known as "Johnny Unitas's bodyguard" because he was an excellent pass blocker, Parker retired after the 1967 season. In 1973, he became the first pure offensive lineman elected to the Pro Football Hall of Fame.

Considered by many the greatest all-around running back in NFL history, Walter Payton holds career records with 16,726 rushing yards and 110 rushing touchdowns in 13 seasons with the Chicago Bears. He was also an outstanding blocker and receiver.
Courtesy Chicago Bears

Walter Payton—A Little All-American at Jackson State, the 5-foot-10, 203-pound Payton joined the Chicago Bears in 1975 but didn't become a full-time starter until his second season. He then led the NFC in rushing for five straight seasons. Also an excellent receiver and blocker, Payton was named conference player of the year in 1976 and NFL player of the year in 1977, and he won the 1985 Bert Bell Trophy as the league's most valuable player.

When he retired after the 1987 season, Payton held NFL records with 16,726 rushing yards, 110 rushing touchdowns, 10 seasons in which he gained more than 1,000 yards, and 275 rushing yards in a game. He was inducted into the Pro Football Hall of Fame in 1993.

Joe Perry—Perry played football at Compton Junior College and in the navy before joining the San Francisco 49ers of the All-America Football Conference in 1948. The 6-foot, 200-pounder led the league with 10 touchdowns on only 77 rushing attempts as a rookie.

The 49ers entered the NFL in 1950, after the AAFC folded. Nicknamed "Joe the Jet," Perry was the league's rushing leader in 1953 and 1954. After spending 1961 and 1962 with the Baltimore Colts, Perry returned to the 49ers for one season before retiring. He was elected to the Pro Football Hall of Fame in 1969.

Pete Pihos—An end and fullback at Indiana, Pihos entered the NFL with the Philadelphia Eagles in 1947. He was an All-Pro as a two-way end in 1948 and 1949, when the Eagles won NFL championships. Pihos was an All-Pro defensive end in 1952, then moved to the offensive unit and won All-Pro honors the next three years.

He retired after the 1955 season and was inducted into the Pro Football Hall of Fame in 1970.

Jerry Rice—Rice joined the San Francisco 49ers out of Mississippi Valley State in 1985. He led the NFL with 1,570 reception yards in his second season and set a record with 22 touchdown catches in 1987. Sure-handed and strong, the 6-foot-2, 200-pound Rice is a dangerous runner who often turns a short pass into a long gain.

Rice caught 11 passes for 215 yards and a touchdown to be named most valuable player in San Francisco's 20–16 victory over the Cincinnati Bengals in Super Bowl XXIII. After the 1993 season, he held the NFL record with 117 touchdown receptions.

John Riggins—After breaking Gale Sayers' school rushing records at Kansas, Riggins went to the New York Jets in 1971. A 6-foot-2, 230-pounder with speed, he became a free agent in 1976 and signed with the Washington Redskins.

He sat out the 1980 season in a salary dispute but returned in 1981 and was named most valuable player in Super Bowl XVII, after the 1982 season, when he rushed 38 times for 166 yards, including a 43-yard touchdown run, to lead Washington to a 27–17 win over the Miami Dolphins.

Riggins rushed for 1,347 yards and a record 24 touchdowns to win the 1983 Bert Bell Trophy as the player of the year. He retired after the 1985 season with 11,352 yards and 104 touchdowns rushing. Riggins was inducted into the Pro Football Hall of Fame in 1992.

Jim Ringo—Ringo joined the Green Bay Packers out of Syracuse University in 1953 and went on to set a record by starting 182 consecutive games at center. A five-time All-Pro with Green Bay, he was traded to the Philadelphia Eagles because of a salary dispute in 1964 and he retired after the 1967 season.

Ringo was elected to the Pro Football Hall of Fame in 1981.

Andy Robustelli—A nineteenth-round draft choice out of Arnold College, the 6-foot, 230-pound Robustelli became a starting defensive end with the Los Angeles Rams in 1951 and was an All-Pro each of the next two seasons. An outstanding pass rusher, he was traded to the New York Giants in 1956 and won the Bert Bell Award as the NFL's player of the year in 1962.

An All-Pro five times with the Giants, he retired after the 1964 season and was inducted into the Pro Football Hall of Fame in 1971.

Bob St. Clair—An end at the University of San Francisco and Tulsa University, St. Clair became an offensive tackle with the San Francisco 49ers in 1953. The 6-foot-9, 265-pounder captained the team from 1957 through 1964, when he retired. He blocked ten field goal attempts, a league record, in 1956. St. Clair was elected to the Pro Football Hall of Fame in 1990.

Barry Sanders won the Heisman Trophy in 1988 and was the NFL's rookie of the year as a running back with the Detroit Lions in 1989. He has rushed for more than 1,000 yards in each of his six professional seasons. *Courtesy Detroit Lions*

Barry Sanders—Sanders entered the NFL draft after winning the Heisman Trophy as a junior at Oklahoma State in 1988, when he gained a record 2,628 yards. He was the NFL's rookie of the year with the Detroit Lions in 1989, gaining 1,470 yards and scoring 14 touchdowns.

A combination of speed, strength, and incredible cutting ability have allowed the 5-foot-10, 205-pound Sanders to gain more than 1,000 yards in each of his professional seasons, and he's been a three-time All-Pro.

Gale Sayers—An All-American at Kansas in 1963 and 1964, Sayers was the NFL's rookie of the year with the Chicago Bears in 1965, when he scored a record 22 touchdowns and gained 2,272 yards rushing, receiving, and returning kicks. He was the NFL leader in rushing and kickoff returns in his second year.

After missing most of the 1968 season with a knee injury, Sayers again led in rushing with 1,032 yards in 1969. A recurrence of the knee problem forced him to retire in 1971 with a total of 9,435 yards and 56 touchdowns. In 1977, at the age of 34, he became the youngest player ever elected to the Pro Football Hall of Fame.

Joe Schmidt—The 6-foot-2, 220-pound Schmidt joined the Detroit Lions in 1953 out of the University of Pittsburgh. As Detroit's middle linebacker for thirteen seasons, he was an All-Pro eight times. Schmidt retired after the 1965 season and coached the Lions to a 43–34–7 record from 1967 through 1972. He was elected to the Pro Football Hall of Fame in 1973.

Sterling Sharpe—Sharpe was an All-American at South Carolina in 1987 and became a starting wide receiver for the Green Bay Packers the following year. He led the NFC with 90 receptions in 1989. The 6-foot-1, 205-pounder is very similar to Jerry Rice in strength and in his ability to run with the ball after the catch.

Sharpe set a record with 106 receptions in 1992 and he broke that with 112 catches in 1993. Through the 1994 season, he had 595 receptions for 8,134 yards and 65 touchdowns.

Art Shell—Shell joined the Oakland Raiders in 1968 out of Maryland State-Eastern Shore. The 6-foot-5, 285-pounder was a starting offensive tackle for the Raiders until a knee injury forced his retirement in 1982. A three-time All-AFC selection, he took over as the Raiders' head coach in 1989.

Only the second black coach in NFL history and the first since 1922, he guided the team to the AFC championship game in 1990, but they lost to the Buffalo Bills. He was inducted into the Pro Football Hall of Fame as a player in 1989.

Don Shula—After spending seven seasons in the NFL as a defensive back, Shula was an assistant coach for five years before taking over the Baltimore Colts in 1963. He had a 71–23–4 record in seven seasons there, including the 1968 NFL championship. Shula went to the Miami Dolphins in 1970.

The Dolphins won consecutive championships in 1972 and 1973 and the 1972 team won all seventeen of its games. In 1993, Shula became the winningest coach in NFL history. He currently has a 325–158–6 record.

In 1993, coach Don Shula of the Miami Dolphins achieved his 325th victory to set an NFL record. *Courtesy Miami Dolphins*

O. J. Simpson—The winner of the 1968 Heisman Trophy at Southern California, Simpson wasn't an immediate star in the NFL because the Buffalo Bills used him as a part-time player for his first three seasons. But he was installed as a starter at running back in 1972, when he led the NFL in rushing.

The 6-foot-1, 212-pounder in 1973 became the first player ever to rush for more than 2,000 yards in a season. He was named the AP's male athlete of the year. After rushing for more than 1,000 yards during the next three seasons, a knee injury slowed Simpson in 1977. He finished his career with the San Francisco 49ers in 1978 and 1979.

Simpson retired with 11,236 rushing yards and a total of 76 touchdowns. A member of the College and Pro Football Halls of Fame, he was accused of murdering his ex-wife and a friend of hers in 1994.

Mike Singletary—Singletary joined the Chicago Bears in 1981 out of Baylor. As Chicago's middle linebacker, he led the defense that overwhelmed opponents in 1985, when the Bears lost only one game and beat the New England Patriots 46–10 in Super Bowl XX.

An All-Pro from 1983 through 1986, the 5-foot-11, 230-pound Singletary was UPI's defensive player of the year in 1984 and 1985. He retired after the 1992 season with 44 career interceptions, 19 quarterback sacks, and 12 fumble recoveries.

Bruce Smith—At Virginia Tech, Smith won the 1984 Outland Trophy as the best college lineman. He was the first player chosen in the 1984 college draft, by the Buffalo Bills. With Buffalo the 6-foot-4, 273-pounder has become one of the dominant defensive lineman in the NFL.

Bruce Smith won the 1984 Outland Trophy as the nation's best collegiate lineman and he then became one of the NFL's dominant defensive players with the Buffalo Bills, averaging more than 12 sacks a season. *Courtesy Buffalo Bills*

He has used his quickness and speed to average more than 12 sacks a season during his career, even though he missed parts of three seasons because of injury and a substance abuse suspension.

Emmitt Smith—Smith was an All-American halfback at Florida in 1989 and he joined the Dallas Cowboys the following season. After gaining more than 900 yards as a part-time player, he became a starter in 1991, when he led the NFC with 1,563 yards rushing.

The 5-foot-9, 210-pound Smith emerged as the league's best all-around running back in 1992. After leading the league in rushing and helping Dallas to a Super Bowl title, he held out in 1993. The Cowboys lost their first two games, signed Smith, and won another Super Bowl. Smith again led the league in rushing and he became the first player ever named most valuable player in the regular season and the Super Bowl.

Jackie Smith—A 10th-round draft choice out of Northwestern Louisiana State, Smith joined the St. Louis Cardinals in 1962 and took over as the starting tight end two seasons later. Twice an All-Conference selection, the 6-foot-4, 230-pounder retired after playing with the Dallas Cowboys in 1978. He was the all-time leading receiver among tight ends with 480 receptions. Smith was inducted into the Pro Football Hall of Fame in 1994.

Bart Starr—After starting as a freshman at Alabama, Starr was only a part-time player during his last three seasons, when Alabama concentrated on a running attack. He joined the Green Bay Packers in 1956 and took over as the team's starting quarterback in 1960. The Packers won six division titles, five NFL championships, and the first two Super Bowls during the next eight years. A very accurate passer, Starr was the NFL passing champion in 1962, 1964, and 1966, and he once threw 294 consecutive passes without an interception. He was named the MVP in Super Bowls I and II, completing 29 passes in 47 attempts for 452 yards and 3 touchdowns. Starr retired after the 1971 season and coached the Packers to a 52–76–2 record from 1975 through 1983. He was inducted into the Pro Football Hall of Fame in 1977.

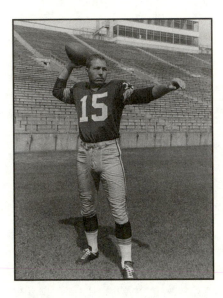

Green Bay quarterback Bart Starr was named most valuable player in the first two Super Bowls. He guided the team to five NFL championships in eight years. *Hank Lefebvre Photo/ Collection of Lee L. Lefebvre*

Roger Staubach—The Heisman Trophy winner as a junior quarterback at Navy in 1963, Staubach had to spend four years in service before joining the Dallas Cowboys in 1969. He became the starter in 1971 and was named NFL player of the year that season, when he led the Cowboys to a 24–3 win over the Miami Dolphins in the Super Bowl.

Twice the NFL passing champion and a three-time All-Pro, Staubach also quarterbacked the Cowboys to their second Super Bowl victory, after the 1977 season. He retired after the 1979 season with 22,700 passing yards and 153 touchdown throws. Known as "Roger the Dodger" because of his scrambling ability, Staubach ran for 20 touchdowns. He's a member of the College and Pro Football Halls of Fame.

Ernie Stautner—Stautner served in the Marines before becoming a starting tackle at Boston College for four years. He joined the Pittsburgh Steelers in 1950. The 6-foot-2 Stautner weighed only 235 pounds, but he was very quick. The Steelers often moved him to defensive end in passing situations because of his ability to rush the quarterback.

Stautner retired after the 1963 season and was elected to the Pro Football Hall of Fame in 1969. For more than twenty years, he was the defensive coordinator for the Dallas Cowboys.

Jan Stenerud—A native of Norway, Stenerud went to Montana State on a skiing scholarship. He didn't play college football, but he impressed the Kansas City Chiefs in a tryout and became the team's place kicker in 1967. He was with the Green Bay Packers from 1980 through 1983 and the Minnesota Vikings in 1984 and 1985.

Stenerud set a record by kicking 16 consecutive field goals in 1969 and he had 22 in 24 attempts in 1981, setting another record with a 91.7 percentage. In 1991, he became the first pure kicking specialist elected to the Pro Football Hall of Fame.

Ken Strong—Strong captained the New York University team in 1928, when he led the nation with 160 points. He joined the NFL's Staten Island Stapletons the following season and went to the New York Giants in 1933. The league's leading scorer that season and an All-Pro the following year, Strong scored 17 points when the Giants beat the Chicago Bears 30–13 for the 1934 championship.

After spending two years with the New York Yanks in the American Football League, Strong sat out the 1938 season and returned to the Giants in 1939. He then retired, but came back in 1944 and remained with the Giants as a kicking specialist through 1947. Strong scored 496 NFL points and was inducted into the Pro Football Hall of Fame in 1967.

Joe Stydahar—After captaining the West Virginia team in 1935, Stydahar joined the Chicago Bears as a starting tackle. He was an All-Pro from 1937 through 1940. Stydahar served in the Navy during World War II and returned to the Bears for a final season in 1946.

Known as "Jumbo Joe," the 6-foot-4, 230-pound Stydahar took over as coach of the Los Angeles Rams in 1950 and guided them to the 1951 NFL championship. He also coached the Chicago Cardinals in 1954 and 1955. Stydahar was inducted into the Pro Football Hall of Fame in 1967.

Fran Tarkenton—Tarkenton passed for four touchdowns and ran for another in his first game with the Minnesota Vikings in 1961, out of the University of Georgia. A great scrambler and leader, he was Minnesota's starting quarterback until 1967, when he was traded to the New York Giants.

He returned to the Vikings in 1972 and led them to three Super Bowl appearances, but they lost all three times. The consensus player of the year in 1975, Tarkenton retired after the 1977 season with a record 47,003 passing yards and 342 touchdowns. He also ran for 32 touchdowns. Tarkenton was elected to the Pro Football Hall of Fame in 1986.

Charley Taylor—A running back at Arizona State, Taylor joined the Washington Redskins in 1964 and was moved to wide receiver in 1966, when he led the NFL with 72 catches. At 6-foot-3 and 210 pounds, he had excellent speed and was a dangerous runner after catching the ball.

He led the league again with 70 receptions in 1967. A shoulder injury forced him out for all of 1976 and he retired after the 1977 season with 649 catches, a record at the time, and 79 touchdown receptions. Taylor also scored 11 touchdowns as a running back. He was inducted into the Pro Football Hall of Fame in 1984.

Jim Taylor—Taylor joined the Green Bay Packers in 1958 out of LSU and became the team's starting fullback the following year. A rugged, durable runner, he was a key member of the Packer offense, in large part because of his blocking ability. Though light for a fullback at 215 pounds, Taylor successfully took on defensive tackles to help the famed power sweep work consistently.

A 1,000-yard rusher from 1960 through 1962, Taylor was named NFL player of the year by the AP in 1962, when he led the league with 1,174 yards and a record 19 rushing touchdowns. He went to the New Orleans Saints in 1967 and retired after that season with a total of 8,597 yards and 93 touchdowns. Taylor was inducted into the Pro Football Hall of Fame in 1976.

Lawrence Taylor—Known as "L. T.," Taylor was an All-American linebacker at North Carolina in 1980. With the New York Giants in 1981, the 6-foot-3, 240-pounder was named the NFL's rookie of the year and the AP defensive player of the year. He won the AP award again in 1982, and he was chosen the NFC defensive player of the year by UPI in 1983 and 1986.

Exceptionally fast, Taylor was a six-time All-Pro and the best player on a Giant defense that helped the team win two Super Bowl championships. He retired after the 1993 season.

Derrick Thomas—Thomas won the Butkus Award as the nation's best college linebacker at Alabama in 1988 and he became a starting outside backer with the Kansas City Chiefs the following season. At 6-foot-3 and 242 pounds, Thomas has been a very effective blitzer because of his outstanding speed.

He set a record with 7 sacks in a game in 1990, when he led the NFL with 20 for the season. Through 1993, Thomas had 65 sacks and 12 fumble recoveries in five seasons.

Thurman Thomas—A second-round draft choice of the Buffalo Bills in 1988 out of Oklahoma State, Thomas took over as a starter at running back in his second season. Much like Emmitt Smith, his counterpart in Dallas, he's an excellent runner who also catches the ball well.

The 5-foot-10, 198-pounder gained more than 2,000 all-purpose yards in 1991 and 1992. The NFL player of the year in 1991, Thomas has unfortunately played poorly in Buffalo's four consecutive Super Bowl losses. Through 1994, he had a total of 12,116 yards and 66 touchdowns.

The first great professional star was Jim Thorpe, shown here attempting a field goal with the Canton Bulldogs in 1920. Thorpe served that year as the president of the new American Professional Football Association, which became the National Football League in 1922. *Courtesy Pro Football Hall of Fame*

Jim Thorpe—Part Irish, French, and American Indian, Thorpe entered Carlisle Indian School in Pennsylvania in 1907, left in 1909, and returned in 1911. He scored 25 touchdowns and 198 points in 1912, when he also won the pentathlon and decathlon at the Stockholm Olympics. He was stripped of his medals for having played professional baseball; they were finally returned to his family in 1983, thirty years after his death.

Thorpe joined the Canton Bulldogs for $250 a game in 1915. He played for several pro teams through 1926, and he was also a major-league outfielder from 1913 through 1919. A hard runner and tackler and an outstanding kicker, Thorpe was named athlete of the half-century by AP in 1950 and he became a charter member of the Pro Football Hall of Fame in 1963. He also belongs to the Olympic and the National Track and Field Halls of Fame.

Y. A. Tittle—Tittle entered pro football with the Baltimore Colts of the All-America Football Conference in 1948 after playing at LSU. The Colts entered the NFL in 1950 but folded after one season and Tittle went to the San Francisco 49ers, where he became the starting quarterback in 1952.

UPI's player of the year in 1957, Tittle was traded to the New York Giants in 1961. He helped lead New York to three straight division championships and was named the AP player of the year in 1963. He retired after the 1964 season with 33,070 passing yards and 242 touch-down passes. Tittle was elected to the Pro Football Hall of Fame in 1971.

George Trafton—The original "big bad Bear," Trafton left Notre Dame after being suspended from football for playing professionally. He joined the Decatur Staleys in 1920. The team moved to Chicago the following season and became the Bears in 1922.

Named the center on unofficial All-Pro teams three times, the 6-foot-2, 235-pounder was outstanding on both offense and defense and he developed a reputation as a dirty player who was hated by opponents and fans of rival teams. Trafton retired after the 1932 season and was inducted into the Pro Football Hall of Fame in 1964.

Charlie Trippi—Trippi was a triple threat tailback in the single wing at Georgia, the Maxwell Award winner as the nation's top college player in 1946. He signed an unprecedented four-year, $100,000 contract with the Chicago Cardinals in 1947 and he promptly led the team to the NFL championships, scoring touchdowns on runs of 44 and 75 yards in the Cardinals' 28–21 win over the Philadelphia Eagles.

An outstanding breakaway runner, Trippi was also a fine passer who played quarterback for two seasons before returning to running back in 1953. He spent his final two seasons as a defensive back. Trippi accounted for a total of 7,241 yards and 37 touchdowns. He also threw 16 touchdown passes and punted for a 40.4-yard average. Trippi was elected to the Pro Football Hall of Fame in 1968.

Emlen Tunnell—After serving in World War II, Tunnell played at the University of Iowa and joined the New York Giants as a safety man in 1948. Nicknamed "Emlen the Gremlin," the 6-foot-1, 200-pounder had outstanding speed and was a constant threat to score on interception and kick returns.

Tunnell went to the Green Bay Packers and retired after the 1961 season with a record 79 interceptions. He scored 4 touchdowns on interception returns, 5 on punt returns, and 1 on a kickoff return, accounting for 4,706 total yards. In 1967, Tunnell became the first black player and the first defensive specialist inducted into the Pro Football Hall of Fame.

Bulldog Turner—Turner joined the Chicago Bears in 1940 after playing at Hardin-Simmons College in Texas. The 6-foot-2, 232-pound Turner immediately took over as the team's starting center. A powerful blocker and outstanding linebacker, he led the NFL with 8 intercep-tions in 1942 and in 1947 he returned an interception 96 yards for a touchdown.

A seven-time All Pro, Turner retired after the 1952 seasons and entered the Pro Football Hall of Fame in 1966.

Johnny Unitas—One of the greatest quarterbacks in history, Unitas played at the University of Louisville and was with a semi-pro team when the Baltimore Colts signed him in 1955. He took over as the starter in his second season. Unitas became instantly famous when he guided the 80-yard touchdown drive that beat the New York Giants 23–17 for the 1958 NFL in the first-ever overtime game.

Unitas led the Colts to a second title in 1959, when he won the Bert Bell Trophy as the league's player of the year. He also won that award in 1964 and 1967 and was a five-time All-Pro. Unitas was traded to the San Diego Chargers in 1973 and retired after one season there. He passed for 40,239 yards and 290 touchdowns and was elected to Pro Football Hall of Fame in 1979.

Norm Van Brocklin—Van Brocklin was Oregon's starting quarterback for three years and he joined the Los Angeles Rams in 1949. He threw four touchdown passes in his first start. After winning the 1950 NFL passing championship, Van Brocklin set a record by passing for 554 yards in a game in 1951.

His 73-yard touchdown pass gave the Rams a 24–17 win over the Cleveland Browns for the 1951 championship, and he won passing titles again in 1952 and 1953. Van Brocklin went to the Philadelphia Eagles in 1958 and was named the player of the year in 1960, when the Eagles won the NFL title. He retired after that season with 23,611 yards passing and 173 touchdown passes. He later coached the Vikings and Falcons.

Van Brocklin was inducted into the Pro Football Hall of Fame in 1971.

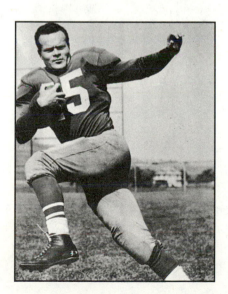

Steve Van Buren of the Philadelphia Eagles rushed for a record 1,146 yards in 1949. Though known as a power runner, he also had outstanding speed and was often used as a kick returner. *Courtesy Philadelphia Eagles*

Steve Van Buren—After leading the nation in scoring with 110 points at LSU in 1943, Van Buren joined the Philadelphia Eagles. He led the NFL in rushing in 1945 and set a record with 1,146 yards in 1949. The 6-foot, 210-pound Van Buren had such great speed for his size that he was often used as a kick returner.

A five-time All-Pro, Van Buren scored the only touchdown in Philadelphia's 7–0 win over the Chicago Cardinals for the 1948 championship, and he had 196 yards in their 14–0 championship win over the Rams in 1949. He retired after the 1951 season and was elected to the Pro Football Hall of Fame in 1965.

Doak Walker—Walker was an All-American halfback at SMU from 1947 through 1949 and he won the 1948 Heisman Trophy. The versatile 5-foot-11, 170-pounder joined the Detroit Lions in 1950, led the league in scoring, and was rookie of the year.

He retired after the 1955 season. In his relatively brief career, he scored 534 points, including 12 touchdowns rushing, 21 on pass receptions, 1 on a punt return, and 2 on interception returns. Walker also threw 2 touchdown passes, punted for a 39.1 average, kicked 49 field goals, and converted 183 extra point attempts. He was elected to the Pro Football Hall of Fame in 1986.

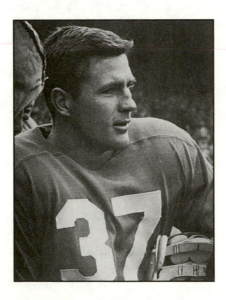

One of the most versatile players in NFL history, halfback Doak Walker won the 1948 Heisman Trophy and was rookie of the year with the Detroit Lions in 1950. He scored 534 points in just six seasons. *Courtesy Detroit Lions*

Herschel Walker—One of the most heralded running backs in college history, Walker won the Heisman Trophy in 1982, his junior year at Georgia. An All-American three times in football and twice in track, he left school to join the New Jersey Generals of the U. S. Football League in

1983 and was the league's player of the year in 1985, its final season. Walker's rather troubled NFL career began in 1986, when he joined the Dallas Cowboys, who sent him to the Minnesota Vikings during the 1989 season in a controversial trade involving six players and twelve draft choices. He went to the Philadelphia Eagles as a free agent in 1992. Through 1993, Walker ranks 20th in NFL history with 13,031 all-purpose yards.

Bill Walsh—Walsh graduated from San Jose State in 1954, coached high school football, and was a college and pro assistant until 1977, when he took over at Stanford. After a 17–7–0 record there, he became head coach of the San Francisco 49ers in 1979.

Bill Walsh coached the San Francisco 49ers to three Super Bowl victories in ten seasons. He was the architect of the "West Coast offense," which features ball-control through short passes. *Courtesy San Francisco 49ers*

Using a ball-control passing game, Walsh guided the 49ers to a 102–59–1 record and three Super Bowl championships in ten seasons. After a year as a TV commentator, he returned to Stanford in 1990. Walsh was inducted into the Pro Football Hall of Fame in 1993.

Paul Warfield—One of the great deep receivers in NFL history, Warfield was a running back at Ohio State before becoming a wide receiver with the Cleveland Browns in 1964. He was traded to the Miami Dolphins in 1970. Though he caught only 43 passes in 1971, he led the league with 11 touchdown receptions.

Warfield went to the Memphis Southmen of the World Football League in 1975. That league folded, and he played for the Browns in 1975 and 1976 before retiring. He averaged 20.1 yards and scored 85 touchdowns on his 427 career receptions and was elected to the Pro Football Hall of Fame in 1983.

Bob Waterfield—A single-wing tailback at UCLA, Waterfield joined the Cleveland Rams as a T-formation quarterback in 1945, when he became the first rookie to be named the NFL's most valuable player. He threw two touchdown passes when Cleveland beat Washington 15–14 in the championship game.

The team moved to Los Angeles the following season and won another championship in 1951, with Waterfield and Norm Van Brocklin splitting the quarterback job. Waterfield retired after the 1952 season with 11,849 passing yards and 98 touchdowns. He punted for a 42.4-yard average, scored 495 points as a kicker, and had 20 interceptions in five seasons as a two-way player. He was inducted into the Pro Football Hall of Fame in 1965.

Arnie Weinmeister—The 6-foot-4, 235-pound Weinmeister joined the New York Yankees of the All-America Football Conference out of the University of Washington in 1948. An all-league selection at defensive tackle in 1949, he went to the New York Giants the following season, after the AAFC folded.

Surprisingly fast for his size, Weinmeister was an All-Pro four times before going to the Canadian Football League in 1954. He retired after two seasons there and was elected to the Pro Football Hall of Fame in 1984.

Randy White—White won the 1974 Outland Trophy as the nation's best college lineman at Maryland in 1974 and was the Dallas Cowboys' first draft choice. He became a starting defensive tackle in his second season. The 6-foot-4, 245-pounder, who was known as "Manster," half man and half monster, was UPI's NFC defensive player of the year in 1978, and he was an All-Pro from 1978 through 1982. He retired after the 1988 season. White was inducted into the Pro Football Hall of Fame in 1994.

Reggie White—An All-American defensive end at Tennessee in 1983, the 6-foot-5, 285-pound White spent a season with the Memphis Showboats of the U. S. Football league before joining the Philadelphia Eagles in 1985. He led the NFL with 21 sacks in 1987 and 18 in 1988.

White became the league's highest paid defensive player when he signed a four-year, $17-million contract with the Packers in 1993. He surpassed Lawrence Taylor as the NFL's career sack leader that season.

Bill Willis—After three seasons as a starting guard at Ohio State, Willis spent a year in service and then joined the Cleveland Browns of the All-America Football Conference in 1946. The 6-foot-4 Willis weighed only 210 pounds, but he became an outstanding defensive middle guard because of his speed and agility.

Known as "the Cat," he sometimes jumped over blockers who tried to take him low. An all-AAFC choice from 1946 through 1948, Willis was a four-time All-Pro after the Browns joined the NFL in 1950. He retired after the 1953 season and was inducted into the Pro Football Hall of Fame in 1977.

Larry Wilson—Wilson became a free safety with the St. Louis Cardinals in 1960 after being a two-way player at Utah. In his second season, he ran the first safety blitz and recorded an 11-yard sack. He had another sack later in the game.

A four-time All-Pro, the 6-foot, 190-pound Wilson led the NFL with 10 interceptions in 1966. He retired after the 1972 season with 52 interceptions and 5 touchdowns. Wilson was elected to the Pro Football Hall of Fame in 1978.

Alex Wojciechowicz—One of the "Seven Blocks of Granite" at Fordham, Wojciechowicz was an All-American center in 1936 and 1937. He joined the Detroit Lions in 1938 as an offensive center and defensive linebacker. Very fast at 6-foot-2 and 235 pounds, he intercepted 7 passes in 1944.

During the 1946 season, he went to the Philadelphia Eagles, who used him mostly as a linebacker. He played for NFL champions in 1948 and 1949 and retired after the 1950 season. Wojciechowicz was elected to the Pro Football Hall of Fame in 1968.

Willie Wood—Wood was a quarterback at Southern California and he joined the Packers as a free agent in 1960. The 5-foot-10, 185-pounder became the starting free safety in his second season and led the NFL with 9 interceptions in 1962. He retired after the 1971 season with 48 career interceptions and 4 touchdown returns. He also had 2 touchdowns on punt returns.

Wood was inducted into the Pro Football Hall of Fame in 1989.

Steve Young—A left-handed quarterback, the 6-foot-2, 205-pound young was an All-American at Brigham Young in 1983. He entered pro football with the Los Angeles Express of the U. S. Football League. When the league folded after the 1985 season, he joined the Tampa Bay Buccaneers.

Young was traded to the San Francisco 49ers in 1987 and he became the team's starter after Joe Montana was injured in 1991. He was named the NFL's player of the year in 1992, when he was the league's top rated quarterback. Through 1993, Young had passed for 15,900 yards and 105 touchdowns. He had also rushed for 2,676 yards and 20 touchdowns.

Young was traded to the San Francisco 49ers in 1987 but didn't become the team's starter until after Joe Montana was injured in 1991. The NFL's Player of the Year in 1992, when he was the league's top rated quarterback, Young won the award again in 1994. He led the 49ers to a 49–26 victory over the San Diego Chargers in Super Bowl XXIX after that season.

10

Best and Worst Moments

November 7, 1920—George Trafton of the Decatur Staleys (who became the Chicago Bears in 1921) deliberately landed with both knees on Rock Island center Harry Gunderson, who had to leave the game with a broken hand, a cut lip, and a cut over his eye. After the game, 5,000 infuriated Rock Island fans chased Trafton and his teammates to the bus.

December 4, 1921—At half-time of the first pro football game ever played in New York City, the great Jim Thorpe of the Cleveland Indians and Charlie Brickley of Brickley's Giants engaged in a kicking contest that got more publicity than the game itself. It ended in a 6–6 tie, but Thorpe's 55-yard drop kick beat Brickley's best effort, a 50-yard place kick. Thorpe also had a 42-yard field goal in Cleveland's 17–0 victory.

October 13, 1922—The Rock Island Independents set an NFL record that still stands by scoring nine rushing touchdowns in a 60–0 victory over Evansville. Jimmy Conzelman had five of them, a record until 1929.

November 29, 1922—A free-for-all erupted in the first quarter of the Thanksgiving Day game between the Chicago Bears and Chicago Cardinals after player-coach George Halas and halfback Joey Sternaman of the Bears picked up Cardinal quarterback Paddy Driscoll and threw him violently to the ground. Driscoll then slugged Sternaman. Not only did players come off both benches to get into the melee, but more than a hundred fans stormed out of the stands. With the help of police, officials finally broke up the many fights that were going on. Driscoll, Halas, and Sternaman were thrown out of the game. The Cardinals went on to win 6–0.

November 4, 1923—On a muddy field at Sportsman's Park in St. Louis, Cub Buck of the visiting Green Bay Packers punted a record 19 times. A 6-foot, 259-pound tackle out of the University of Wisconsin, Buck also got the game's only score, a 20-yard field goal, in Green Bay's 3–0 victory over the St. Louis All-Stars.

December 6, 1925—A crowd of 73,651 showed up at the Polo Grounds in New York to see Red Grange and the Chicago Bears play the New York Giants in a post-season exhibition game. It was by far the largest crowd to attend a professional game at that time and the gate receipts pulled the Giants out of the red and into the black. The Bears beat the Giants 19–7.

October 16, 1927—After leaping in an unsuccessful attempt to catch a pass, Red Grange of the New York Yankees caught his cleats in the turf and suffered a badly damaged knee when George Trafton of the Chicago Bears fell on him. Grange refused surgery, missed the entire 1928 season, and was, in his own words, "just another halfback" for the rest of his professional career.

November 6, 1929—The first night game in NFL history was played at Kinsley Park in Providence. Led by Ernie Nevers, the Chicago Cardinals beat the Providence Steam Roller 16–0. Nevers scored 10 points and passed for the other 6.

November 28, 1929—Ernie Nevers scored a record six rushing touchdowns and kicked four conversions to account for all of the Chicago Cardinals' points in a 40–7 win over the Chicago Bears. That's still the NFL record. A week earlier, he'd scored all 19 points in a win over the Portsmouth Spartans.

December 15, 1929—Benny Friedmann of the New York Giants threw a 27-yard touchdown pass to beat the Bears 14–9 in the final game of the season, at Chicago's Wrigley Field. It was his 20th touchdown pass of the season, a record until 1942.

December 6, 1931—John V. McNally, Jr., who played under the name "Johnny Blood," caught a 32-yard touchdown pass from Bo Molenda in the Green Bay Packers' 7–6 loss to the Chicago Bears. It was his 10th touchdown reception of the season, still the NFL record for a running back. Despite the loss, the Packers won their third straight championship.

December 18, 1932—The Chicago Bears and Portsmouth Spartans met for the NFL championship after tying for first place. Moved indoors to Chicago Stadium because of heavy snow and bitter cold, the game was played on a field that stretched only 60 yards from goal line to goal line. The goal posts were moved from the end lines to the goal lines. Despite the shortened field, the teams failed to score until the Bears got a touchdown late in the fourth quarter, and a safety shortly afterward sealed a 9–0 victory. Because of the publicity generated by the game, the league decided to split into two divisions in 1933 to set up an annual post-season playoff.

September 24, 1933—One of the most famous collisions in NFL history took place between the league's two best fullbacks in the Chicago Bears 14–7 win over the Green Bay Packers. Green Bay's 205-pound Clarke Hinkle smashed into Chicago's 230-pound Bronko Nagurski and Nagurski had to leave the game with a broken nose, one of the few times he was ever forced out of action. Nagurski was better known for knocking opponents out of the game.

December 17, 1933—The New York Giants, Eastern Division champions, faced the Chicago Bears of the Western Division at Soldier Field in the first true NFL championship game. It was an exciting contest, with seven lead changes. The Giants took a 21–16 lead on a broken play in the fourth quarter. Fullback Ken Strong, trapped behind the line of scrimmage on a planned run, lateraled to tailback Harry Newman, who scrambled around and finally threw an 8-yard touchdown pass to Strong. The Bears won 23–21 when Bronko Nagurski threw a pass to end Bill Hewitt, who lateraled to Bill Karr. Karr went into the end zone to finish a 32-yard touchdown play.

October 28, 1934—The Detroit Lions rang up their seventh consecutive shutout, an NFL record, by beating the Cincinnati Reds 38–0. The streak ended on November 4, when the Pittsburgh Pirates (now the Steelers) managed a touchdown, although Detroit won the game 40–7. The Lions ended up losing their last three games of the season and finished second to the Chicago Bears in the Western Division.

November 29, 1934—The first national broadcast of an NFL game was carried on the CBS Radio Network. The Chicago Bears beat the Detroit Lions 19–16 in Detroit on Thanksgiving Day and went on to compile the first perfect regular-season record in league history, a 13–0 mark.

December 8, 1934—The Bears seemed likely to finish a perfect season with an NFL title when they took a 10–3 half-time lead over the New York Giants on a frozen field at the Polo Grounds. During the break, New York coach Steve Owen had his players switch from cleats to sneakers for better traction. The Giants went on to win 30–13 in what went down in pro football history as the "Sneakers Game."

August 25, 1939—The Pittsburgh Pirates and Green Bay Packers played the only doubleheader in NFL history at City Stadium in Green Bay. The first game ended in a 7–7 tie and the Packers won the second, 17–0. Quarters were only 10 minutes long in the two exhibition games.

September 15, 1940—The Detroit Lions and Chicago Cardinals played the most boring game in league history, appropriately on neutral ground, at Buffalo's War Memorial Stadium. "Fighting" to a scoreless tie on a muddy field, the teams accounted for a total of only 30 yards and 7 first downs. Detroit completed the only pass of the game, for 26 yards, but lost 10 yards rushing. To add injury to insult, a number of players had to be treated for alkali burns caused when the lime used to mark the field mixed with rain water.

October 27, 1940—In the first field goal attempt of his NFL career, Lee Artoe of the Chicago Bears kicked a 52-yarder, the second longest in league history. He had earlier missed an extra point attempt in Chicago's 37–21 win over the New York Giants. Artoe tried only nine other field goals and made only one more in his seven professional seasons.

December 8, 1940—Davey O'Brien of the Philadelphia Eagles set three records by completing 33 passes in 60 attempts for 316 yards in the last game of his brief professional career. O'Brien, who had been Sammy Baugh's successor at Texas Christian, retired from pro football at twenty-three after just two seasons.

December 8, 1940—The Chicago Bears beat the Washington Redskins 73–0 in the NFL championship game at Griffith Stadium in Washington. Fullback Bill Osmanski began the rout by scoring on a 68-yard run on Chicago's second play from scrimmage. The Bears were the only NFL team using the T formation at the time, but their lopsided victory persuaded most other teams to begin using the T within the next few years.

October 19, 1941—NFL umpire Charles W. "Chick" Rupp shot himself in the hand with the gun used to signal the end of a period during a game between the New York Giants and Pittsburgh Steelers at the Polo Grounds. Though the cartridge was a blank, he had to spend several days in the hospital and never officiated another NFL game.

November 14, 1943—The Giants held a Sid Luckman Day for the visiting Chicago Bears' quarterback, who was a New York native and a graduate of Columbia University. Luckman responded with a record 7 touchdown passes and 433 yards through the air in Chicago's 56–7 victory.

December 26, 1943—The Bears beat the Washington Redskins 41–21 for the NFL title, but the score could have been much closer if it hadn't been for Bronko Nagurski. After five years in retirement, Nagurski had returned to play tackle during the regular season. Because of injuries, he was moved to fullback for the championship game. His 3-yard touchdown run gave Chicago a 14–7 half-time lead. More important, the Bears faced five short-yardage situations on fourth down and the 35-year-old Nagurski got them the first down every time.

December 15, 1945—The Cleveland Rams beat the Washington Redskins 15–14 in what was probably the strangest NFL championship game ever played. Washington's Sammy Baugh threw a first-quarter pass that was caught up in a strong wind. The ball hit a goal post and went into the end zone. Under the rules of the time, that was a safety that gave Cleveland a 2–0 lead. After Washington went ahead 7–2, Cleveland scored a touchdown in the second quarter. Bob Waterfield's extra-point attempt hit the cross bar and popped over to make the score 9–7. Both teams scored touchdowns in the second half, and Waterfield missed that conversion, but the Rams won because of the wind-blown safety and the fluke extra point.

March 21, 1946—Halfback Kenny Washington signed with the Los Angeles Rams, becoming the first black player to be on an NFL roster since 1933. Another black, end Woody Strode, signed with the Rams later that year and two black players, guard Bill Willis and fullback Marion Motley, joined the Cleveland Browns of the new All-America Football Conference.

December 15, 1946—New York Giants' fullback Merle Hapes was indefinitely suspended for failing to report a bribe attempt but quarterback Frank Filchock was allowed to play in the NFL championship game against the Chicago Bears. Chicago won the game 24–14 and Filchock was given an indefinite suspension immediately afterward. His suspension was lifted in 1950, Hapes's in 1954.

September 25, 1948—Tackle Stan Mauldin of the Chicago Cardinals died two hours after his team beat the Philadelphia Eagles 21–14. He had suffered a heart attack immediately after the game and he died in the dressing room after being hooked up to an artificial lung.

November 28, 1948—After a touchdown put the AAFC's San Francisco 49ers ahead of the Cleveland Browns, 20–10, Joe Vetrano was ready to place kick the extra point. But the bad snap eluded his holder. Vetrano picked the ball up and drop-kicked the conversion. It was the last successful drop kick in pro football history, and probably the last such attempt.

November 13, 1949—Halfback Gene "Choo Choo" Roberts of the New York Giants caught 7 passes for 212 yards and 3 touchdowns when the Giants beat the Green Bay Packers 30–10. Three weeks earlier, he had caught 4 passes for 201 yards and 3 touchdowns. No other NFL running back has ever had more than 200 yards on pass receptions in a game.

September 16, 1950—Amid doubts that they could compete in the NFL after winning four straight championships in the defunct All-America Football Conference, the Cleveland Browns faced the defending champion Eagles in the first game of the season, at Philadelphia. The Browns proved they were for real by whipping the Eagles 35–10.

September 24, 1950—Quarterback Jim Hardy of the Chicago Cardinals threw a record eight interceptions in a 47–7 loss to the Philadelphia Eagles. That's still the NFL record. Hardy also lost two fumbles for a total of ten turnovers.

December 3, 1950—End Tom Fears of the Los Angeles Rams caught 18 passes in a 51–14 victory over the Green Bay Packers, still the NFL single-game record.

December 24, 1950—The Cleveland Browns climaxed their first year in the NFL by beating the Los Angeles Rams 30–28 in one of the most exciting championship games in history. The Rams led 7–0 and 14–7 before the Browns took a 20–14 lead in the third quarter. Los Angeles went ahead again, 21–20 and then 28–20. The score was 28–27 when the Browns took over on their own 32-yard line with less than two minutes to play. With 28 seconds left, Lou Groza kicked a 16-yard field goal for the victory.

September 28, 1951—Norm Van Brocklin of the Los Angeles Rams passed for a record 554 yards against the New York Yanks.

November 25, 1951—Halfback Edgar "Dub" Jones of the Cleveland Browns tied an NFL record by scoring 6 touchdowns in a 42–21 win over the Chicago Bears. He scored the last five times he touched the ball.

December 16, 1956—In the Western Conference championship game, Chicago Bear defensive end Ed Meadows knocked Detroit Lion quarterback Bobby Layne out with a concussion on a late hit in the second quarter. Layne had handed the ball off to running back Gene Gedman, who was being tackled seven yards downfield when Meadows made the hit, throwing Layne violently to the ground. There was no penalty, but Meadows was later thrown out of the game for punching another Lion. The Bears won 38–21.

December 27, 1958—The Baltimore Colts beat the New York Giants 23–17 in the first overtime game in NFL history to win the league championship. The Colts took over on their 20-yard line after a punt and marched 80 yards in 12 plays, with Alan Ameche scoring the winning touchdown on a 1-yard run.

October 30, 1960—"The Violent World of Sam Huff," the New York Giants' middle linebacker, ran on the CBS News show *The Twentieth Century* at 6:30 P.M. By wiring Huff for sound during training camp and an exhibition game, the telecast gave fans their first real close-up look at pro football in the days before instant replays and isolated cameras.

November 20, 1960—With the Philadelphia Eagles leading the New York Giants 17–10 late in the fourth quarter, New York halfback Frank Gifford caught a short pass and was hit by cornerback Don Burrough and linebacker Chuck Bednarik. Gifford was knocked unconscious and fumbled the ball. The Eagles recovered. Bednarik celebrated exuberantly, bringing boos from the fans at Yankee Stadium. He later explained he'd been celebrating the fumble recovery. Gifford spent several days in a hospital with a severe concussion and retired temporarily the following year, but he returned to the Giants to play three more seasons as a wide receiver. The Eagles went on to win the NFL championship.

November 27, 1960—The Denver Broncos lost seven of their last eight games in the AFL's first season. In the only one they didn't lose, they were trailing the Buffalo Bills 38–7 with less than five minutes left in the third quarter. Then NFL castoff quarterback Frank Tripucka led the team to four touchdowns and a field goal to gain a 38–38 tie.

December 26, 1960—The veteran Philadelphia Eagles and the young, emerging Green Bay Packers met for the league title at Philadelphia. The story of the game was Chuck Bednarik, who played 58 minutes as a center on offense and a linebacker on defense. His tackle forced Packer halfback Paul Hornung out of the game in the third quarter. With the Eagles leading 17–13 and time running out, Packer fullback Jimmy Taylor caught a short pass and was headed for the goal line, but Bednarik made a sure tackle and sat happily on Taylor's back when the game ended. Bednarik announced his retirement after the game, as did Norm Van Brocklin, who had become the first quarterback to lead two different teams to NFL championships. This was the only loss the Packers suffered in ten playoff games during Vince Lombardi's regime.

September 11, 1961—Not much was expected of the expansion Minnesota Vikings in their first NFL season. But, in their first game they beat the Chicago Bears 37–13. It was also the first game as a head coach for Minnesota's Norm Van Brocklin and the first pro game for quarterback Fran Tarkenton, who passed for four touchdowns and ran for another.

September 17, 1961—In the second quarter of a game between the New York Giants and St. Louis Cardinals at Yankee Stadium, Larry Wilson of the Cardinals sacked Giant quarterback Charlie Conerly for an 11-yard loss. It was the first time the safety blitz was used. Wilson had a second sack later in the game and the underdog Cardinals won 21–10.

December 23, 1962—With the score tied 17–17 in the AFL championship game, the Dallas Texans and Houston Oilers went into overtime. Dallas coach Hank Stram told his captain, Abner Haynes, to take the wind if he won the toss. Haynes won, but elected to kick off, thinking he could also choose which goal to defend, and Houston got both the ball and the wind. Fortunately for Haynes, neither team scored in the first overtime and Dallas won 20–17 in the second overtime period.

April 17, 1963—NFL Commissioner Pete Rozelle announced that halfback Paul Hornung of the Green Bay Packers and defensive tackle Alex Karras of the Detroit Lions had been suspended indefinitely for betting on pro football games. He also said that neither had ever bet against his own team. Both were reinstated for the 1964 season.

January 5, 1964—Keith Lincoln of the San Diego Chargers rushed for 205 yards, caught passes for 123 yards, and completed a 20-yard pass in San Diego's 51–10 victory over the Boston Patriots for the AFL championship. Lincoln scored touchdowns on a 67-yard run and a 25-yard reception.

October 25, 1964—Jim Marshall, a fine end on the Minnesota Vikings "Purple People Eaters" defense, picked up a fumble against the San Francisco 49ers and ran 62 yards into the end zone—the wrong end zone. The result was a safety and 2 points for the 49ers. Fortunately for Marshall, the Vikings won anyway, 27–22, in a game that also featured five fumbles, five interceptions, and a touchdown run with a fumble recovery by Minnesota's other defensive end, Carl Eller.

December 26, 1965—The Baltimore Colts faced the Packers for the NFC championship in Green Bay without a quarterback. Halfback Tom Matte filled in ably and an aroused Baltimore defense played so well that the Colts led 13–10 with less than two minutes to play, when Green Bay's Don Chandler attempted a 22-yard field goal to tie the game. Chandler shook his head in disgust as his kick swerved to the right. But the field goal was ruled good, despite Baltimore's protests, and the Packers went on to win 16–13 in overtime. The following season, the height of the goal posts was increased from 10 to 20 feet above the crossbar.

November 27, 1966—The Washington Redskins beat the New York Giants 72–41 in the highest scoring game in NFL history. With only seven seconds remaining, Washington kicked a 29-yard field goal to break the former regular season record of 70 points by a single team.

January 15, 1967—The first Super Bowl, formally the AFL-NFL championship game, matched the NFL's Green Bay Packers against the AFL's Kansas City Chiefs before a crowd of 61,946 at Los Angeles Coliseum. Televised by both CBS and NBC, it was close for two periods, but the Packers broke it open with three touchdowns in the second half to take a 35–10 victory.

September 24, 1967—Jim Bakken of the St. Louis Cardinals kicked a record 7 field goals in a 28–14 victory over the Pittsburgh Steelers.

December 31, 1967—In a game that became known as the "Ice Bowl," Bart Starr scored on a quarterback sneak with sixteen seconds left to play as the Green Bay Packers beat the Dallas Cowboys 21–17 for the NFL championship. The field in Green Bay was frozen and the wind chill factor was minus 50. Two previous running plays had failed to gain any yardage because the back slipped just as he got the hand-off, so Starr and Packer Coach Vince Lombardi decided to run the same play with Starr carrying the ball quickly into the hole instead of handing-off. The touchdown play made right guard Jerry Kramer famous because of his key block on Cowboy defensive tackle Jethro Pugh.

November 17, 1968—The Oakland Raiders scored two touchdowns in the last 50 seconds to beat the New York Jets 43–32 in the famous "Heidi" game. With the Jets winning 32–29, NBC elected to leave the game in order to show the movie *Heidi* at 7 P.M. The network got so many calls from angry fans that the switchboard broke down.

January 12, 1969—Although the Baltimore Colts were favored by as much as three touchdowns over the New York Jets in Super Bowl III, Jet quarterback Joe Namath guaranteed victory. He completed 17 of 28 passes for 206 yards, running a ball-control offense that combined with a strong defense for a 16–7 win, the first by an AFL team.

September 21, 1969—Rookie Steve O'Neal of the New York Jets set an NFL record with a 98-yard punt against the Denver Broncos. With the ball on New York's 1-yard line, O'Neal got off a kick that sailed over the punt returner's head. It landed at about the Denver 30 and rolled dead at the 1.

November 2, 1969—Two of the worst teams in pro football, the New Orleans Saints and the St. Louis Cardinals, met in a meaningless game at St. Louis. It ended up in the record books. The Saints won 51–42 and each quarterback, Charlie Johnson of the Cardinals and Billy Kilmer of the Saints, threw six touchdown passes, one short of the NFL record. The total of twelve is the record for both teams in a game.

November 8, 1970—Tom Dempsey of the New Orleans Saints kicked a 63-yard goal with 2 seconds left to beat the Detroit Lions 19–17. The kick broke the former NFL record by 7 yards. Dempsey, who was born with no toes on his right foot, was cut by the Saints before the 1978 season but he spent nine more seasons in the league, with four other teams.

January 17, 1971—Sportswriters called it the "Stupor Bowl" and the "Stumble Bowl" after Baltimore and Dallas met in the first Super Bowl after the AFL-NFL merger. There were six fumbles and six interceptions, plus a blocked extra point. Baltimore scored its first touchdown when a pass slid off the fingers of a wide receiver, was touched by a defensive back, and caught by tight end John Mackey, who turned it into a 75-yard play. Fittingly, an interception with one minute to play set up the winning field goal in Baltimore's 16–13 win.

August 14, 1971—Shades of Chick Rupp (see October 19, 1941). It was only an exhibition game between the Washington Redskins and Denver Broncos, but it's still worth noting that line judge Gene Barth shot himself in the rear while putting the timing gun into his back pocket in the officials' dressing room. He worked the game, anyway, and didn't have the wounds treated until he went home afterward. It was Barth's first NFL game. He went on to become a highly regarded referee.

October 17, 1971—Pittsburgh wide receiver Dave Smith caught a pass well behind the Kansas City Chiefs' defense and was headed for a touchdown when he decided to spike the ball. But the spike came on Kansas City's 5-yard line, the ball rolled through the end zone, and the Chiefs were awarded possession at their own 20-yard line on the resulting touchback.

December 10, 1972—In the last game of the season, running back Dave Hampton almost became the first Atlanta Falcon to rush for 1,000 yards. He gained a yard against the Chiefs to reach the 1,000-yard plateau and the game was stopped so he could be presented with the ball. On his next attempt, he lost 6 yards. Hampton got just one more carry and gained only 1 yard to finish the game and the season with a total of 995.

December 23, 1972—The Oakland Raiders were beating the Pittsburgh Steelers 7–6 with five seconds to play in the AFC championship game when Pittsburgh quarterback Terry Bradshaw, rolling to his right to avoid a sack, threw the ball downfield. It caromed to running back Franco Harris, who ran it in for a 32-yard touchdown that gave Pittsburgh a 13–7 win. The Raiders protested vehemently that the ball had been touched only by another Pittsburgh receiver, which would have made it incomplete, but replays clearly show it bounced off the shoulderpad of Raider defensive back Jack Tatum.

January 14, 1973—Going into Super Bowl VII, the Dolphins had won sixteen consecutive games, fourteen during the regular season and two in the playoffs. Led by the "No-Name Defense" and a ball-control offense that featured the running and blocking of halfback Jim Kiick and fullback Larry Csonka, with the dangerous Mercury Morris occasionally replacing Kiick for a change of pace, Miami beat Washington 14–7 to complete a perfect 17–0 season. An otherwise rather dull game was enlivened by "the pass" thrown by Miami kicker Garo Yepremian, a soccer player from Cyprus. When his 42-yard field goal attempt was blocked early in the fourth quarter, the ball came back to Yepremian. He ran frantically toward the right sideline, then threw the ball downfield. Not far downfield. It was intercepted by Mike Bass, who ran 49 yards for Washington's only score.

October 21, 1973—Defensive end Fred Dryer of the Los Angeles Rams set an NFL record by scoring two safeties in a single game against the Green Bay Packers. Only eleven players, including Dryer, have ever scored two safeties in a season.

January 18, 1976—After a string of nine less-than-super Super Bowls, the Steelers and Cowboys gave stirring performances in Super Bowl X. Dallas, the first wild-card team to get into the game, led 10–7 at the end of the third quarter. Pittsburgh closed to 10–9 with a safety on a blocked punt, then went ahead 15–10 on two field goals. The big play was a 64-yard touchdown pass from Terry Bradshaw to Lynn Swann, giving the Steelers a 21–10 lead when the extra point try failed. Dallas came back with a touchdown and got the ball back with less than a minute and a half to play, but ran out of time. The two teams accounted for 609 yards of offense.

November 20, 1977—Walter Payton of the Chicago Bears set a record by rushing for 275 yards against the Minnesota Vikings. He broke the record held by O. J. Simpson, who had twice gained 273 yards in a game.

August 12, 1978—In an exhibition game, wide receiver Darryl Stingley of the New England Patriots leaped in vain for a high pass and was hit by the Oakland Raiders' Jack Tatum when he came down. Tatum's shoulder hit Stingley in the face mask and Stingley dropped to the ground. He suffered two broken vertebrae in his neck and was totally paralyzed.

September 10, 1978—The Oakland Raiders were at the San Diego Chargers' 14-yard line, losing 20–14 with 10 seconds left in the game, when quarterback Ken Stabler was apparently sacked. He intentionally fumbled the ball forward, tight end Dave Casper batted it into the end zone and recovered it there for a touchdown. The extra point won the game. As a result, the NFL adopted a new rule in 1979: If the ball is fumbled forward on a fourth-down play and is recovered by a member of the offensive team other than the player who fumbled, it's returned to the point where the fumble occurred.

January 21, 1979—In Super Bowl XIII, the Pittsburgh Steelers led the Dallas Cowboys 21–17 at the end of the third quarter. Pittsburgh had a second-and-five at its own 45-yard line when Terry Bradshaw threw a long pass toward Lynn Swann, who was well covered by Benny Barnes. Barnes seemed to have a shot at an interception when they collided. To the disbelief of the Cowboys, Barnes was called for interference at the Dallas 23-yard line. Pittsburgh scored shortly afterward and ended up winning 35–31. Barnes later received an apology from the NFL office for the call.

November 4, 1979—In the worst offensive performance in NFL history, the Seattle Seahawks lost 24–0 to the Los Angeles Rams before a hometown crowd of more than 62,000. Seattle's offense held the ball for less than 15 minutes, had net yardage of *minus* 7 yards, picked up only one first down, and never got beyond its own 42-yard line. The Seahawks ran thirty-two plays, and only nine of them gained yardage, including two completions in seventeen attempts. Meanwhile, the Rams recorded six sacks for a total loss of 55 yards.

January 20, 1980—In their fourth appearance, the Pittsburgh Steelers became the first team to win four Super Bowls with a 31–19 win over the Los Angeles Rams. The Rams led 13–10 at the half and 19–17 after three quarters, but Terry Bradshaw's 73-yard touchdown pass to John Stallworth and a 1-yard touchdown run by Franco Harris gave Pittsburgh the victory.

December 7, 1980—The New Orleans Saints took a 35–7 half-time lead over the San Francisco 49ers, but San Francisco came back to tie the game in regulation and win it in overtime, 38–35. The comeback was led by a young quarterback named Joe Montana, who less than two years before had brought Notre Dame back from a 23-point deficit in the third quarter to a 35–34 Cotton Bowl victory.

January 25, 1981—With a 27–10 win over the Philadelphia Eagles, the Oakland Raiders became the first wildcard team to win a Super Bowl. A lot of media attention was focused on the presentation of the trophy to Oakland's managing general partner, Al Davis, by NFL Commissioner Pete Rozelle. There had been bad feelings between the two since the AFL-NFL merger, but both performed graciously during the ceremony.

September 13, 1981—Backup defensive back Roy Green of the St. Louis Cardinals was sent in as a wide receiver in the second quarter against the Dallas Cowboys and caught a 60-yard touchdown pass on his only offensive play of the game. The following week, he became the first NFL player since 1957 to have an interception and a touchdown catch in the same game. Green became a full-time receiver in 1982.

January 30, 1983—Trailing 17–13 early in the fourth quarter of Super Bowl XVII, the Washington Redskins decided to go for the first down on fourth and inches at the Miami Dolphins' 43-yard line.

John Riggins broke through the short-yardage defense and went all the way for a touchdown. The Redskins ended up winning 27–17.

November 18, 1985—In a nationally televised Monday night game, the New York Giants blitzed Washington Redskin quarterback Joe Theismann on a flea flicker play and all three linebackers hit him. Theismann's right leg bent sickeningly before it snapped, breaking the tibia and fibula just above the ankle. The injury ended his 12-year career with the Redskins.

December 1, 1985—The Minnesota Vikings were trailing the Philadelphia Eagles 23–0 with $8\frac{1}{2}$ minutes remaining in the game. They scored four touchdowns to win 28–23 in one of the greatest comebacks in NFL history.

September 21, 1987—The NFL Players Association went on strike after the second week of the season. Two weeks later, the league fielded teams made up almost entirely of free agents. The strike ended after three weeks of play by the "scab" teams.

December 6, 1987—Joe Montana of the 49ers completed his first 17 passes against the Packers to set an NFL record of 22 consecutive completions. He had completed his last 5 passes in a game against the Steelers the previous week.

January 31, 1988—Doug Williams, the first black quarterback to start in the Super Bowl, threw four touchdown passes as the Washington Redskins scored a record 35 points in the second quarter and went on to beat the Denver Broncos 42–10. The Redskins set several Super Bowl records: 310 yards passing by Williams, 193 yards on receptions by Rickey Sanders, 204 yards rushing by Timmy Smith, and 602 net yards by the offense.

January 22, 1989—Losing 16–13 to the Cincinnati Bengals with 3:10 left in the Super Bowl, the San Francisco 49ers mounted a 92-yard drive, culminating in a 10-yard touchdown pass from Joe Montana to John Taylor for a 20–16 victory. San Francisco wide receiver Jerry Rice, who had 11 catches for 215 yards and a touchdown, was named the game's MVP.

November 17, 1991—Detroit Lion guard Mike Utley suffered a broken neck vertebra in a game against the Los Angeles Rams. Utley gave his teammates a "thumbs up" symbol as he was carried off the field but, after surgery the following day, he remained paralyzed from the neck down.

November 29, 1992—Dennis Byrd, a defensive lineman for the New York Jets, was partially paralyzed by a broken neck vertebra suffered in a collision with teammate Scott Mersereau. Coming little more than a year after a similar injury to Detroit's Mike Utley, the accident raised questions about whether the NFL should adopt new rules or equipment, or both, to protect players.

December 27, 1992—Sterling Sharpe of the Green Bay Packers caught six passes in a 27–7 season-ending loss to the Minnesota Vikings. His total of 108 receptions broke Art Monk's record of 106 receptions, set in 1984.

January 3, 1993—After struggling late in the season, the Buffalo Bills trailed the Houston Oilers 35–3 in the third quarter of the AFC wild-card playoff game. And their starting quarterback, Jim Kelly, was sidelined by an injury. Backup Frank Reich calmly threw four touchdown passes to lead his team to 35 second-half points and a 41–38 overtime victory, the biggest comeback in NFL history. In 1984, Reich had engineered college football's biggest comeback at the University of Maryland, pulling out a 42–40 win over Miami of Florida after a 31–0 half-time deficit.

January 30, 1994—For the first time, the same opponents met in the Super Bowl two years in a row. The Dallas Cowboys beat the Buffalo Bills 30–13 for their second straight victory. It was a record fourth consecutive Super Bowl loss for Buffalo.

Index